A Very Brief History of
Eternity

~

Frontispiece. Ouroboros, ancient symbol of eternity. Seventeenth-century engraving by Lucas Jennis, in an alchemical treatise.

Carlos Eire

A Very Brief History of
Eternity

~

PRINCETON UNIVERSITY PRESS
PRINCETON AND OXFORD

Library of Congress Cataloging-in-Publication Data

Eire, Carlos M. N.
A very brief history of eternity / Carlos Eire.
p. cm.
Includes bibliographical references (p.) and index.
ISBN 978-0-691-13357-7 (hardcover : alk. paper)
1. Eternity—History of doctrines. 2. Civilization, Western. I. Title.
BT913.E74 2010
236'.21—dc22
2009022951

British Library Cataloging-in-Publication Data is available

This book has been composed in Minion text with
Helvetica Neue Condensed Display
Printed on acid-free paper. ∞
press.princeton.edu
Printed in the United States of America
1 3 5 9 10 8 6 4 2

Contents

Illustrations

Acknowledgments

The idea for this book emerged unexpectedly on a crowded and noisy train, on a dimly lit December afternoon, as I was returning home from a meeting of the Virginia Seminar on Lived Theology. We were still getting acquainted with one another, the members of this group, and wrestling with how each of us might best conceive of a project that would shed light on the ethical, pragmatic dimension of religious belief. I don't think it was anything specific that anyone said during those three days that forced the idea out of its hiding place in my brain; it was just the overall effect of sustained thinking in the company of incredibly gifted and affable individuals that did the trick, I think.

Of course, any book that shows up in such a way has been gestating for years, invisible to the inner eye. All of my life, for as long as I can remember, I have puzzled over death, which has always struck me as the greatest injustice of all, and so senseless. Maybe it has something to do with all those executions I saw broadcast on live television when I was a small boy in Havana, courtesy of Fidel Castro's revolutionary "justice." Maybe not: perhaps I was already thinking this way before Fidel rolled into town and Che started killing people right and left simply for having the wrong ideas in their heads. But it's not the source of the obsession that matters; rather, it's the simple fact that my scholarly work has been informed by it for the past thirty-five years, in one way or another.

This fixation has also affected my personal life, of course, but this isn't the place to dwell on that. Let's just say that it's made me feel out of sync, especially at sporting events, where everyone else seems to care so much about mere numbers on a scoreboard. The only thing I seem to understand and appreciate in sports is talk of sudden death overtime, and that's not out of any interest in the outcome of the game; it's all about the metaphor.

Until that December afternoon, what I hadn't realized was that, in addition to contemplating death and extinction a bit too much, I'd also been keeping a close eye on its opposite, eternity. Then, after I saw that pinpoint of light, another insight followed, overwhelming in its lucidity: I saw the big circle. I realized that my own behavior has been determined in large measure by how I think about my eternal fate, day in and day out, and that all of my thinking on eternity has been inextricable from the cultural matrix in which I have lived. And then I realized that we are all about ends, we human beings: whether they are small ends, such as some instantaneous gratification, or some larger end, such as revolution, death, retirement, or some hope of an afterlife, we structure our choices according to some end, and many of our ends are determined by our cultures. And what end could be bigger than eternity, especially in a culture that has been predominantly Christian for centuries?

I realized, as a group of very noisy Catholic schoolgirls filled the train with their voices, that the concept of eternity was an essential component of the history of Western civilization, a large piece of the puzzle that had vanished from view. Eternity had a history and history had eternity in it, at least in the West, and hardly anyone seemed to notice. It mattered little that those plaid-skirted schoolgirls and no one else on the train seemed remotely conscious of eternity at that moment. No one seemed too aware of the electric current that propelled the train, either, or of the so-called self-evident truths and unalienable rights that allowed them all to pursue happiness freely, attend a private school, and choose between the *New York Post* and the *New York Times*. The deeper that something is embedded in your daily routine, the harder it is to see it or to appreciate its historical contingency.

Eternity had a history, it dawned on me, as did those unalienable rights; and maybe it was high time for someone to write about it, concisely, for even when it's absent from view, eternity can make a hell of a difference. As a historian of religion and a specialist in the early modern period—when the concept of eternity underwent a major redefinition—I knew that eternity had definitely played a role in the shaping of the West.

So I began to think about this history of eternity.

One thing led to another, and before too long I was discussing this project with Fred Appel, at Princeton University Press, who encouraged me to pursue it. Then I received an invitation to deliver the Spencer Trask Lectures at Princeton, in November 2007, and those three lectures became the framework for this book. I would like to thank Fred for making this book happen, for without his encouragement and his wise counsel it might have never seen the light of day or taken its present shape. I also thank those on the Public Lectures Committee at Princeton who extended the invitation and made my visit so enjoyable and productive.

In addition, I thank all those who have read drafts of this work and improved it with their advice, especially the two sharp-eyed readers who commented on the first draft of this book, and the third reader, who set me straight about astrophysics. A special thank you also goes out to Charles Marsh, a long-time friend, who created the Seminar for Lived Theology, and to all of the members of this circle, who have inspired and challenged me over the past four years and whose friendship I treasure: Mark Gornik, Patricia Hampl, Susan Holman, Alan Jacobs, and Charles Mathewes.

I also thank my agent, Alice Martell, whose advice, support, and encouragement have been essential from start to finish.

And, fittingly, as the page proofs were being readied for inspection, travel brought this project—and these acknowledgments—to an end at a location as unlikely as the train on which it had all begun. While visiting what used to be East Germany, I ended up, quite by chance, at a singularly bad spot, perhaps one of the worst on earth: a street in Berlin where the remains of two totalitarian empires converge, and where one can easily feel overwhelmed, even choked, by terminal temporality and the presence of evil. There, at one of the few remaining stretches of the Berlin Wall, a fellow traveler captured my image. Behind me stands the only surviving Nazi building in Berlin, the former headquarters of the Luftwaffe, which was converted after Hitler's demise into the seat of the repressive communist government of the so-called German Democratic Republic. To my left, on the other side of the crumbling relic of the Wall, once stood the building that housed the Gestapo and its torture chambers. I could think of no better author photo to use, for one of the central arguments in this book is that when we lose eternity as a horizon we can end up with totalitarian, materialistic nightmares. And that spot, right there, is as nightmarish a testament to materialism gone mad as one could ever hope not to find. All during this trip I'd been taking photos of my own shadow, at different locations. Thank you, Kayla Black, for insisting that I return home with something more than that, and for capturing that poignant slice of eternity, so shadow-free.

And finally, as always, I thank my lovely wife, Jane, for so many things large and small, which would add up to a very long list. Eternal thanks, always. *Per omnia saecula saeculorum.*

A Very Brief History of
Eternity

1

Big Bang, Big Sleep, Big Problem

> The death of any human being is an outrage; it is the out-
> rage par excellence, and all attempts to diminish this out-
> rage are contemptible, no more than opium for the masses. . . .
> Death is the unacceptable. The annihilation of one memory
> cannot be compensated for by the existence of the universe
> and the continuance of life. The death of Mozart, despite
> the preservation of his work, is an utterly evil thing.[1]

Why dawdle? Let's stare the monster in the eye, close up, right away: this book amounts to nothing, and so do you and I, and the whole world. Less than zero.

So the experts tell us.

These pages and all the words in them will burn up and vanish into oblivion some day, along with every word ever written, every trace of our brief existence and that of every living creature that has ever squirmed on the face of the earth or in its waters.

So we might as well revel in brusqueness.

Never mind that you and I are both headed for certain death, or that our species might face extinction. That's not the worst of it. No. Ponder this: not a speck will be left of you and me; no trace at all. And no number of progeny we engender, and no amount of technological marvels they invent, will make any difference either. Nothing can thwart the ultimate ecological and cosmic crisis.

Figure 1.1. Gustave Doré, illustration for Dante Alighieri's *Divine Comedy* (1861), *Paradiso*, canto 31, verses 1–3, showing the empyrean or highest heaven, where God dwells eternally. For many centuries, eternity was conceived of not just as some other dimension beyond time but also as a location: eternity was identical with the highest heaven above the stars, also known as the empyrean heaven. Dante's fourteenth-century epic poem, *The Divine Comedy*, is a tour of the afterlife: hell, purgatory, and heaven. Widely acknowledged as one of the greatest masterpieces in all of literature, *The Divine Comedy* reflected, shaped, and reinforced medieval conceptions of eternity and their cultural role.

In this scene, at the apex of the cosmos, God is seen as a brilliant light, surrounded by a swarm of very orderly angels. The image draws on nineteen centuries of tradition, and even more, for the circle is an ancient universal symbol for eternity. The fact that this image looks like a depiction of the Big Bang is no accident, even though neither Dante nor Doré knew anything about it.

Five centuries separate the poet Dante from the illustrator Doré, but both faced an equally daunting challenge: representing eternity itself, the source and the ultimate destiny of human existence, as understood in the Christian West.   *Source: La divina commedia di Dante Alighieri*, ed. Eugenio Camerini, illustr. Gustave Doré (Milan: E. Sonzogno, 1869), vol. 3.

First, about a billion years from now—whether or not humans still exist—the sun will grow hot enough to evaporate our oceans, burn away the atmosphere, and incinerate all living organisms. Forget global warming, the melting of the polar ice caps, the depletion of the ozone layer, the shrinking of the glaciers, the swelling of the oceans, the inevitable reversal of magnetic fields, and all the dire predictions that bombard us nowadays, ceaselessly. Forget any other cataclysm anyone might forecast, even a collision between earth and a comet or a giant asteroid. This solar flare-up will be the real deal, the mother of all disasters. Global incineration.

Then, to add insult to injury, in five billion years or so the sun will balloon into a red giant and consume what is left of the earth. Shortly afterward, relatively speaking, this bloated sun will extinguish itself and shrivel into a dark, dwarfish cinder, a pinpoint shadow of its former self, adrift in an ocean of subatomic particles. Planetary and solar annihilation.

But that's not the end of the story. It gets worse. Even if our progeny manage to colonize other planets in distant galaxies and evolve into a smarter, less violent species, even if they manage to prolong their lives for centuries or millennia, or eradicate pain, poverty, and disease, or find a way to live in constant ecstasy, certain annihilation lies in store for them.

Since our material universe is in perpetual flux, ever expanding, it's bound to vanish, in one way or another. Scientists propose several models for the eventual destiny of the cosmos, none of which is comforting. Whichever fate ultimately befalls the whole shebang depends on how fast the universe is actually expanding relative to how much matter it contains—something that has not yet been determined. But no matter where it's headed, exactly, our universe is in for a very rough and tragic ride.

One possibility is that the universe will expand forever and suffer a "cold death," as physicists call it, reaching a temperature of absolute zero. This is the Big Freeze, which could also be called the Big Stretch or the ultimate Big Sleep. Eternal dissipation: a cold, lonely, and dark eternity, ever abounding in nothingness. Linked to this is the highly paradoxical proposition that an ever-expanding universe will eventually slow to an infinitesimally minimal crawl as a result of maximum entropy. Physicists speak of this as "heat death," but I suppose it could also be called the Big Whimper. This, too, sounds awful: an eternal now in which nothing happens. Another possibility is that the universe will stop expanding and collapse on itself and disappear, in a monstrous self-immolation. Cosmic annihilation: no more time and space. As there was a Big Bang, so will there be a Big Crunch.

But that may not be the end of everything.

For all we know, the Big Crunch could be only the prelude to another Big Bang, and then another Big Crunch, and so on, and so on, forever and ever, ad infinitum and therefore also ad nauseam. For all we know, this is how it has always been and ever will be: bang and crunch, always and forever: Yes, the Big Yo-Yo, known in earlier ages as the eternal return.

These are the endings that our scientists propose, ever mindful of their disagreements and of the humbling fact that their grand theories, like those of historians, are somewhat tentative, subject to revision. But in many ways, even before there were astrophysicists or telescopes or microwave probes or infrared spectrophotometers, human beings seemed to intuit the impending doom, fitfully.

About 2,700 years ago, the prophet Isaiah said that our earth would one day vanish, and that it would "not be remembered, nor come into mind" (Isaiah 66:15).

Seven hundred years later, one of the books of the Christian New Testament would be more explicit: "The day of the Lord will come as a thief in the night; in the which the Heavens shall pass away with a great noise, and the elements shall melt with fervent heat, the earth also and the works that are therein shall be burned up" (2 Peter 3:10).

The Zoroastrian magi of Persia, the astrologers of the Mayas and the Aztecs, the shamans of the Hopi voiced similar predictions about cosmic doom, as have clairvoyants and kooks of all sorts, all around the world, at different times, down to our own day.

It's an outrage. *C'est un scandale, le scandale par excellence.*

So much for my property and yours, or the Louvre, the Vatican Library, Disney World, the pyramids of Giza, the Great Wall of China, or any of the kitsch sold at these tourist traps. So much for all precious gems, every tombstone at every cemetery, every monument, every fossil hidden from view, and every coin ever minted. So much for all family photos, lovingly kept dust-free, and those old home movies and videotapes painstakingly transferred to digital video disks. So much for everything, including this book, of course, and your socks and underwear.

Everything will turn to nothing. And there will be no one there to witness this epic ontological reversal. Nobody. No one. No consciousness, so they say; nothing there, nothing left behind. Not a thing.

Nihil. Nada. Nichts. Rien.

The same question asked of the tree in the forest could be raised here: If the universe vanishes and no one notices, will it have ever existed? But that is a very bad question, *une question mal posée,* as some aging existentialist might say. A better question for us human beings—we who are painfully aware of our own mortality—is this: What are we to make of our brief existence, both personal and collective?

As individuals, we blink on and off in the vortex of time with appalling evanescence, each of us, much like a firefly's butt on a warm summer night. We come and go like waves on a beach, as my wife's brother John said recently, at an old cemetery on the banks of the Hudson River, while we were depositing his father's ashes in a perfectly square niche in a massive wall containing hundreds of other such repositories, all duly graced with identical plaques that record not just the names of the deceased (including a man and wife *forever* saddled with the surname *Outhouse*) but also the very symmetrically paired dates of their birth and death. Burial grounds have a unique way of conveying the message we prefer to ignore. Relative to the age of the universe, it could be said that we hardly even register as ripples in a rain puddle, or that we barely exist at all. What is a decade compared to 13.6 billion years, the estimated age of the universe? What is it compared to the time the universe has yet left to exist? What is a century? A millennium? Come to think of it, what, really, is a measly 13.6 billion years?

Not much.

Any length of time, when measured against eternity, amounts to little. Next to nothing: not even as small as the period at the end of this sentence when measured against infinite space. If you have ever had a really lousy job, a job you loathed but could not afford to quit, then you know how pathetically brief every coffee break can seem. Well, imagine a fifteen-minute coffee break in hell that comes around only every 13.6 billion years. "*Kaffeepause, jetzt, schnell!*" Imagine how brief that would seem. Well, now imagine a 13.6-billion-year coffee break in a hell that is eternal. Same difference, more or less: still pathetically short, still next to *nothing*, really. Hardly worth it.

And what might eternity be? Is it anything other than a purely abstract concept, totally unrelated to our lives, or worse, a frightfully uncertain horizon, best summed up by Vladimir Nabokov: "The cradle rocks above an abyss, and our common sense tells us that our existence is but a brief crack of light between two eternities of darkness"?[2]

We loathe death, even pledge our love forever, and yet only very few of us can hope to last for one paltry century. Jeanne Calment (1875–1997), the woman with the longest confirmed life span in history, lived for only 122 years and 164 days, which adds up to a mere 44,724 days. What is that? Less than the wink of an eye, so to speak. An old vinyl record spinning at 33.3 revolutions per minute for a mere 24 hours will gyrate 47,952 times on its turntable. So, despite the fact that someone took the time and trouble to count them, Madame Calment's days on earth amount to less than one full day in the life of a vintage "long-playing" record, a device that did not exist when she was born and was already obsolete when she died. In 1988, a hundred years after the event, at the age of 113, she could still recall meeting at Arles the now famous but then ignored painter Vincent van Gogh, whom she described as "very ugly, ungracious, impolite, and crazy."[3] We are staggered by the thought that someone could have lived so long, and could still remember an encounter with someone long dead, whose work can only be seen in museums or purchased for millions of dollars. Nonetheless, her 44,724 days are but an insignificant sliver of time, less noticeable than a snowflake atop Mount Everest.

As for the human race altogether, the proportions of its existence are no better: as insignificant as an eyelash bobbing on the ocean. We humans have only been writing down our history haphazardly, for about five thousand years. That is an incredibly brief amount of time. Chances are that when she met van Gogh back in 1888, Jeanne Calment was within a stone's throw of the Roman amphitheater at Arles, which was already ancient and revered as a relic, despite its continual use as a Provençal bullring. Ancient Rome might seem very distant to you and me, but we would only need about fifteen Jeanne Calments, laid end to end, chronologically, to take us back to the days when gladiators killed each other in that arena. Imagine fifteen people in a room. It's a very small number. The ideal number for a college seminar. Now try to imagine forty people. That is the number of Jeanne Calments required to take us back to the dawn of civilization in Sumeria during the Uruk period, and to some old Mesopotamian lady who could remember Gilgamesh as "very ugly, ungracious, impolite, and crazy," with bad breath to boot. Forty is a small number of people, too, hardly enough customers for a fine restaurant on any night of the week.

The farther back one reaches into the past for some sense of proportion in the history of the human race as a whole, the more ephemeral that history seems, the more life-denying its relative nothingness. Before Sumerians devised writing for record keeping they had already been farming for about two thousand years. Imagining two thousand years of history without any written record of what happened is very difficult for any historian, perhaps for most people who give it any thought. What happened to all those people, during all that time? Imagining twenty or forty or a hundred thousand years without records, or without farming or cities, is even harder.

Experts now say that our species, *Homo sapiens*, appeared in Africa about a quarter of a million years ago, and that, oddly enough, we are all descended from one woman, as the authors of Genesis claimed way back when myths ruled the day.[4] This means we have no record of what happened to this woman's progeny, our kin, for roughly 245,000 years. The Paleolithic age, when all we had were crude stone tools, at best, covers the greatest portion of our time on earth, or roughly ninety-eight percent of human history. That is also around 2,050 Jeanne Calments or so, if we choose to reckon time according to the longest confirmed life span. If we include our immediate hominid ancestors—Neanderthal, *Homo erectus*, Australopithecus, and so on—we can go back a million years, or two, which amounts to more than 8,000 to 16,000 Jeanne Calments, roughly the number of students at many top-notch research universities. Contending with such a thought is impossible. Forget it; the mind reels.

What is my life span or yours, compared to so many others that are lost in an inconceivable, impenetrable fog? And what are all human lifetimes compared to the age of the earth, or of the universe? As nothing, really. Chances are that you are familiar with the following attempt to make sense of our place on earth: If the history of our planet is reduced to a twenty-four-hour scale, with 00:00 hours equal to 4,600,000,000 years ago and 24:00 equal to our present time, then the most rudimentary life would appear at 4:10, land-dwelling plants at 21:31, dinosaurs at 22:46, and *Homo sapiens* at 23:59:59.3, a split second before midnight. Your lifetime and mine do not even register on such a scale, except as the smallest of fractions, with enough zeroes after the decimal point to make a seasoned accountant dizzy. The same is true of our Ur-mother, Eve, and every one of our Paleolithic ancestors.

Yet when we lay eyes on art from the Paleolithic age, we peer into a very distant mirror, and thousands upon thousands of years seem to evaporate, instantly. We know these cave dwellers were our kin, and we are stunned. They weren't knuckle-dragging troglodytes or half-beasts but men and women with thoughts and emotions and abilities like ours.[5] Their genius, buried in silence, lost to time, can only be guessed at, but here and there it has survived, along with evidence of cannibalism: the Venus of Willendorf (22,000 BCE); the cave paintings at Chauvet (30,000 BCE), Altamira (18,000 BCE), and Lascaux (16,000 BCE). Some might even say, as did the ancient Romans and Greeks, that those early years of human history were a golden age, an ideal stage. After visiting the caves at Altamira and seeing its antediluvian paintings, Pablo Picasso supposedly exclaimed, "after Altamira, all is decadence." Some would like to agree with this quip, or to believe it was really uttered by Picasso.[6] Others who contemplate the leftovers from cannibalistic feasts also found in such caves, however, might agree with Thomas Hobbes, who described life in those times as "solitary, poor, nasty, brutish, and short,"[7] or with St. Augustine, who argued that there is a beast raging within all of us, itching for mayhem at all times. Some of us might be more comfortable with ambivalence, and a quotation from Dickens: "It was the best of times, it was the worst of times."[8]

And there's the rub: apparently, these sublimely ambiguous physical signs point to a rejection of the brevity and brutishness of life. Many experts think that the cave paintings and the fertility figurines were religious in nature, and an attempt to transcend mundane existence. Paleolithic burial customs lend credibility to this hypothesis, for the caring respect shown to the dead, and the ritualistic behavior implied by such care, point to a belief in something beyond the material world.[9] Acceptance of the brevity and finality of human life, and of the limitations of nature, was apparently as much of a quandary for them as it is for us. Contemplating a yawning abyss of nothing after the loss of dear ones, then, could have been as tough on our cave-dwelling ancestors as it is on us, even if they ate their enemies. Perhaps tougher, for they lacked spices and antibiotics, and didn't have three hundred channels of television programming to distract them. And no cocktails, either.

Thinking and feeling that one *must* exist is part and parcel of human experience. Conceiving of *not being* and of *nothingness* is as difficult and as impossible as looking at our own faces without a mirror. As Miguel de Unamuno put it almost a hundred years ago, "Try to fill your consciousness with the representation of no-consciousness and you will see the impossibility of it. The effort to comprehend it causes the most tormenting dizziness."[10] Strict materialists would say that this does not necessarily point to the existence of some transcendent reality beyond the physical universe, to which we are attuned as a species, or as individuals. They would most likely say that nature has encoded us to think and feel this way, or that it is simply impossible to imagine our own nonexistence because our brains are not equipped for such a task, and never will be.[11] And they are probably one hundred percent correct in making that assumption. All life on earth is programmed to survive, and thrive, and reproduce. Occasionally, nature goes berserk and living beings kill themselves, be they lemmings, beached whales, or anguished artists, such as Vincent van Gogh, who may or may not have been troubled by his own churlishness. But the vast majority of living organisms go on living and struggling to thrive, even as others die by the thousands, or hundreds of thousands, or even millions. If you doubt this, simply consider that over 150,000 people die every day on planet earth. That is about one per second, or over twice the number killed by the atomic bomb the United States dropped on Hiroshima on August 6, 1945. If the Nazis had been able to achieve that same death rate in their extermination camps, it would have taken them only forty days to kill six million people. Do the math, and you might begin to wonder why you are still alive. The grim reaper is the ultimate workaholic.

Death always intrudes rudely, uninvited; very few living beings ever consciously seek it out, even when they refuse to wear seatbelts and smoke three packs of cigarettes a day. Scientists affirm this concept, emphatically and without question. This is why no credible scientist has yet attributed the extinction of any species to mass suicide. Human beings in particular are not exempt from this encoding, which is crucial to the survival of all life on planet earth. We even pass laws making suicide a crime.

Nonetheless, the fact that our preference for life over death is a survival tactic genetically encoded by nature in every fiber of our being does not necessarily make death seem any less rude to us, or repulsive, or scandalous, or unfair. And it is precisely this incongruity, this chasm between what we are compelled to feel and what we know must happen, that makes death seem so heinous and unnatural, and worthy of our contempt. And this scorn is perhaps one of our chief unquestioned assumptions, universally embraced. Who, for instance, would not resonate with one of the most famous poems of our time?

> Do not go gentle into that good night,
> Old age should burn and rave at close of day;
> Rage, rage against the dying of the light.[12]

Countless texts, both ancient and modern, offer us proof that human beings have been raging for a very long time. Sixteen centuries ago, when the Roman Empire was teetering on the brink of collapse, St. Augustine of Hippo gave voice to this sensibility, and to the ultimate unquestioned assumption, saying to his congregation: "I know you want to keep on living. You do not want to die. . . . This is what you desire. This is the deepest human feeling; mysteriously, the soul itself wishes and instinctively desires it."[13] Three and a half centuries ago, in the earliest days of the so-called scientific revolution, one of the brightest minds of that day, Blaise Pascal, burned and raged against the human predicament with icy logic. Ambushed by death at an early age, he left behind only formidable fragments of what would have been an even more formidable book on the human need for transcendence. Many of these fragments touch on the absurdity and unfairness of our mortality. One in particular sums up his moral outrage over the extinction of human life:

> Man is only a reed, the weakest in nature; but he is a thinking reed. There is no need for the whole universe to take up arms to crush him; a vapour, a drop of water is enough to kill him. But, even if the universe were to crush him, man would still be nobler than his slayer, because he knows that he is dying and the advantage the universe has over him; *the universe knows none of this*.[14]

This is but one side of the coin, so to speak. In addition to raging, we human beings have also tried to transcend death in positive ways. No matter how brief our collective presence on earth has been, relatively speaking, we human beings have sought to do more than simply survive, thrive, and reproduce, as our DNA impels us to do. We have also imagined more than this, more than the birthing, eating, digesting, reproducing, and dying. Human beings have imagined something beyond material existence, something beyond space and time. Inchoately and precisely, and in myriad ways, human beings have imagined an enduring life, some state of being beyond constant flux and evanescence. Human beings have imagined *eternity*, a permanent state of being. Whether by means of rituals and symbols or of clear, cold logic—or anything in between—we as a species have been intuiting or imagining or constructing very elaborate and sometimes elegant conceptions of *forever*, of permanence and endurance: we have imagined and even pined for whatever is the opposite of transience and impermanence and the nothingness from which we came, which always engulfs us, on all sides. In some cases this eternity has been actually experienced. Or at least some claim to have glimpsed it, for real. Poets and mystics, especially, make their rounds of eternity with embarrassing frequency. Take the Welshman Henry Vaughan, for instance, who penned these lines in the seventeenth century:

> I saw Eternity the other night
> Like a great Ring of pure and endless light
>   All calm as it was bright;
> And round beneath it, Time, in hours, days, years,
>   Driven by the spheres,
> Like a vast shadow moved, in which the world
> And all her train were hurled.[15]

At an opposite extreme, even a great skeptic such as Bertrand Russell, philosopher and mathematician, could find an odd sort of comfort in believing that our existential quandary could give meaning to life, and sustain all our thinking and striving. "Brief and powerless is Man's life; on him and all his race the slow, sure doom falls pitiless and dark," Russell was proud to admit. Yet this was no reason for despair. On the contrary, he proposed, "only within the scaffolding of these truths, only on the firm foundation of *unyielding despair*, can the soul's habitation henceforth be *safely* built."[16] Safety in despair: if that is not a leap of faith, nothing else is.

Russell may have had no patience for eternity, but nonetheless exemplified an innate human trait. One could just as easily refer to our race as *Homo credens* rather than *Homo sapiens*. What makes us unique among all living organisms on earth is not just the fact that we are rational, the fact that we *know*, and have managed to figure out many details of the structure of the physical universe, but also the fact that we seek coherence and meaning, that we imagine and we *believe:* the inescapable fact that we tend to be grossly dissatisfied and offended by the thought that we came from nothing and to nothing shall return. Perhaps even more significant is the fact that we as a species tend to find the very concept of *nothing* and the thought of *not existing* unimaginable and abhorrent, that we are disturbed by our own awareness of mortality, and conceive of existence beyond the here and now, *forever.*

That, precisely, is the subject of this book: how conceptions of *forever,* or eternity, have evolved in Western culture, and what roles these conceptions have played in shaping our own self-understanding, personally and collectively. In essence, this is a book about belief, about the ways in which the unimaginable is imagined and reified, or spurned, and the ways in which beliefs relate to social and political realities. Its subject is the largest subject of all, which has taxed minds great and small for centuries, and will *forever* be of human interest, intellectually, spiritually, and viscerally. Interpret *forever* as you wish.

Essential Boundaries and Definitions

When dealing with eternity—the ultimate boundless subject—the first order of business should always be the drawing of boundaries. What, exactly will be covered? What will not? Which approach will be taken? Which will not? What should the reader expect, or not expect? In other words, what this book is and what it is not needs to be made crystal-clear at the outset, for eternity is a subject that raises large expectations. Defining our scope and limits is an essential first step, and in order to do this, one has to establish not only what the book seeks to do, but also what it will definitely avoid.

This is a survey of the major ways in which an abstract concept has played a role in the development of Western culture. In other words, this is history, pure and simple. It is not philosophy or theology, even though it will deal with philosophers and theologians. I am a historian, and my own peculiar obsession has always been the intersection of intellectual and social history. One of the chief assumptions I have tried to challenge in all my work is the conceit that ideas matter very little or not at all in human history, that mentalities or collective thoughts and beliefs are mere symptoms, perhaps even involuntary reflexes or passive epiphenomena, flotsam and jetsam, meaningless effluvia in the septic tank of class conflict, bobbing on the surface of a swirling gurge of natural, economic, and political forces. Right up front, at the very start, the reader should know that I reject any history that overlooks the dynamic relation that often exists between beliefs and behavior. As I see it, a material determinism that excludes ideas is as wrongheaded as that type of intellectual history, now nearly extinct, that traces ideas from mind to mind over the centuries and assigns causality to disembodied thoughts. I speak from experience. Having lived under a doctrinaire Marxist-Leninist totalitarian regime that saw class struggle as the sole determining factor in all of history and sought to eradicate all "intellectuals," and having lost some of my family to its dungeons and firing squads simply because they dared to challenge dialectical materialism in public, I am especially sensitive to the dangers of reductionism, and especially of the material determinism that some historians accept unquestioningly.

More specifically, all of my work has focused on the way in which realms beyond those experienced by the senses have been imagined, and how these imaginings relate to social, cultural, and political realities and to people's behavior. This complex interrelationship of belief and material environments is hard to pin down, as far as terminology is concerned. What we are dealing with here is not simply *ideology*, for that is a term that normally refers to abstract concepts alone.[17] Neither is it *mentalities,* or *mindsets* or *worldviews,* for these terms refer to attitudes and habits of mind and behavior, with only vague references to the way in which environments and minds shape one another.[18] It is not *social theory* either, for that, too, has more to do with abstract thinking and certified experts than with anything else.[19] Very recently, Charles Taylor has used the neologism *social imaginary* to describe how people imagine their social existence, what expectations they share, and "the deeper normative notions and images which underlie these expectations." But what we are dealing with here is not exactly what Taylor's newly minted *social imaginary* has in mind.[20]

This book explores the nature and function of one concept and of how it evolved in one particular culture, that of Western Europe and of those of its colonies in which native cultures were eclipsed. Our main concern here is eternity as it pertains to human existence, not eternity as abstractly conceived. In other words, we will not focus so much on the universe itself, which came into existence long before humans entered the scene and could continue to exist without humans, as on the concept of eternal life for humans. This, then, is an existential, anthropocentric history of eternity, a history of how humans in the West have tried to insert themselves into the largest picture of all, and how they have dealt with a formidable conceptual imbalance: namely, that while it is certainly possible to conceive of an eternal universe without human beings, it is utterly impossible to conceive of eternal life for humans without an eternal universe. Consequently, since our prime concern is really the place humans have tried to conceive for themselves in eternity, this history will be quite different from that which an astrophysicist or a philosopher might write. Our focus will be eternity solely as it pertains to humans. You may be tempted to ask, Is this then more a history of immortality than eternity? My answer to that would be "no, not necessarily," owing to the conceptual imbalance just mentioned: that immortality, in and of itself, cannot be conceived of apart from some eternal realm.

The idea for this project emerged from a seminar funded by the Lilly Foundation, in which I have taken part since 2005: The Project on Lived Theology.[21] Terms such as *lived religion* and *lived theology* have gained acceptance over the past decade in several disciplines, not in spite of their vagueness but precisely because of it.[22] In essence, the concept of a "lived" set of religious beliefs acknowledges the two-way symbiosis that constantly takes place between the abstractly conceived and the concrete realities of life in the material world. And this acknowledgment is left wide open, allowing for a wide range of approaches. We are a long way from a universally accepted definition of this intentionally ambiguous term, but its broad contours are at least recognizable: "lived" theology is no mere list of doctrines, and "lived" religion is no mere code of ethics or set of rituals, viewed as the sole framework of human behavior. Lived religion is always in sync with specific environments, responding directly to certain circumstances and at the same time giving shape to its environment, in a constant exchange. Speaking of this relationship as *symbiotic*, much as one would in biology, thus seems perfectly appropriate.

What, you may ask, is the difference between *lived religion* and *lived theology*? Suffice it to say that lived theology applies more directly to beliefs and ethics, and lived religion has a broader reach which includes rituals and symbols along with the beliefs and ethics. You may also ask, why not speak of *lived beliefs* rather than lived theology or lived religion? My answer would be that beliefs are covered by lived theology, especially in the case of religions that have well-developed doctrines and theological traditions. In the case of those religions that lack formal theologies, however, or of societies such as our own, which are secularized, to speak of lived beliefs might be more appropriate. For instance, throughout the democratic nations of the industrialized world, the equality of all human beings is a shared *belief*, not necessarily based on any theology. In Puritan New England or Afghanistan under Taliban rule, in contrast, everyone was forced by law to live out a specific *theology*.

As far as this book is concerned, I would prefer to speak of lived beliefs, for a simple reason: we are dealing here with about four thousand years of history, give or take a few centuries. This means we have a very broad focus across a vast landscape, covering many different cultures and time periods, tracing the evolution of ideas and paradigms rather than theology per se, which, as normally understood, refers to the formal belief system of one specific religion or tradition.

To study "lived" beliefs is to delve into one of the most deeply entrenched dichotomies in modern and postmodern thought: that which distinguishes between "material factors" and "ideas." This binary template is most often applied when historians deal with causality. At its most extreme, this dichotomy is turned into an antagonistic either/or proposition, and when this happens it is usually the case that the material factors will be proposed as the "real" causal agent, while the ideas are curtly dismissed as a response, or a by-product of the material factors. This reductionism is not only wrongheaded but dangerous, for it lessens the value of one of the things that make us human beings who we are, and in the process provides a template for dehumanization, especially of the sort exalted by totalitarian regimes. Ideas are part and parcel of human existence, and so are beliefs. And they do make a difference. Sometimes, a hell of a difference. The fact that they are invisible and unquantifiable does not necessarily mean that they are inconsequential. Human behavior is all about the interaction of mind and environment, and it is not a simple one-way relation, in either direction. Charles Taylor, who is a philosopher rather than a historian, has summed up this interdependence succinctly:

> What we see in human history is ranges of human practices which are both at once, that is, "material" practices carried out by human beings in space and time, and very often coercively maintained, and at the same time, self-conceptions, modes of understanding. These are often quite inseparable. . . . Just because human practices are the kind of thing which make sense, certain "ideas" are internal to them; one cannot distinguish the two in order to ask the question, which causes which.[23]

In sum, this book takes it for granted that lived beliefs are that nexus between the abstract and the concrete: they are the manifestation of convictions that in some way or another proclaim a higher, transcendent reality beyond the physical universe and the here and now—a reality that promises all the order and purpose that seems to be missing among mortals in time and space. Allow me to provide but one brief concrete example of what tends to be meant by lived religion: it is the last will and testament of Father Juan de Talavera Salazar, written in Madrid in 1587, in which the priest named his own eternal soul as *heredera universal*, or sole heir of his earthly estate. "It is fitting that my soul should now enjoy the fruits of my labor," he declared, "and that my earnings all be spent in masses and sacrifices, so that through these devotions and through His mercy, God my redeemer may save me." Sinking everything he had earned into something totally beyond this world, as into some eternal retirement plan, this priest (ostensibly an exploiter who foisted false beliefs on the masses, according to Marxist historians) expected a real return on his investment.[24] His choice was not at all unusual. In fact, it was commonplace, and expected: His will—a legally binding document—made eternity a crucial part of the Spanish economy. So did every other will in Spain at that time, for it was required of all testators to include some minimum number of mass requests. Multiplied millions of times over, in will after will, such bequests made eternity a very real thing in his day and age.

So, to move as quickly as possible from the abstract to the concrete, and back again: this book explores how that transcendent higher reality has been conceived in the West, and how such conceptions relate to social, political, and economic structures, and even to specific lives, such as that of Father Juan de Talavera Salazar. Since there is no concept more central to the definition of transcendent reality in the West than that of eternity, it cries out for attention, especially from historians who seek to study lived religion.

A brief history of a large subject, like a good map of a large area, needs to be brutally succinct, and to condense and generalize fiercely while paying careful attention to all the essential details. It is a perilous venture for any scholar, for our profession values details, with good reason. Fortunately, we also value surveys and summaries, because we know that they serve an indispensable purpose of their own: after all, a life-sized map of the world would not only be useless but insanely cumbersome. Fully aware of the dangers involved, I have structured this book according to the most easily recognizable paradigm shifts that have occurred in the history of a single concept. "Paradigm shifts" are those moments in history when thinking changes irreversibly. It is a term that was first applied to the history of science to describe a change in basic assumptions that realigns all subsequent thinking, such as the so-called Copernican revolution, after which it became impossible for anyone to propose that the sun orbits the earth without being taken for a fool. Paradigm shifts occur not just in science but also in belief systems, even though when it comes to beliefs, the older interpretations can survive and even thrive alongside the new ones. When it comes to belief, then, a paradigm shift does not necessarily kill off older ways of thinking—although that can happen sometimes, as with polytheism in Europe—but it does certainly bring about the existence of a rival interpretation of reality.[25] Each of the chapters, then, traces one of four distinct periods, from ancient times to the present, each of which is distinguished by a different dominant paradigm, or conception of eternity. The periods covered by each chapter are not of equal length, but the chapters tend to focus equal attention on each period, more or less. Chronological symmetry has never been a pattern in the development of civilization (one need think only of the technology developed in the past century alone), but we historians are nonetheless compelled to impose a certain degree of symmetry on our summaries of the past so it can make more sense, much like cartographers who stretch and bend real landscapes in order to make intelligible maps of complex subway systems.

First, in chapter two, we cover roughly a thousand years, tracing the development of Western concepts of eternity back to their Greek and Jewish roots, up until the collapse of the Western Roman Empire (fifth century BCE–fifth century CE). The main focus of this chapter is the early development of Christian notions of eternity, viewed simultaneously as a rupture with the past and continuing expression of some of its most salient features. Chapter three covers the medieval period, a millennium during which eternity was tightly woven into the very fabric of Western society (500–1500). Chapter four traces and analyzes the early modern period, roughly two centuries during which the medieval synthesis of time and eternity was challenged and overturned (1500–1700). This chapter looks closely at those changes that this pivotal rupture with the past brought about—changes that marked a transition to modernity and continue to have an effect on us. Chapter five takes us from the Enlightenment of the eighteenth century up to the present day, a period during which the impact of eternity on Western civilization has steadily declined or almost disappeared. The final chapter takes stock of the impact that the decline of eternity has on us who live in the secularized West and offers some reflections on the ways in which we cope with the big problem that is at the heart of all thinking on eternity and will therefore never vanish from view: that of our own mortality. Naturally, this last chapter is somewhat different from those that preceded it, and more like the introduction you have just read: meditative in tone and approach, it seeks to situate the main subject in our own immediate historical context.

A few basic points need to be touched on before delving into the history of eternity. First and foremost, one has to admit that the concept of eternity has boundaries as complex and bewildering as those of the old Holy Roman Empire, and that the word *eternity* can be understood in various ways.[26] Three of the most common definitions of eternity are:

1. As time without beginning or an end, or *sempiternity*.
2. As a state that transcends time wholly and is separate from it.
3. As a state that includes time but precedes and exceeds it.

In addition, *eternity* is often linked to the concept of *infinity*, or confused with it. Normally, in common speech, infinity is understood as endless space and eternity as endless time, but infinity can also be applied to time and eternity to space, often inappropriately or carelessly. In Western history, eternity also became inseparable from conceptions of God, who tends to be ascribed both eternity and infinity, along with prescience, or foreknowledge of all events. Moreover, in Western history eternity has also been given a human dimension, insofar as it touches on conceptions of an afterlife, and beliefs about heaven, hell, apocalyptic millennia, the New Jerusalem, and whatever else might follow earthly existence. This overlapping meaning could be very vague, even totally devoid of religious substance, as in the novel and film entitled *From Here to Eternity*. Or it could lead to speculation about what may lie between time and eternity, and the invention of terms such as *aeviternity*, which applies to angels and demons; or to the development of doctrines such as that of *purgatory*, where souls are cleansed of their sins after death on some time scale that is vastly different from that of earth.

This book will not plot a way out of this terminological labyrinth. Not at all. But it will definitely encompass all of these conflicting and overlapping approaches to eternity, and analyze their role in the history of the West. Similarly, this book will not seek to answer metaphysical, epistemological, and ontological questions, much less those of dogmatic or systematic theology. But it will definitely try to make sense of this question: What difference has eternity made in history? What difference might it make for us now? To anyone who asks "Is time contained within eternity, or outside of it?" or "How can humans have free will if God has fore-ordained everything from before the beginning of time?" or "What was the eternal God doing before he made time and space?" I can only respond as a historian. Which means that when it comes to philosophy and theology, the best I can do is to quote St. Augustine. When faced with that last query just mentioned, here is what he said: Before God created heaven and earth, he was busy designing hell for people who ask such questions.[27]

To imagine eternity is to venture beyond the world of sense experience, to ponder the unimaginable, to contemplate the ultimate. Eternity is beyond comprehension, but not beyond the mind's grasp. It is no mere logical conundrum, something contradictory or fantastic, such as a square circle. Neither is it a "hiccup of gross irrationality," as some extreme materialists like to argue.[28] Eternity is a real logical possibility, with many dimensions; it is as much an epistemological and metaphysical question as a scientific or even ethical and political one. Eternity is a subject closely linked to religion, philosophy, psychiatry, and astrophysics, but not limited to them. It is a subject without boundaries, of as much interest to the faithful on their knees as to atheists and agnostics who analyze images of the outer reaches of the universe sent back to earth by the Hubble telescope. Eternity is at once an abstract idea and a practical concept, a puzzle for logicians and cosmologists and a goal for individuals and societies; to grapple with it is to search for meaning and purpose, or ultimate justice, even if one is not conscious of the fact. Given the vast size of the subject and the stakes at hand—both personal and cosmic—none of this should be surprising.

Measured against eternity, all time seems outrageously insufficient. What is a billion years but a fraction of an infinite number, or of something much greater, beyond number? Or, even worse, just a fraction with a beginning and an end, something sandwiched at both ends by nonexistence? Any history of eternity, then, no matter how long or short, is ridiculously brief when measured against eternity itself. Another way of putting this is to say that the only definitive history of eternity would be an eternal one, without beginning or end. And that would be as useless as a life-size map of the earth. So, perhaps, since anything short of that is insufficient, and our time on earth runs out too quickly, a brief account seems best. When one also considers that all books and everything else are *as nothing* and will one day vanish completely into oblivion, then the "perhaps" can vanish too.

In the meantime, as you and I wait for our inevitable end, all we have is time, and time can seem very precious—even if it is *as nothing*. Some, like Sigmund Freud, might say it is all the more precious for precisely that reason. Time has relative value not only when measured against eternity, but also against itself. Who has not felt this? Even Albert Einstein admitted it, when trying to explain the concept for which he is best known. "When a man sits with a pretty girl for an hour, it seems like a minute," he said. "But let him sit on a hot stove for a minute—and it's longer than any hour. That's relativity."[29]

So let us move along, and make the best of the ticking of the clock. I don't know about you, but I can't wait *forever,* and I rage, rage against the tick, tick, tock, and anything else so pathetic, so much a reminder of the Big Sleep and the grim reaper's inexorable approach.

Eternity Conceived

In principio

Some time in the twelfth century, an English cleric from Lincoln named Philip embarked on a pilgrimage to Jerusalem, which was then considered the holiest place on earth, and the most direct and intense link to heaven and eternity. Like many other pilgrims of his day, Philip never made it to the Holy Land, or back home. But the reasons for his failure were somewhat unique. Much to his surprise, he had found a superior destination in Champagne, of all places, at the relatively new Cistercian monastery headed by Bernard of Clairvaux. Writing to the bishop of Lincoln to explain why his canon Philip would not be returning, St. Bernard had the confidence to say:

> He [Philip] has taken a short cut and arrived quickly at the place of his destination. . . . He has entered the holy city, he has chosen his heritage with those of whom it is rightly said: "You are no longer exiles or aliens; the saints are your fellow citizens, you belong to God's household" (Ephesians 2.19). . . . Therefore, rather than a curious spectator, he is a devout inhabitant and an enrolled citizen of Jerusalem, not of this earthly Jerusalem to which Mount Sinai in Arabia is related, which is in bondage with her children, but of that free Jerusalem, which is above. . . . And if you insist on knowing: this is no other than Clairvaux. She herself is Jerusalem, affiliated to the Jerusalem which is in Heaven, by the complete devotion of the mind, by the imitative way of life and by a spiritual affinity.[1]

Figure 2.1. Ouroboros swallowing its tail, from a fifteenth-century Greek alchemical manuscript. The Ouroboros, also spelled Ourorboros, Oroborus, or Uroborus, is one of the most ancient symbols of all, found in many cultures. It depicts a serpent or dragon devouring its own tail and forming a circle. The word *ouroboros* derives from the Greek ουροβόρος, "tail-devourer." It has multiple meanings but is most often interpreted as a symbol of eternity and infinity, especially of a cyclical nature: creation out of destruction, life out of death, eternal renewal and destruction.

This symbol shares in the symbolic meaning of the circle, with an added organic twist, blending a perfect geometrical shape with a biological entity that represents nature and the physical world. Circles represent eternal life and perfection and serve as barriers, or boundaries between the inside and the outside. The Ouroboros has a long history of use in religion, magic, and alchemy. In the twentieth century the psychologist Carl Jung identified it as a central archetype of great significance to the human psyche.

Western conceptions of eternity, like the Ouroboros, have deep roots in antiquity and in basic human psychology. Moreover, ancient non-Christian ideas, symbols, and rituals concerning eternity could also survive alongside Christian ones, as evidenced by this image. To fully understand eternity in the West, then, one must begin with the distant past.

In other words, Philip was freed from all earthly responsibilities and even certain vows because Bernard's monastic community had gained him entrance to eternity. Simply put, he was now beyond time and space, within the precincts of the heavenly Jerusalem. Whether or not he was still physically present on earth, a few hundred miles south of Lincoln, or still had bad teeth, or kidney stones, or dirt under his fingernails, made absolutely no difference: he was in another dimension by "spiritual affinity."

St. Bernard's rhetorical gambit speaks volumes, any way one looks at it. The mere fact that he could employ such outrageously inflated language with the bishop of Lincoln, hoping to be understood, shows clearly that the concept of eternity—which was inseparably joined to that of heaven or the New Jerusalem or paradise or any eschatological or apocalyptic projection beyond earthly historical time—held a central place in their way of thinking, and also their way of life. Eternity was no mere abstraction or metaphor but rather the ultimate destination, as real as legal obligations, or money, or death. Eternity was an ineffable mystery, to be sure, but of no less value in human interaction than material objects such as crowns, precious gems, contracts, wool, salted fish, produce, and plows. In fact, to say it was not as "valuable" or as "real" as anything is to sell the concept short, and to surrender totally to anachronisms and present-day assumptions. Among the elites who ruled back then, eternity was constantly invoked as a superior reality, higher in value than temporal existence. And that metaphysical conceit was not only part and parcel of social, cultural, political, and economic life but also a highly charged touchstone for strife between church and state, or even within the church itself.

But how did things get to be that way? Why aren't they still like that? How did eternity emerge in the West as something more than a mere concept? How did eternity materialize as a fourth dimension and an organizing principle for life, and then gradually disappear? What difference does that make for us?

To answer these questions, we must go back to the beginning—not the absolute beginning, but just the start of the arc that we can trace through written texts in the ancient cultures from which the West arose. It is not just all that we have time for but literally all we have. And this chapter must be more intensely focused on ideas than on lived religion, for two reasons: first, because it is essential to understand the architecture of the conceptual structure of Christian thinking on eternity, and second, because we don't have as much evidence about lived religion in this period as we do in later ones.

This chapter, therefore, might seem unlike the first: much more technical in nature and less informal in tone. This is inevitable. Ancient philosophical and religious concepts of eternity are distant enough from our twenty-first-century mindset as to seem somewhat alien, though not necessarily incomprehensible, much like one's mother tongue spoken with a very thick foreign accent. As you read this chapter please keep in mind that later chapters will be less focused on the introduction of basic terms and distinctions. And as we move from abstractions about eternity to its concrete manifestations in everyday life, what has been covered in this chapter—remote as it might seem at first—should prove invaluable in comprehending our own day and age.

Eternity in Antiquity: Jerusalem and Athens

In Western culture, the concept of eternity has always been closely related to that of God, or his realm, heaven. Two

streams joined to form a single tradition: that of Greek philosophy and that of Jewish monotheism. Asking which is
more important would be foolish, for in many ways, one
cannot conceive of Christianity or its eternity without either
Athens or Jerusalem.

So let us begin with Jerusalem.

The desire for immortality is as ancient as civilization,
perhaps even as old as the human species itself. In ancient
cultures, the realm of the divine was often conceived of as
that of immortality, which is not the same thing as eternity,
for eternity is more than simply having no end: it is also having no beginning. *Eternity*, as such, was too much of an abstraction. Ancient myths were all about beginnings, and they
tended to speak of gods begetting gods, and even of gods
intermingling with humans, and of humans who either at-
tained or lost the gift of life immortal. One the oldest texts
on earth, *The Epic of Gilgamesh* (ca. twenty-seventh century
BCE), is such a tale; it relates the story of a partially divine
man's failed quest for immortality.[2] Myths were only part
of the total picture, however, inseparable as they were from
symbols and rituals that permeated daily life and punctuated
major transitions, including death. As everyone knows, the
ancient Egyptians had a very keen interest in life beyond this
world and did their utmost to ensure a safe passage, so much
so, in fact, that they are known to us chiefly through their
pyramids, temples, and mummies, the relics of their belief in
life after death. So, even if we remember the ancient Egyptians for their rituals and symbols rather than their myths, we
must grant that they exemplify a society and culture deeply
affected by its conception of time and mortality.[3]

Western conceptions of eternity have deep roots that
reach back to tales such as that of Gilgamesh, and the earliest pyramids in Egypt, and even further back. But, as anyone

who has pulled up a plant by the roots knows—to stretch this metaphor—the farther one gets from the main stem, the harder it is to number the roots, and the more bewildering their complexity. The roots we can trace most clearly when it comes to the subject of eternity in Western culture are Jewish ones, especially those that can be plainly seen in the Hebrew scriptures (the Old Testament of the Christian Bible).

Ancient Jewish conceptions of God, time, and eternity tended not to be very abstract, at least not until around the fourth century BCE, after all the books of the Hebrew scriptures had already been written. Experts tell us that Jewish thought and culture were profoundly affected by the so-called Babylonian exile in the sixth century BCE, when tens of thousands of Jews were forced to spend decades abroad, among the enemies who had pillaged and destroyed their homeland. One of the most significant changes, it has been argued, is the way in which Jews expanded their conception of God and eternity after being exposed to the tenets of Zoroastrianism, a dominant religion in Persia and the Babylonian Empire.[4] But it is not so much in tracing the genealogy of Jewish monotheism that one finds its essence. What matters most about the religion of the ancient Jews, as far as eternity is concerned, is the uniqueness of its conceptual structure, especially in a world where belief in a multiplicity of deities was the norm, and in which *belief*, in and of itself, was far less important than ritual. The exclusivity of the Jewish God also ran against the syncretistic grain of the ancient world, where the truth claims of one people's religion or any cult did not necessarily cancel out those of others but could instead be mixed and remixed in dizzying ways. Israel's God, Yahweh, was a jealous deity who brooked no compromise or intermingling of any sort: He alone was supreme, and true; all other deities and their rituals were false.[5] His personal name, יהדה (YHWH, or Yahweh), which means "I am who am," occurs more than 6,800 times in the Hebrew scriptures. It was a name so sacred, and so beyond normal speech, as to be considered the "Ineffable Name" or "Unutterable Name," or simply "*the* Name" (*Hashem*). In ancient times, only the high priest of the Temple in Jerusalem could utter the name, once a year, on Yom Kippur, the Day of Atonement. The practice arose, then, of substituting the word *Adonai* ("my Lord") in its place. This meant, of course, that whatever Yahweh revealed to his people, the Jews, was the ultimate truth. All others were in error, and their symbols, rituals, and truth claims mere illusions.[6] Even in the face of Zoroastrianism, a religion with only two deities, one good and one evil, Yahweh's ontological uniqueness reigned supreme.[7]

The Jewish God was radically "other" in yet another singular way: Yahweh forbade all depictions of himself. Nothing divine was to be depicted and incorporated into ritual. "Thou shalt not make unto thee any graven image, or any likeness of any thing that is in Heaven above, or that is in the earth beneath, or that is in the water under the earth."[8] The fact that Jews had no religious symbols, and especially no icons of their deity, made him all the more mysterious, and more removed from this world. And this abstraction—a God who is beyond representation—made it logically necessary to conceive of everything divine as radically "other," including the divinity's relation to earthly time. At a time when religion was all about symbols and rituals, as well as about multiple deities, the Jews stood out as unique—or at least were supposed to. We all know that the Hebrew scriptures are filled with accounts of how Yahweh's chosen people disappointed him repeatedly by hankering for some idols to worship.

Naturally, Jewish conceptions of Yahweh were never static, or carved in stone (even if his commandments were), and one can see this reflected clearly in the Hebrew scriptures, where various traditions are layered one upon the other, and the God who reveals himself is inseparable from a people who grow and develop and change over time.[9] But one constant characteristic of Jewish monotheism that is not fundamentally altered with the passage of time, even when one takes into account earliest Jewish beliefs that simply placed Yahweh *above* other gods, is a belief in Yahweh's exclusive and superior oneness, and in his monopoly on Truth, with a capital "T." As the psalmist put it, "For Yahweh is good; his mercy everlasting; and his truth endures to all generations."[10] This joining of truth, revelation, and eternity was not elaborated on in the Hebrew scriptures but simply reasserted many times, unphilosophically. Yet this did not mean that Jewish conceptions of eternity and the divine were unsophisticated. It is very clear that Yahweh, the singular deity of the ancient Hebrews, gradually acquired personal and transcendent characteristics that placed *him* (rather than *it*) above space and time. The Hebrew God was not just there *in principio*, bringing everything into being, but also beyond comprehension, and also beyond time. As the psalmist put it, "Before the mountains were born, the earth and the world brought forth, from eternity to eternity you are God. A thousand years in thy sight are but as yesterday when it is past, and as a watch in the night."[11]

And if God was eternal, perhaps his covenant with his chosen people, too, could share in this dimension of his being. Although scholars disagree on how it was that belief in the resurrection of the dead emerged in rabbinic Judaism, and to what extent this belief was normative, there is no denying that this belief was part and parcel of the culture of the Second Temple period (536 BCE–70 CE), and that it was most definitely upheld by the Pharisees, from whom it was passed on to Christianity. Some have recently argued that belief in the resurrection of the dead and in the immortality of the resurrected was not a sudden invention of the Second Temple rabbis but rather a teaching that developed slowly and unevenly, and that it became inseparably linked to belief in the ultimate truth of God's promises among those who accepted it. After all, so ran one line of reasoning, if God is truly good and not a liar, then his promises to his people will have to be fulfilled in some way other than in this world, where death, disease, injustice, and national catastrophes such as the destruction of Jerusalem by its enemies seem to negate them, constantly. In other words, resurrection became an ethical and theological necessity among some rabbis, including, of course, Jesus and St. Paul.[12]

So, even though ancient Jewish thinkers were not given to abstractions or to thinking philosophically, and even though Jewish religion was very focused on rituals and proscriptions that reified the uniqueness of the Jewish people and of their bond with the one true God, the very concept that underlay this religion was, in fact, a momentous abstraction, with profound universal implications: the very idea that there was a single, monolithic "reality," controlled by the single deity who had brought it into being. Moreover, the very name of God, "I am who am," was a tautology with profound philosophical implications, which would eventually be unpacked by Jews and non-Jews alike. Add to that the conceit that this lone creator and ruler of all had struck an exclusive pact with only one people on earth, granting them direct access to the Truth, and the abstraction gets no less abstract, but it certainly becomes less open to universal acceptance. To become universal, Yahweh's eternity needed to become even more abstract and detached from any specific community. This is where the Greeks come into the picture.

So, on to Athens.

For the pagan philosophers of antiquity, especially in ancient Greece, from the seventh century BCE onward, eternity was related to questions of time, perfection, and the emergence of the physical world, not to questions about a jealous God with an unutterable name who revealed himself to one tribe alone. Incongruously, although Greek philosophers belonged to a culture in which polytheism and religious syncretism were the norm, and in which all conceptions of reality received their ultimate expression through myth, symbol, and ritual rather than through sacred scriptures or logical discourse, Greek philosophers were nonetheless able to arrive at conceptions of a single, monolithic "reality" in ways that dovetailed with those of the Jews, but without the hulking presence of their jealous Yahweh. It is no small marvel, but also no accident, that concepts from these two radically different cultures would one day merge, giving rise to Christian—and Western—eternity, despite resistance from some Christians who would have preferred no such merging, such as Tertullian, a third-century North African, who carped, "What has Athens to do with Jerusalem?"[13] The very idea that such a thing as reality exists and that it can be apprehended not only links these two traditions but is the very foundation of all traditional Western conceptions of time and eternity.

Classical philosophy touched on the subject of eternity from various vantage points, posing interrelated questions. Interested as they were in dissecting the fabric of the world, and even the structures of their own thought, the ancient Greek philosophers distinguished between the kind of thinking one could do about physical world—which included mathematics, geometry, astronomy, botany, and so on—and the kind of higher, more abstract thinking one could do to make sense of the natural order: thinking that analyzed the very fabric of that order, plumbing the nature of reality itself. Eventually, this sort of thinking would be called *metaphysics*, that is, thinking about what lay beyond (Greek: *meta*) the physical order and gave it its structure and its existence.

By asking questions about the very fabric of reality, outside the context of pagan mythology, Greek philosophers could not avoid dealing with something as basic as time. What was it? Why did everything have to happen sequentially? Why were motion, flux, and impermanence the very structure of our physical world? Why was it that "you cannot step twice into the same river," as Heraclitus put it in the fifth century BCE? Could there be some existence not determined by flux? If this world is all about coming into existence, constantly changing, and ceasing to exist, how does the whole cycle begin? What made it begin? Could there be some sort of existence without beginning and end? Without diminution or lack of any kind? A state of *being* rather than *becoming*? And so on, question begetting question, answers giving rise to more questions.

When it came to metaphysics, then, Greek thinkers honed in on the concepts of permanence, endlessness, and perfection vis-à-vis impermanence, sequential time, and mutability. In addition, questions arose about the very nature of existence, or being. Why is there something instead of nothing? What does it mean to "be," especially in light of the fact that all is in flux? Is there anything that simply "is" without beginning or end, or change, or wear and tear? With great subtlety, Greek philosophers then began to focus on the difference between "necessary" and "contingent" being, that is, between what always "is" and what is not. Eventually, thinking about such questions would be dubbed *ontology*, that is, the study of being (Greek: *ontos*, being). Such abstract thinking, and such careful parsing of questions and categories of thought, allowed for the concept of eternity to emerge in Greek philosophy, despite the absence of a lone creator god upon whom all depended for existence. Understanding how Greek thinkers developed various "logies" (Greek: *logia*, knowledge, or science of) that honed thinking ever more precisely, looking at reality from multiple vantage points, is crucial not only to understanding how classical philosophy worked but also to apprehending the structure of abstract concepts such as eternity, for eternity is not at all within the realm of space, form, and number, like a triangle in a geometrical theorem, but by definition is totally beyond that. Its "beyondness," or transcendence, then, is its very reality. Consequently, eternity depends entirely on thinking, and more precisely on the ways in which it is thought about.

This is why one may say: no ontology, no eternity. At least not the eternity that was conceived in the West. And the same should be said for other Greek "logies," such as *epistemology* (thinking about the very process of thinking; that is, how do we know what is true?) and *teleology* (thinking about and determining the end or purpose of anything). When it came to epistemology, self-reflexive questions needed to be raised about the ways in which the human mind—limited as it is by sense perception and its finitude—could grapple with thinking about that which is limitless. And teleological questions also had to be raised, for when thinking about the order of things, and their proper end or fulfillment, one must necessarily examine why they came to exist in such-and-such a way in the first place and how the "such-and-such" relates to time and flux.

At the most basic level, metaphysical and ontological questions concerning eternity remained closely linked to metaphorical or mythological language rather than to theology for the Greek philosophers, but nonetheless bordered closely on religion. Questions about the origin of the cosmos and its relation to time naturally encompassed the question of what being or entity or dimension might exist necessarily, above and beyond time. Perhaps the cosmos itself was eternal, without beginning or end? Moreover, such questions were always framed in reference to human existence, for Greek philosophy seldom lost sight of that essential point of reference. So it was that epistemology was as crucial as teleology, for questions about how one discerns the truth are linked to questions about the mind's capacities; and so it was that teleology was as essential as ontology, for questions about the proper end of human existence always loomed large in all speculation about eternity. And, so it was, too, that ethics, another branch of philosophy, entered into the picture.

Philosophical inquiry into the nature of existence could never be uncoupled from questions about the ultimate fate of human beings. In probing what the nature and purpose of human life might be, death always loomed large over every question mark. Was the proper end of humanity limited to physical existence? Were we humans capable of transcending death, of immortality? If so, then how did physical life on earth relate to whatever may follow it? Or to whatever may have preceded it? Such questions invariably led to questions about behavior, and morality, and about justice, rewards, and punishments. Consequently, ethics, too, entered into view when pondering eternity.

The two Greek philosophers who had the greatest influence on Western notions of eternity were Plato (ca. 428–347 BCE) and Aristotle (ca. 384–322 BCE), and of these two Plato was the most important. Of course, it would be absurd to claim too much for either of them. No philosopher ever thinks in a vacuum: they not only influence one another through constant disputation, they also reflect on ideas and attitudes that are part of their cultural, social, and political ambiance. What Plato and Aristotle did that sets them apart is that they set paradigms for thinking and behaving that ended up having a greater influence on the course of Western history, not just among the intellectual elites, but also on society in general. This can be explained in great part by the fact that they ended up having a more profound influence on the development of Christianity than their philosophical colleagues and rivals.

This should not be surprising. In ancient times, the line between what we would call religion and philosophy was very blurry. Philosophers founded schools and gathered disciples, establishing traditions that were elaborated on and passed down for generations. Some of these philosophical schools might seem very similar to religious cults from our postmodern point of view, since many were wholeheartedly devoted to living out their precepts. The followers of Epicurus (341–270 BCE), for instance, referred to him as *soter*, or "savior," convinced as they were that his teachings rescued them from ignorance and deception. Terms and concepts developed in some of these philosophical schools would help shape the Christian religion when it first emerged in the first century. The Gospel of John, for instance, depends heavily on the Stoic school and its concept of the *Logos*, that is, the "reason" or "word" that permeates the universe and gives it its order. The opening lines of John's Gospel identify the person of Jesus Christ as *Logos*, or "Word": "In the beginning was the *Logos*, and the *Logos* was with God, and the *Logos* was God. . . .Through him all things were made; without him nothing was made that has been made. . . . And the *Logos* became flesh and made his dwelling among us."[14]

This is not to say that Jews and Christians bought their Greek philosophy wholesale, or wrapped in identical, tidy packages. No, they took only bits and pieces from the Greeks. So, while the Stoic *Logos* was turned into Jesus Christ, other aspects of Stoic thought were tossed away. One of the most significant Stoic teachings rejected by Christians was that of cyclic history, or the "eternal return." According to this Stoic teaching, the cosmos underwent constant cycles of conflagration (*ekpyrosis*) back into Zeus and of radiations of new worlds out from him. As the Stoic Chrysippus of Soli (ca. 280–ca. 207 BC) put it, "Socrates and Plato will exist again and every man with his friends and his fellow citizens; he will suffer the same and do the same. Every city, every village and field will grow again. And this restoration will not happen once, but the same will return without limit and end."[15] Saint Augustine would ridicule this idea in his *City of God* as utterly preposterous.[16] In the nineteenth century, Friedrich Nietszche would attempt to resurrect it. But what matters the most here is not the idea of the eternal return but the fact that Jews and Christians adapted only certain aspects of Greek philosophy, and that it is only what they chose to accept—and how they accepted it—that ultimately made a difference in Western culture. And the two philosophers who would be favored above all others would be Plato and Aristotle.

So, on to Plato, first.

Plato (428–348 BCE), a disciple of Socrates (469–399 BCE), owed much to his mentor, and also to earlier Greek thinkers who had arrived at the conclusion that there must be some ultimate, underlying principle governing all of existence. Among these earlier thinkers, Plato was especially indebted to Xenophanes (b. 570 BCE), who proposed that a single eternal unity permeated the universe and governed it by its thought, and Parmenides (b. 511 BCE), who argued that everything outside of such an eternal unity—everything mutable and multiple—was less than "real." Plato conceived of existence in hierarchical terms, with eternity as a "higher" or "superior" realm, outside of time, in which were contained the eternal forms or ideas that were the source of the physical universe, the world of multiplicity and mutability. In his dialogues *Timaeus, The Republic,* and *Phaedo,* Plato contrasted these higher, eternal forms with their inferior pale reflections in the material world. Time itself was part of creation, inseparable from the world of motion, mutation, and becoming. In *Timaeus,* Plato conceived of time as "the moving image of eternity," and of eternity as timeless duration, or sempiternity. In *The Republic,* especially, he laid the foundations for a dualistic metaphysics in which everything in the world of time and motion was deemed inferior.

In what are perhaps the best-known four or five pages in all of his writings, Plato used allegory to illustrate his dualism, saying that the world we inhabit can be compared to a deep, dark cave, where we are all chained to the back wall, unable to perceive what is really happening beyond the cave's mouth. Since we are all chained to the wall from birth, we mistake the sounds and shadows that are dimly perceptible within the cave for reality, totally ignorant of the world outside, where the sun shines and people walk free. Anyone who escapes and sees what lies beyond the cave would instantly recognize that reality was very different, and that the world left behind was not only truly inferior but an appalling deception (an allegory reinterpreted for the digital age by brothers Larry and Andy Wachowski in their three *Matrix* films). As Plato put it, philosophers were the escapees, those who knew there was a superior, *intelligible* realm beyond sense perception, an eternal realm of *real* existence, of *being* rather than *becoming.* "The visible realm should be likened to the prison dwelling," says Plato. The purpose of life, our *telos* or proper end, lies beyond what we can see and touch. Life should be focused, then, on an "upward journey and the study of things above" rather than on the visible realm.[17]

Of course, if our telos, or proper end, lies beyond this world, there must be some part of us other than our bodies capable of reaching that goal. Plato's dualism applied not just to the visible and invisible realms but also to the human self, which was composed of body and soul. As Plato saw it, the *real* self was the soul (*psyche*), which was deathless and indestructible but had somehow fallen from the intelligible realm to a lower level of existence. How the immortal soul came to be trapped in a mutable body Plato did not care to explain, save by allusion to myths. His main concern was not explaining how the soul got here but rather how it could escape back to its true home, the eternal, intelligible realm. The process of returning was difficult, Plato admitted, but not impossible. Above all, it required an "upward" thrust for the soul, a detachment from visible and temporal existence. "I can't conceive of any subject making the soul look upward," said Plato, "except one concerned with that which *is*, and that which is invisible."[18]

In *Phaedo*, Plato expanded upon this conception of human beings as eternal in origin and destiny and of the soul as the ultimate identity, emphasizing the inferiority of the body and its role as a temporal prison for the eternal soul. "The soul reasons best when none of the senses troubles it," he said, "but when it is most by itself, taking leave of the body and as far as possible having no contact or association with it in its search for reality."[19] Making eternity the goal of human existence, and assigning it a huge ontological advantage over temporality, at the expense of the body and the physical world, Plato bequeathed to the West a conceptual package that not only would be ambivalently embraced but would become an essential component of its complex and somewhat self-contradictory identity. Among other things, by reducing the body to a nuisance and an obstacle to the true eternal destiny of the human soul, all physical pleasure was made suspect. Plato's description of what awaits a purified soul can sound very familiar to anyone who has heard of the traditional Christian heaven, precisely because that heaven is its offspring. A pure soul, said Plato, "makes its way to the invisible, which is like itself, the divine and immortal and wise, and arriving there it can be happy, having rid itself of confusion, ignorance, fear, violent desires and the other human ills."[20] Plato thus elevated humanity to a very lofty suprasensual destiny, but at a certain cost: the denigration of all things visible and temporal. Which, by the way, explains not only the root meaning of the expression "platonic relationship" but also why good Platonists have always shunned loud shirts, trendy footwear, and tattoos.

A few centuries after his death, Plato's metaphysics were further refined along monotheistic lines by some of his followers, who are usually called Platonists.[21] Among these, none were more important than Philo, a Jewish contemporary of Jesus (ca. 15 BCE–50 CE), and Plotinus (ca. 185–254), a pagan, both of whom hailed from Alexandria, Egypt, arguably the most cosmopolitan city of the ancient world, a melting pot seething with religious and philosophical ferment. Their most significant contribution was to conceive of the source of creation and time itself as a single being that was completely above and beyond time, timeless rather than sempiternal. Philo, a Jew, naturally ascribed this timelessness to Yahweh, the God of the Torah, who was One and without distinctions, and slightly less jealous and wrathful than in days of yore. Plotinus conceived of a more complex divine triad: the One (eternal transcendent being), the Nous (mind), and the Psyche (soul). Both conceptions proved to be enormously influential for Christian thinkers. In fact, were it not for the influence of Christian Platonists who accepted these assumptions and passed them on, such as Origen (185–254), Clement of Alexandria (150–215), Gregory of Nyssa (335–394), and Augustine of Hippo (353–430), we wouldn't need to deal with Plato at all.[22]

Christianity and Western culture would also owe a large debt to Aristotle, one of Plato's pupils and colleagues. Aristotle's contribution was less mythopoetic than Plato's and less dualistic in outlook, and its impact was also less direct, or pervasive. Another way of saying this is that Aristotle's eternity was more of a concept than a destination, and therefore also something one might puzzle over rather than long for. Aristotle would come to have an enormous influence on medieval Christian philosophy and theology, but his impact on the shaping of eternity would apply more to learned circles. Contrasting necessary and contingent existence on purely logical terms, Aristotle conceived of eternity as an absolute ontological necessity: if anything exists at all, it must be derived from something that has eternal existence. In other words, in order for anything to exist, there must be a source of being that exists necessarily, for all times. As Aristotle saw it, then, the universe itself was sempiternal, successive, but without beginning or end.

Unlike Plato, Aristotle was perfectly content to accept the visible world as *real* on its own terms and eternity as a realm that does not exist beyond and outside the physical realm. His arguments for proving the necessity of eternity were all based, in one way or another, on three premises:

1. Concerning matter: that *something* cannot come from *nothing*. (And therefore, whatever exists must be derived from an eternally existing substratum.)
2. Concerning motion: that infinite regressions are illogical and impossible. (And therefore, everything that moves must get its motion from one single, eternal cause, not from some endless string of causes.)
3. Concerning time: that self-contradictions are illogical and impossible. (And therefore, there cannot be anything *before* time.)

Although Aristotle was no monotheist, Jews and Christians would find a natural fit between the person of the Hebrew God Yahweh—"I am who am"—and Aristotle's eternal, necessary cause of all being.

But it would take a very long time for that association to be made. And such rarefied arguments, while formidable in and of themselves, carried little ethical weight (unlike Plato's take on the body and its needs, for instance), and did not therefore help determine one's outlook toward material existence or one's behavior. For this reason, precisely, Aristotle's eternity ended up being that of the philosophers and theologians—a great set of conceptual tools for elites, rather than bricks and mortar for the construction of Christian society. And for the same reason, good Aristotelians have always tended to care less for poetry than for true-or-false or multiple-choice exams in metaphysics. As someone who was subjected to dozens of such tests in college, I can vouch for their earnestness.

But we are getting ahead of ourselves. Before we can begin to make sense out of Athens and Jerusalem as sister cities, we have to know how the distance and differences between them were bridged.

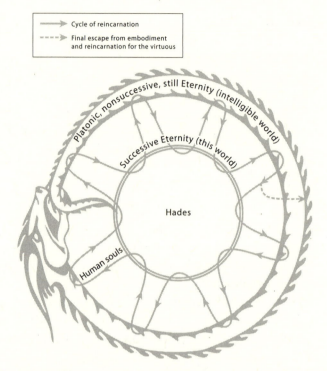

Figure 2.2. Cyclical eternity. This diagram attempts to capture the platonic understanding of the cosmos. In it, human souls cycle in an infinite loop, up and back from nonsuccessive eternity to this world. Eternity, or Plato's intelligible world, is represented by the Ouroboros (see figure 2.1).

Belief in reincarnation, also known as metempsychosis or the transmigration of souls, was fairly common in antiquity, as it still is in some Asian religions. Some early Christians adopted this belief, including the great Alexandrian philosopher-theologian Origen. Although it was explicitly condemned in the fifth century, this belief would also be adopted by several medieval Christian sects: the Paulicians, Bogomils, and the Cathars (also known as Albigensians).

Early Christianity: Martyrs and Philosophers

Merging Yawheh, the personal God of the Hebrews, with the ultimate principles of the Greek philosophers may not have been too difficult for some Christian thinkers, but this assimilation was not at all tidy. From the earliest days of the Christian religion, the issue of eternity was inextricably joined to that of salvation and the afterlife, since the promise of eternal bliss for humans was the most fundamental Christian claim. This paradoxical conjoining of the eternal with the temporal—this elevation of the mutable, contingent creature from time to eternity—was the very essence of the Christian message, but it was nonetheless inchoately expressed.

Adding fuel to the fire, so to speak, and making the smoke thicker, the earliest Christian message sought to convey at once a fulfillment of Jewish prophecies and a deep rupture in Jewish history. Somehow, for some mysterious reason, the Jews had rejected their promised Messiah, or savior, who had come to rescue not just the Chosen People but all humans from sin and death. That was the essence of the Christian message: all of the earliest Christian texts are heavily indebted to Jewish messianism, but at the same time they also proclaim that the Jews, as a people, had missed their Messiah, and that their religion had been eclipsed. Woven tightly into the fabric of the Christian message, one finds Jewish and non-Jewish notions of time and eternity. But neither the oral tradition nor the sacred texts cherished by Christians went beyond elementary, unexamined propositions. Moreover, overlapping and seemingly contradictory images of the afterlife abounded. In dozens upon dozens of Gospel texts, Jesus speaks of a "kingdom" to come, or a "kingdom of heaven" or a "kingdom of God." Forty other New Testament texts promise "resurrection," or belief in the reconstitution of corpses. Scores of other passages promise "eternal life," or speak of "eternal punishment." In one key text the crucified Jesus promises to the thief next to him an immediate entry into a better realm without any explicit mention of eternity: "Amen I say to you, today you will be with me in paradise."[23] Another key New Testament passage is at once explicit and vague about the life to come: "For we know that if our earthly dwelling, a tent, should be destroyed, we have a building from God, a dwelling not made with hands, eternal in Heaven."[24] Many other texts are filled with apocalyptic expectations, suggesting the imminent end of the whole world and a final judgment of the entire human race; while others yet hint at personal, individual judgments at the moment of death, such as the parable of the beggar Lazarus and the rich man who would not feed him.[25]

Yet no matter how fragmentary or inchoate its teachings on the afterlife might have been, the New Testament as a whole did convey one message very clearly and forcefully: earthly time was an inferior, flawed, passing phase of human history that was about to end. The promise of the kingdom of God involved a cosmic change from time to eternity, which entailed nothing less than the total annihilation of the present order.

> Then I saw a new Heaven and a new earth. The former Heaven and the former earth had passed away. . . . I also saw the holy city, a new Jerusalem, coming down out of Heaven from God. . . . I heard a loud voice from the throne saying, "Behold, God's dwelling is with the human race. He will dwell with them and they will be his people and God himself will always be with them . . . and there shall be no more death, or mourning, wailing or pain, for the old order has passed away."[26]

This significance of this conception was immeasurable, for it is difficult to find any Christian teaching, symbol, or ritual that is not in some way dependent on this assumption that the end of time is always potentially imminent. So, while the message itself was shrouded in mystery, its meaning was very clear: the redemption offered by Christ will be totally fulfilled through the irruption of a new, eternal cosmic order: a "new heaven and a new earth." Until that change occurs—that is, until humans live in eternal, resurrected bodies in a new cosmos—redemption is incomplete. In Paul's letter to the Romans, one of the oldest Christian texts, the redemption of every individual and of the cosmos as a whole are meshed inseparably in a common expectation, and in belief in a bodily resurrection and an eternally embodied life:

> We know that all creation is groaning in labor pains even until now; and not only that, but we ourselves who have the firstfruits of the Spirit, we also groan within ourselves as we wait for adoption, the redemption of our bodies.[27]

These texts, though very significant, are only part of the story. Ancient Christians encountered the sacred more often through ritual than through the reading of sacred scriptures. In fact, rituals informed the sacred texts themselves, as evidenced by Paul's letters, which are full of prayers and exclamations from common worship. And it was there, in their communal worship, that Christians encountered densely packed basic concepts repeatedly, including conceptions of eternity. The most significant prayer is also one of the most ancient, and can be traced to the first century: the simple *doxology* (praise) that ascribes eternal glory to God "forever and ever" (literally: "for ages of ages"; *toùs aiônas tôn aiónon* in Greek, *in saeculae saeculorum* in Latin).[28]

Throughout the first century and well into the second, the earliest Christians had to sort through their very rich and also somewhat dissonant teachings on salvation (that branch of theology known as *soteriology*), all of which, in one way or another, were directly related to their teachings on the end of life and the transition from time into eternity (that branch of theology known as *eschatology*). It was a mixed message: salvation was offered here and now through Jesus, but not completely. Not yet. Almost all experts now agree that the first generation of Christians expected the return of Jesus and the final judgment within their lifetime (an event which the New Testament refers to as *parousia*), and that when this failed to occur, they had to adjust to that harsh reality, and to the uncertainty that came with it.[29] Focusing on the end times and the transformation of the earth gradually gave way to focusing on the death of every individual, that is, on the way in which time would end for every Christian, one by one. This gradual transformation depended on an inchoate sense of the person and work of the savior, Jesus Christ, as beyond time, and of the individual Christian's relation to Christ as a participation in eternity. Through every Christian, history itself was transcended, even though history itself marched on, stained in the blood of the martyrs. Given the fact that persecution was an ever-present reality, martyrdom acquired a prominent place among Christians, and every such act of self-sacrifice came to be seen as an immediate point of entry to eternal life, not just for the individual who died but for the entire community. The interdependence of beliefs, circum-stances, and behavior in this case is enormously difficult to untangle: as persecution made martyrdom inevitable, so did belief in eternal life through self-sacrifice make persecution inevitable, even necessary, creating a circular, self-sustaining dynamic. One of the earliest Christian documents, *The Mar-*

tyrdom of Polycarp (mid-second century), relates how death could be viewed as a birth and the charred remains of the martyrs as manifestations of eternal life:

> So we took up his bones, more precious than costly stones and more valuable than gold, and laid them away in a suitable place. There the Lord will permit us . . . to gather together in joy and gladness to celebrate the day of his martyrdom as a birthday.[30]

Other early documents also give us a very clear glimpse of the way in which Christians embraced martyrdom as an immediate entry into eternity, and of the assumptions that made that embrace possible. Take, for instance, these lines from a letter written by Ignatius of Antioch on the eve of his martyrdom, sometime between 98 and 117 CE, as he awaited his entry into the "immortal love feast" promised by Jesus:

> I shall be a convincing Christian only when the world sees me no more. Nothing you can see has real value. Our God Jesus Christ, indeed, has revealed himself more clearly by returning to the Father. . . . Let me be fodder for wild beasts—that is how I can get to God. . . . I would rather that you fawn on the beasts so that they may be my tomb and no scrap of my body be left. . . . Then I shall be a real disciple of Jesus Christ when the world sees my body no more. . . . What a thrill I shall have from the wild beasts that are ready for me! I hope they will make short work of me. I shall coax them on to eat me up at once and not hold off. . . . Do not stand in the way of my coming to life. . . . Do not give back to the world one who wants to be God's. . . . I do not want to live any more on a human plane.[31]

Strong stuff. Not exactly appropriate reading for young children in Sunday school nowadays, when warning labels are affixed to *Sesame Street* videos, admonishing all good parents to shield their children from the horrors of Oscar the Grouch's bad temper and the Cookie Monster's penchant for stuffing his face with unhealthy, fattening snacks.[32] Yet this gory ethic of martyrdom was all the rage among early Christians precisely because their sensibilities were attuned to death and suffering and unimaginable violence as the entry to eternal bliss, as exemplified by their crucified savior, Jesus. Eternity was no mere concept for them, no distant realm. It was an immediate destination, a painful heartbeat away. The difference between them and Aristotle and Plato, and their abstract disquisitions on time and eternity, could not have been greater or more necessary, given the inescapable reality of persecution. Moreover, given the appeal of Christianity, which grew by leaps and bounds in the second and third centuries, one is led to conclude that martyrdom and eternity were inseparably linked. The adage coined by Tertullian in the third century, "The blood of the martyrs is the seed of the Church," could just as easily have been worded in two alternative ways: "belief in eternity is the seed of persecution" or "persecution is the seed of belief in eternity."[33]

It is precisely in the painful reality of persecution that we have our most solid evidence of a lived religion suffused with eternity, not just as a hope or belief but as a tangible reality. From the very start, as evidenced in the *Martyrdom of Polycarp* cited above, Christians began to venerate relics, and to mingle intimately with their dead. As points of contact with eternity, relics fulfilled many functions at once, but above all they reified the link between earth and heaven, time and eternity. The tomb inscription of St. Martin of Tours (fifth century) declared this linkage boldly: "Here lies Martin, the bishop, of holy memory, whose soul is in the hand of God; but he is fully here, present, and made plain by miracles of every kind."[34] As in the case of Polycarp, the martyr was at once a member of the Christian community on earth and of the celestial, eternal community in heaven: the relics themselves were "more precious than costly stones and more valuable than gold." In Polycarp's day, under persecution, this comparison with gems and precious metals was metaphorical. But as soon as persecution ceased and the emperors became Christian, the value ascribed to relics shifted very rapidly from the metaphorical to the economic realm.

Enshrined in costly receptacles known as reliquaries, which were most often made of gold or silver and bedecked with precious stones, relics became treasures, literally, and a focal point of the medieval economy throughout all of Christendom. Relics also sacralized the landscape, dotting it with entry points to eternity: the churches in which they were housed could eventually become pilgrimage sites, attracting thousands of travelers and creating networks large and small of paths to the sacred, which, in essence, were not too dissimilar from our modern tourist industry. One vestige of this ancient business that is still thriving is the "camino de Compostela," or "way of St. James," which runs along multiple paths that converge along the northern rim of Spain. This network of roads, which is dotted with medieval churches and shrines, attracts tens of thousands of tourists and pilgrims of all sorts, even atheists, who are eager to experience the thrill of the past rather than a foretaste of eternity on their way to the shrine of St. James the Apostle in Galicia, at the westernmost edge of the European continent.[35]

Relics also played a prominent role in court ritual, as avatars of eternity that legitimized the rank and authority of all earthly rulers. Relics also supposedly healed the sick and protected whole communities from natural disasters. It could be said that in many cases, the dead saints in heaven were the only doctors to be found on earth, and their relics the only medicine. In addition, relics also attracted some of the largest financial investments made by the elites of church and state, since appropriate reliquaries and shrines had to be built for them. In Rome itself, as in Constantinople and Jerusalem, and countless other sites, the costliest materials and the work of the finest, best-paid artists and craftsmen were lavished on these points of contact with eternity. Soon enough, by the sixth century, many of the values ascribed to relics began to migrate to their images as well, creating yet another dimension in symbol and ritual—and in the economy—of the Christian world. This is why so much of the artistic heritage of the West from the fourth to the seventeenth century is connected in one way or another to the cult of the saints.

Religion doesn't get more lived than this. Neither does eternity.

But Christians eventually got their turn at lofty scholarly discourse too, after persecutions ceased in 313, thanks to Emperor Constantine's conversion. By that time some Christians were highly educated and very familiar with Greek philosophy, especially with Platonism. Even while persecutions raged, Christians had made it their business to build bridges between Athens and Jerusalem, especially in the Egyptian port city of Alexandria, which not only housed the ancient world's largest library but also teemed with philosophical schools. One leading light of the Alexandrine Christian academy, Origen, was a living link between Athens and Jerusalem, and thus with philosophical dialectics and martyrdom. According to tradition, Origen not only studied with Ammonius Saccas, the same Platonist who taught the great Plotinus, but also lost his father to martyrdom in 202, and earnestly longed for the same fate. A towering intellect and a pioneer on many theological and philosophical issues, the

author of *On First Principles*, in which he laid down fundamental hermeneutical (interpretive) guidelines for the interpretation of the Bible, Origen also wrote *An Exhortation
to Martyrdom* in 235, and, during the persecution of Decius
in 250, eventually succumbed to injuries suffered under torture, earning himself the martyr's crown.[36]

Crossing over from an ethic of martyrdom to philosophical discourse, then, was obviously not much of a stretch
for early Christians. Their world-denying, body-distrusting
ethic could just as easily deal with eternity in blood-soaked
arenas, which were viewed as its antechamber, as in the
rarefied intellectual atmosphere of late antique academies.
Among the first to make a full transition, right after the end
of the persecutions, was another Platonist, St. Gregory of
Nyssa (335–94), who strove to make the proper distinctions
between time and eternity as a philosopher, eagerly trying
to argue that human beings, despite their temporality and
finitude, were indeed capable of enjoying eternal bliss.[37] Employing Greek terms such as *aion, chronos, kairos,* and *diastema* to make fine distinctions about different dimensions
of time,[38] Gregory raised Christian theological discourse to
new heights while simultaneously defending the ineffability of God and the capacity of human beings to experience
that ineffable reality.[39] Gregory also placed a very Christian
spin on Platonic notions of eternity by proposing that humans would continually progress in perfection, eternally, in
a process he called *epektasis.* Since there is no limit to perfection, or eternity, Gregory argued, the same applies to virtue,
and progress is never-ending. Many experts consider this his
most sublime contribution to Christian theology.[40]

Gregory of Nyssa was the prototype of the Eastern Christian theologian and bishop in the age of Christian emperors,
ever ready to marshal his philosophical training in the service

of the church. His take on eternity was at once abstract and practical: among other things, Gregory was a consummate man of prayer—a mystic, we would say nowadays—and above all else he was committed to defending the notion that Christianity offered humans the chance of encountering God and becoming God-like.

Yet St. Gregory was no head-in-the-clouds idealist. His take on eternity and perfection may have been influenced by his keen awareness of the imperfections that plagued the Church in his own day. Like many of his fellow bishops in the fourth century, he struggled to overcome paganism, which was still immensely strong, and to enforce a single, unified version of Christian "truth" in a world that was rife with different interpretations of the Christian message. Much of his attention was devoted to writing about the Trinity and defending the eternal nature of the Father, Son, and Holy Spirit against the Arians, followers of an Alexandrine Christian named Arius, who argued that the Son of God could not be eternal. The Arian controversy, which sharply divided the Christian community just as it was emerging from persecution, centered at its most abstract level on the question of eternity: if God the Father had a son, did this not mean that the son came into being *after* the Father? Arians argued that there must have been some interval outside of time when the Son did not yet exist, but Gregory and many others fought against such parsing of eternity and any attempts to speak of "before" and "after" in regard to God the Father and the Son of God.[41]

Gregory's side would win the battle eventually, but the cost would be steep. The Arian controversy would be the first of many great battles Christians fought with one another over the definition of *orthodoxy*, or "true teaching." These were theological controversies with intense social, political, and cultural dimensions that involved much more than mere theologizing, and eventually led to splintering among Christians and the creation of rival churches. Among the many lessons to be learned from Arianism, one of the most significant is the way in which abstract questions related to eternity could have an impact on daily life. If Gregory of Nyssa is to be taken at his word, the streets of Constantinople were abuzz with talk of eternity during the Arian controversy. Here is what he had to say about public interest in theology in that imperial city on the eve of the Council of Constantinople in 381:

> The whole city is full of it, the squares, the market places, the cross-roads, the alleyways; old-clothes men, money changers, food sellers: they are all busy arguing. If you ask someone to give you change, he philosophizes about the Begotten and the Unbegotten; if you inquire about the price of a loaf, you are told by way of reply that the Father is greater and the Son inferior; if you ask "Is my bath ready?" the attendant answers that the Son was made out of nothing.[42]

"Lived theology" or "lived religion" gets no grittier than this.

And speaking of gritty realities, few were as hard to miss during Gregory's lifetime as the growing rift between the eastern and western halves of the Roman Empire and its two capital cities, Rome and Constantinople. Gregory was firmly ensconced in the eastern half, where the Roman Empire would weather the great migrations of peoples from northern Europe that textbooks used to call the "barbarian invasions." Gregory's half of the empire would not only survive, it would also develop along very different lines from the western half. Christians in the surviving remnant of the Roman Empire would gradually drift apart from Rome and its version of

Christianity, for many reasons. Eventually, in 1054, the pope at Rome and the patriarch of Constantinople would break ties with one another, officially recognizing the differences between them as insurmountable. The eastern Christians, who preferred to be known as Orthodox (those who have the true teaching), would end up developing their own approach to just about every aspect of life, independently from their western brethren, who preferred to call themselves Catholic (those who are universal). Except for a few notable crossovers—two of which will be dealt with presently—the eastern Christian take on eternity, rich as it is, ceases to be directly related to the history we are tracing.[43]

So, let us turn back to the West, and Catholic Christianity.

Among the early Western Christians who grappled with the philosophical and theological dilemmas raised by the mingling of Jewish and Greek thought, no one proved more influential than Augustine of Hippo (353–430).[44] A consummate philosopher who did not become a Christian until age thirty-five, after delving deeply into the dualistic religion of Manicheanism (which had affinities with Zoroastrianism) and the philosophical theology of Plotinus, Augustine was obsessed with metaphysics, and especially with eternity and its relation to time. Augustine's conception of eternity was inextricably bound to his thinking on God, and also heavily influenced by the Neoplatonism of Plotinus. Like most Platonists, Augustine had no doubt whatsoever that the ultimate reality was eternal, and wholly above and beyond time. As a Christian and a bishop, Augustine baptized Plotinus, so to speak, converting his Triad into the Christian Trinity, and simply assuming that time was outside and beneath God's eternity. In other words, Augustine's God existed timelessly, without beginning or end, in an eternal now that contained time itself, past, present, and future, and transcended it:

It is not in time that you precede times. Otherwise you would not precede all times. In the sublimity of an eternity which is always in the present, you are before all things past and transcend all things future, because they are still to come.[45]

Divine fullness and eternity are one and the same in Augustine, coinciding as fully as the opposite ends of time: God is not only the *alpha*, the cause of all times, but the *omega*, the endpoint, or telos, of time itself, the sole source and fulfillment of all human longing, and of all of creation itself:

> You are before the beginning of the ages, and prior to everything that can be said to be "before." . . . In you it is not one thing to be and another to live: the supreme degree of being and the supreme degree of life are one and the same thing. You are being in a supreme degree and are immutable. In you the present day has no ending, and yet in you it has its end. . . . Because "your years do not fail" (Ps. 101.28), your years are one Today. . . . And all tomorrow and hereafter, and indeed all yesterday and further back, you will make a Today, you have made a Today.[46]

Augustine's meditations on time and eternity, most fully sketched in the eleventh book of his *Confessions*, were not only a lucid summation of various tendencies in late antique pagan philosophy and early Christian theology but also the foundation of much of medieval thought and piety, and even of the very structure of medieval society. His work synthesized the practical and the speculative, linking physics and psychology, philosophy and theology, and also politics and devotion.[47] Most significantly, Augustine also addressed the question of time in an ethical dimension, turning his rigorously philosophical queries into a meditation on Christian attitudes toward the world. Although he was obsessed with the question of eternity, and admitted that his mind was "on fire to solve this very intricate enigma,"[48] Augustine the Christian bishop felt compelled to transcend mere philosophical speculation, saying: "Lord my God . . . may your mercy attend to my longing which burns not for my personal advantage but desires to be of use in love to the brethren."[49]

And what was of use concerning eternity for Augustine? Nothing less than the claim that earthly time, in and of itself, was so insubstantial and illusory as to border on non-being, and the corollary assumption that human existence could only find fulfillment in eternity. Analyzing the essence of time in ways eerily close to those of some present-day physicists, Augustine came to the conclusion that time could not be defined or even explained. "What then is time?" he asked. "Provided that no one asks me, I know. If I want to explain it to an inquirer, I do not know."[50] But time was much more than an epistemological puzzle for him. It was also an ontological conundrum, uncomfortably close to sheer illusion. "Time flies so quickly from future into past that it is an interval with no duration," he observed. "If it has duration, it is divisible into past and future. But the present occupies no space."[51] Even the simplest and shortest word failed to capture the essence of the present *nunc*, or "now," for the word itself, when thought or uttered, was nothing but part of the unceasing, evanescent flow from the present to the past. In sum, time was nothing other than the past, which was irretrievably gone, and the future, which did not yet exist. "If future and past events exist," he groaned in utter frustration, "I want to know where they are."[52] Augustine's conclusion was as drastic as it was definitive: since "now" is a ceaselessly moving point between future and past, totally ephemeral, time itself is sorely lacking in substance:

Who can measure the past which does not now exist or the future which does not yet exist, unless perhaps someone dares to assert that he can measure what has no existence? At the moment when time is passing, it can be perceived and measured. But when it has passed and is not present, it cannot be.[53]

Abstract as such an insight might seem, it had profound practical implications. Its ultimate significance lay in the ontological claim that existence itself was only fully realized in eternity—and not just in sempiternity, that is, an endless flow from present into past, but in an eternity that transcended time: God's eternal now moment, in which there was no past, present, or future:

In the sublimity of an eternity which is always in the present, you are before all things past and transcend all things future. . . . Your "years" neither go nor come. . . . Your "years" are "one day" (Ps. 89:4; Pet. 3:8) and your "day" is not any and every day but Today, because your Today does not yield to a tomorrow, nor did it follow on a yesterday. Your "Today" is eternity.[54]

For Augustine, this eternity was the only realm in which humans could find true fulfillment. Herein lay the existential and ethical payoff of his meditation on time and eternity: the nature and purpose of human existence—the proper end or telos of every human being—was to reach such a state of being. And since anything less than God was less than eternal, God himself was the ultimate fulfillment of human existence. Hence the crushing urgency of Augustine's plaintive cry to God in the first paragraph of the *Confessions*: "You have made us for yourself, and our heart is restless until it rests in you."[55]

Augustine would not be satisfied with anything less than eternity, and, as he saw it, neither should any other Christian, or any human being. The younger Augustine who wrote the *Confessions* was still too much of a Neoplatonist to ponder an eternal embodied existence, but the older Augustine who wrote *The City of God* came around to see the promise of a resurrected eternal existence as the greatest and most universal of all hopes shared by human beings. "I know you want to keep on living," he said to his readers:

> You do not want to die. And you want to pass from this life to another in such a way that you will not rise again as a dead man, but fully alive and transformed. This is what you desire. This is the deepest human feeling; mysteriously, the soul itself wishes and instinctively desires it.[56]

He was not the first to voice such aspirations, nor was he alone in voicing them, but Augustine was certainly the most eloquent and, eventually, the most influential.

Augustine's longing for eternity had a social dimension; and he was as much a product of his environment as a shaper of it.[57] Conditioned by Manichean, Neoplatonist, and Christian communities to pose questions as he did, and to arrive at certain conclusions, Augustine distilled and passed on what he had learned at a crucial point in Western history, with consummate eloquence, reinforcing tendencies on two levels, intellectually and spiritually. On an intellectual level, Augustine's masterful treatment of time and eternity ensured that Western Christians would conceive of the subject on his terms.

In a very concrete way, Augustine provided medieval Christians with basic metaphysical definitions and the conceptual framework for all discourse on eternity, fixing God's eternity as nonsuccessive and nontemporal, that is, as a present moment extended over a life without beginning or end. A century later, Boethius (ca. 470–524) would pass on this Augustinian definition to many medieval philosophers and theologians, including Thomas Aquinas: "Eternity, then, is the complete, simultaneous and perfect possession of everlasting life."[58] On every level, intellectual, spiritual, and practical, Augustine can also be given a great deal of credit for teaching the West to view all of history and every individual life under the light of eternity, *sub specie aeternitatis,* an outlook consciously and eagerly embraced by many and constantly invoked by church authorities as normative for all.

Augustine's world came crashing down around him, literally, as Rome fell victim to barbarians from the north. As he grew old and outlived many around him, Augustine could not help but notice that the fabric of the Roman Empire was collapsing. Perhaps he saw an affinity between his own body, which grew ever frailer and closer to death, and that of the society in which he lived, which he associated with the world itself. It's tempting to speculate on what effect the advanced rot of the Roman Empire had on Augustine's thinking on eternity, but speculation won't take us very far. Suffice it to say, by the time the Vandals got to the gates of Hippo in 430 and Augustine was on his deathbed, eternity was probably more on his mind than ever. His *City of God* had defended Christianity against pagan charges that it had caused the downfall of the Roman Empire. Rome was collapsing under its own weight, argued Augustine: its own self-love, vices, and shortcomings were to blame, not the abandonment of the old gods, or the "weakness" caused by the Christian ethic of love and the Christian obsession with otherworldly realities. But one has to wonder whether Augustine underestimated the impact of Christian otherworldliness on his civilization and the effect of social disintegration on the Christian longing for eternity.

The world built on the ruins of Augustine's civilization was certainly full of otherworldliness and eternity; brimming over, even. And it is to that world we must now turn our attention.

Eternity Overflowing

If we wish to reach eternal life, even as we avoid the torments of Hell, then—while there is still time, while we
are still in this body and have time to accomplish all these
things by the light of life—we must run and do now what
will profit us forever.[1]

So reads the *Rule of St. Benedict*, written in the late sixth
century for the monastic community of Monte Cassino,
about eighty miles south of Rome. This was a manual that
outlined how monks were to live, work, and pray together,
apart from "the world," under vows of poverty, chastity, and
obedience. Monasteries were all about praying and fasting,
avoiding temptation, praising God, becoming holy, aiming
for undisturbed contemplation of God, and preparing for
eternity. The goal of monasticism was well established by the
time Benedict wrote his rule, and this goal is clearly reflected
in the paragraph above: monastic life was an investment in
eternity. You purify yourself here and now to "avoid the torments of Hell" and "reach eternal life." You "do *now*" what
will "profit" you "forever." Avoiding and gaining, investing,
profiting. It sounds almost like a business venture. And, in
many ways, it was.

Eternity was serious business in the sixth century. Perhaps
the most serious of all.

Figure 3.1. Rose window, Cathedral of Notre Dame, Paris (1250–60).

Rose windows symbolize many things at once and function on various levels—spiritual, intellectual, and emotional. Since the circle is a nearly universal symbol of eternity, rose windows are above all entryways to the divine and infinite.

All stained glass windows in churches reflect the mystical theology of Dionysius the Areopagite, as interpreted by Abbot Suger, who built the first Gothic-style church in the twelfth century, with large stained glass windows that bathed the interior in light of many hues and made the stones seem ethereally light. As Suger put it, the multicolored splendor of stained glass was supposed to transport the faithful "from material to immaterial things," raising them to a state of contemplation in which they would see themselves "existing on some level, as it were, beyond our earthly one, neither completely in the slime of earth nor completely in the purity of Heaven." Much like the circular mandalas found in Asian religion, the rose windows of medieval Europe seek to elevate the mind and spirit to a higher state of consciousness, even beyond space and time.   Photo © Karol Kozlowski/Dreamstime.com.

How it became that way for Christians has already been explained, in part. But the full context into which monasticism fits has yet to be outlined, as does the structure of a way of life that endured for a millennium, suffused with points of contact with eternity. That will be the subject of this chapter. But before we can go any further, we must turn our attention to that world we call the Middle Ages, in which eternity overflowed, for concepts never exist in a vacuum.

By the time St. Augustine died, in 430, the world he left behind was very different from the one he had been born into. Tribes from the north and east, Visigoths, Ostrogoths, and Vandals, had invaded the Roman Empire, wreaking havoc. More were to follow, including Franks, Huns, and Lombards.[2] His own town was not spared, all the way across the sea, in North Africa; soon after he died, Hippo was ravaged by the Vandals, whose name says it all. While many of the barbarians had been recently converted to Christianity, some were Arian Christians, like the Vandals and Visigoths: heretics in the eyes of both Rome and Constantinople. This difference would cause no end of trouble.

As things fell apart, the old Roman aristocracy was still resisting conversion to Christianity, but their opposition meant little in the long run. They could do nothing to stop the ancient temples from being demolished or transformed into churches. And they could do even less to stop the rude northern warlords who insisted on sacking their cities, dismembering their empire, and claiming their places at the top of the social hierarchy.[3]

As the known world collapsed, bit by bit, a new order of things arose in the West, chaotically. This disorderly change would endure for a few centuries.[4] In the East, the empire survived, and continued to thrive during that turbulent time.[5] Naturally, East and West drifted apart, also bit by bit. But they continued to share much. Linking these two very different worlds was the church, a well-ordered institution, and a common faith, which included a similar take on eternity and its relation to time.[6] Throughout this Christian world, certain institutions stood firm, and a certain order prevailed, an order that reflected and reinforced certain otherworldly values. An order in which eternity was "real," one might say, in the sense that it was woven tightly and in innumerable ways into the very fabric of society.

So, let us see in which ways eternity became the warp and woof of the medieval West.

Eternity, Monasticism, and the Mystical Quest

Augustine's legacy was crucial for the development of Western thinking on eternity both at a philosophical level and at a practical level. On the spiritual and ethical plane, Augustine gave expression to certain world-denying sentiments that were an integral part of Christian monasticism, a way of life he much admired and longed to embrace—a way of life that sought to reify Christian thinking on eternity and, at the same time, to blur the line between time and eternity on earth.[7]

The monastic worldview, while firmly rooted in theology, tended to exclude abstract speculation. As Godfrey of St. Victor put it in 1185, concerning theological hairsplitting: "Let us monks leave this question which holds very little interest for us, to the disputations of the scholastics, and devote our attention to other things."[8] What mattered most in the monastic tradition was prayer and the contemplation of God. For Bernard of Clairvaux, monks were Christians who "for a long time have been concerned with celestial realities"

and who constantly "make these the object of their meditations by day and by night."[9] In other words, monks were not
as concerned with figuring out how God was eternal as they
were with experiencing that eternity in the here and now,
as much as possible. Augustine's understanding of the nature and purpose of human existence was of one piece with
monastic ideals, for, as he saw it, nothing but the mystical
quest for union with the eternal God could satisfy the deepest longings of the human heart.

> Lord . . . You are my eternal Father, but I am scattered in
> times whose order I do not understand. The storms of inco-
> herent events tear to pieces my thoughts, the inmost entrails
> of my soul, until that day when, purified and uplifted by the
> fire of your love, I flow together to merge into you.[10]

At the time when Augustine wrote these words, it was commonly assumed by Christians that the surest way to "flow
together and merge with God" was through ascetic disci-
pline and the monastic life. Transcendence was the chief
goal of monks: detachment from "the world" and its fleeting
pleasures, coupled with unceasing prayer and meditation.
Within this monastic frame of reference, heaven and eternity were not some distant horizon, ostensibly, but rather an
imminent threshold within the cloister walls. Celestial themes
abound in monastic literature, often as the central focus of attention. "The contemplative life," said an anonymous monk,
is one "in which one aspires only to the celestial realities, as
do monks and hermits." Entire treatises were devoted to the
subject of eternal bliss, with such revealing titles as *On Celestial Desire*; *On the Happiness of the Celestial Homeland*; *On
Praise of the Celestial Jerusalem*; or *For the Contemplation and
Love of the Celestial Homeland, Which is Accessible Only to
Those Who Despise the World*.[11] Monks may have often fallen

short of their goals, but in their literature, monasticism itself tended to be viewed as realized eschatology—as an entry point to one's eternal destiny. Monasticism could also be viewed on less individualistic terms, as a communal eschatology: even apocalyptic themes could surface, as evinced by St. Bernard's reference to Clairvaux as the heavenly Jerusalem, the ultimate redeemed society.

Monastic literature was filled with numerous accounts of divine epiphanies and references to eternity, including accounts of visions, apparitions, ascents to heaven, and other such phenomena in which the boundaries between earth and heaven collapsed. Accounts of visits by souls in hell or purgatory were also rather common, as were those of raptures, ecstasies, and other brushes with the eternal realm. Many of these accounts tell of communal events rather than personal experiences, mostly in connection with ritual.[12] Prayer and chant were an essential component of monastic life, and a readily accessible connection with eternity. When Bernard of Clairvaux spoke of his monastery as the heavenly Jerusalem, it was not just because of the asceticism observed by the monks but also because of their liturgical life, which mirrored the adoration of God by his angels in heaven and created a bridge to eternity. Bernard was fond of telling his monks that the angels were always among them, accompanying their singing.[13] Another monastic, Mechtild of Hackeborn (1241–1299), claimed she could hear the angelic voices, and once reported that when the cherubim and seraphim took their turn, the chant became so melodious that no harmony on earth could compare with theirs.[14]

Monasticism thrived, in part, due to this promised mingling of heaven and earth in the cloister. It is not at all surprising, then, that one of the most influential voices on heavenly and eternal topics in all of Christian history should have

Figure 3.2. Hildegard of Bingen, *Scivias*, twelfth century—an example of a monastic vision. Monastics often claimed they could receive visions from God and perceive realities beyond space and time. One of the few ever to depict her own visions was Hildegard of Bingen (1098–1179), who claimed she had "a blazing mind longing to soar above the clouds." In this image, the flames engulfing her head represent her connection to heaven. Some historians of medicine have interpreted Hildegard's drawings as depictions of migraine headaches rather than as glimpses of eternity.

emerged from this milieu: Dionysius the Areopagite, who is also known as Pseudo-Dionysius because he faked his identity and pretended to be a first-century Athenian mentioned in the Acts of the Apostles 17:34, who was converted by the Apostle Paul on the Areopagus hill, near the Acropolis. Most experts agree that the four texts authored by Dionysius, known collectively as the *corpus aeropagiticum*, were most probably written in the fifth or sixth century by a Syrian monk who was well versed in Neoplatonism. Shocking as this deceit might seem, especially at the hand of someone writing sublime theology, such ruses were common in that day, when it was still relatively easy to fool one's readers: it was a way of claiming authority when one thought one had a very valuable message to promote. Experts now tell us, for instance, that some of the books in the New Testament make false claims too: the letter to the Hebrews, once thought to be St. Paul's, and the book of Revelation, supposedly written by St. John the Apostle, to name but two. While the real identity of "Dionysius" remains a mystery, the origin of the texts is now clear to us. Aside from the fact that no mention is made of them, anywhere, until the seventh century, the Greek in which they are written can be easily identified by its syntax and vocabulary and by its many similarities to texts by Proclus, a non-Christian Greek Neoplatonist who died in 485. Whoever he was (and some have speculated it could have been a *she*), Dionysius can hardly be blamed for playing fast and loose with time and identity. In the light of eternity, a subject of central significance in these texts, what is a mere five centuries?

The impact of the *corpus aeropagiticum* was immense, not just because of the extra authority lent to the texts by the author's assumed identity but also because of what is contained in them.[15] The four treatises, *On the Divine Names, On Mys-*

tical Theology, On the Celestial Hierarchy, and *On the Ecclesiastical Hierarchy,* compose a systematic theology that delves deeply into the nature of the divine and eternal and the relation between the human intellect and those higher realities. Taken together, they are a metaphysical and epistemological manifesto without equal, a road map of sorts to the cosmos and the human self. Heavily influenced by Neoplatonism, the texts of Dionysius are very focused on symbolic representation, hierarchy, the coincidence of opposites, and the limits of human language.[16] As far as eternity is concerned, one of Dionysius's major contributions was the affirmation of a deep connection between the temporal and eternal, and of the way in which contemplation of things in the visible world can lead the human mind to eternal realities.

Two of the four texts provided a crucial theological foundation for many of the claims made by the Christian church, both Orthodox and Catholic, principally concerning its intercessory role as nexus between heaven and earth, and as the sole gateway to *eternal* salvation. *On Celestial Hierarchies* outlines the composition of the realm of the divine and angelic worlds, eternity itself. Its companion volume, *On Ecclesiastical Hierarchies,* outlines the composition of the church on earth, highlighting its direct affinities with the hierarchies in the eternal realm. According to Dionysius, then, the metaphysical *and* physical are integrally related to one another in the church: it is a visible, material manifestation of the eternal order. Naturally, such a claim rung sweet to the church hierarchy, and, more than that, also helped it to defend the status quo repeatedly, with authority. Dionysius, after all, was taken to be a contemporary of Jesus, as ancient as the New Testament. In the West, Dionysius came in very handy repeatedly in conflicts between church and state, as an authority who defended the superiority of the church over all temporal powers. In the East, in the Byzantine Empire, where the line between church and state was very blurry, Dionysius also helped with church-state matters, but in different ways, as an authority who could be called on to legitimize various arrangements of the system known as *caesaropapism*, in which the emperor played a crucial role in church affairs, almost as pope-emperor, and in which the hierarchical order of the empire itself could be seen as a reflection of the eternal order in heaven.

On the Divine Names is a deconstruction of language itself, with an air of what we now call "postmodernity." Its chief insight concerns the relationship between temporal and eternal realities: the affirmation that any conception that we can have of the eternal God falls short, but, at the same time, can bring us closer to knowing him. In sum, negation and affirmation are equally necessary, and both positive and negative statements about God and eternity need to be transcended. For instance, Dionysius spoke of the "divine darkness" that transcended physical light itself, and of the true illumination of the human mind as immersion in this darkness, this knowing beyond ordinary conceptions. This way of thinking about divine realities would come to be known in Latin as the *via negativa*, or way of negation. In English it would acquire the name of *unknowing*; in Greek it would be called *apophatic* theology, that is, theology that refrains from positive assertions (Greek: *apophanai*, to say no). Arguing that the powers of the human mind are far too limited to comprehend God's transcendence, Dionysius points out how we humans can never apprehend the coincidence of opposites in the divine, which we can only express as contrary polarities: time and eternity, mercy and wrath, freedom and necessity, being and nonbeing, and so on. *On Divine Names* analyzes all of the names given to God in the Bible and argues, simultaneously, that each reveals something about God, but is also woefully inadequate. It would prove to be a very influential book, so influential, in fact, that its authority hardly diminished at all when it was proven by Lorenzo Valla in the fifteenth century that Dionysius had faked his identity.

On Mystical Theology is the briefest of the four treatises but also the densest, probing deeper into the ineffability of God. This text would have a tremendous impact on theology and piety, precisely because it is *not at all* written for beginners or those inexperienced in the mystical ascent. Although it does not have much to say about eternity, per se, its attempt to grasp the "superessential" through paradox is a giant leap into the realm of the eternal and inconceivable:

> I pray we could come to this darkness so far above light! If only we lacked sight and knowledge so as to see, so as to know, unseeing and unknowing, that which lies beyond all vision and knowledge. For this would be really to see and to know: to praise the Transcendent One in a transcending way, namely through the denial of all beings.[17]

Dionysius grapples with epistemology, ontology, and metaphysics, affirming that the eternal and divine can only be apprehended by transcending our normal thinking processes. Referring to the superessential reality as "it," Dionysisus piles contradiction upon contradiction, affirmation upon negation:

> As we climb higher we say this. It is not soul or mind, nor does it possess imagination, conviction, speech, or understanding. Nor is it speech per se. It cannot be spoken of and it cannot be grasped by understanding. . . . It has no power, it is not power, nor is it light. It does not live nor is it life. It is not a substance, *nor is it eternity or time.* It cannot be grasped by

the understanding since it is neither knowledge nor truth. . . .
There is no speaking of it, nor name nor knowledge of it.
Darkness and light, error and truth—it is none of these. It is
beyond assertion and denial.[18]

Part prayer, part theology, part philosophy, *On Mystical Theology* would become a key text for all mystics and many a theologian.[19] As we shall see, despite its abstractness and its esoteric nature, it would have quite an impact on the so-called real world and those within it who yearned to be mystics, and would even indirectly influence the invention of gothic architecture.

So let us return to the so-called real world and its would-be mystics.

Eventually, in the later Middle Ages, especially after 1300, monasticism began to lose its monopoly as a bridge to eternity. As Europe grew increasingly more urbanized and less feudal, religious fervor led some of the laity to imitate the monks by creating quasi-monastic movements such as the Beguines and Beghards or the Brethren of the Free Spirit.[20] And as these movements proliferated, the mystical quest gained popularity. One extreme example can shed light on the ways in which talk about eternity could capture the popular imagination: the case of the preacher known as Meister Eckhart (ca. 1260–1328), who tested the boundaries of orthodoxy with unusual daring.[21]

Meister Eckhart was a Dominican friar and scholar, equally adept in scholastic Latin discourse and vernacular preaching to lay folk. Involved in the spiritual direction of Beguines—lay women who tried to live as monastics without vows or strict cloistering—Eckhart became an immensely popular preacher in Cologne. The focus of most of his sermons was the mystical quest, which he interpreted in novel ways, through extreme paradoxical propositions. Among the various teachings he stressed, none was more significant than that of the spark of the soul, or *fünklein*, which claimed an intensely direct ontological affinity between God and humanity, proposing that all human beings were equally gifted with a divine presence deep in the core of their souls. This *fünklein*, Eckhart claimed, was accessible to all, and could be reached through a process of detachment from the world that did not necessarily require monastic vows or any sort of ritual. Eckhart would be accused of heresy on several counts, including that of pantheism, and therefore became suspect. But his legacy endured through the orthodox writings of some of his disciples, such as John Tauler (ca. 1300–1361) and Jan van Ruysbroeck (ca. 1296–1381), who professed the same teachings in more careful language and thus passed them on to succeeding generations of mystics and would-be mystics.[22] But there is no denying the fact that this highly individualistic brand of mysticism was as potentially dangerous to established authority as it could be potentially conservative. Eventually, this so-called Rhineland mysticism would wend its way through various translations to Spain, Italy, and France, and gain approval as supremely orthodox in the writings of mystics such as St. Teresa of Avila and St. John of the Cross.[23] At another extreme, this kind of mysticism would evolve in the radical branch of the Protestant Reformation, among dissenters such as Thomas Müntzer, a leader of the Peasants' War of 1525, and Sebastian Franck, one of the first Universalist Unitarians, who dismissed the Bible as "the paper pope."[24]

Eckhart's take on eternity was intensely anthropocentric, for he was concerned with eternity only as it touched on human existence and on the possibility of mystical union between the human and the divine. As far as God was concerned, Eckhart followed Augustine closely, assuming that the divine existed in an eternal realm that was above and beyond time. "All time is contained in the Eternal Now-moment," he declared in one sermon.[25] "As long as one clings to time, space, number, and quantity, he is on the wrong track and God is strange and far away," he added.[26] "To say that God created the world yesterday or tomorrow would be foolishness," Eckhart argued, "for God created the world and everything in the one present Now."[27] But as far as human beings were concerned, Eckhart went beyond Augustine, stressing a much closer ontological affinity between creator and creature. Eckhart's God was above all a paradoxical divinity, at once utterly transcendent and immanent. "God is closer to the soul than the soul is to itself," he proclaimed, "and therefore, God is in the soul's core—God and all the Godhead."[28] Distinguishing between "God" as he is in himself and "God" as a human concept, and also between "God" as person and "God" as divine essence (*Gottheit* in German, or *Godness*, translated as "Godhead"), Eckhart proposed that humans had the capacity to transcend time owing to the presence of the "Godhead" within them, in the spark of the soul. Even more shocking, Eckhart proposed a very trinitarian affinity between each human self and God by proposing that all divine realities could be found within the human soul, including the eternal begetting of the Son by the Father: "God's day is the real Now-moment, which for the soul is eternity's day, on which the Father begets his only begotten Son and the soul is reborn in God. Whenever this birth occurs, it is the soul giving birth to the only begotten Son."[29] Eckhart's claims stretched orthodoxy to its limits: "The soul that lives in the present Now-moment is the soul in which the Father begets his only begotten Son and in that birth the soul is born again."[30] Taking his conception of divine-human affinities to their ultimate logical conclusion, Eckhart seemed to delight in extreme propositions: "I am my own first cause," he boasted, "both of my eternal being and of my temporal being. To this end I was born, and by virtue of my birth being eternal, I shall never die. It is of the nature of this eternal birth that I have been eternally, that I am now, and shall be forever."[31]

Meister Eckhart died before he could defend himself against the accusations of heresy leveled against him. Some of those close to the tradition he expressed, however, were less fortunate. Accused of adhering to "the heresy of the Free Spirit," many of those men and women who believed in the radical connection with eternity within each human soul were hunted down, imprisoned, or executed as spiritual anarchists and antinomians.[32] Mystical access to eternity was a highly charged proposition. Without a doubt, all those who could claim access to the Eternal Now-Moment and the divine *fünklein* within them inherently challenged the hierarchical authority of the church, whether they did so explicitly or not.[33] But dissent or potential dissent was not the sole by-product of an intensely vivid claim on eternity in the Middle Ages. Eternity was there for all to grasp, simply by stepping into any church and taking part in its daily rituals.

Christian Ritual: Eternity Reified

Significant as the links to eternity were in the monastic and mystical traditions, they were limited to a select few: the spiritual elites. Nonetheless, the vast majority of Christians had their own access points to eternity, which they also shared with the monastics, as members of the same church. Ritual was one of the chief ways in which Western Christians imagined

and experienced eternity. As the monks had their divine of-
fice to chant day after day, the laity had their liturgies at least
once every Sunday, if not more often, especially in urban areas. The most important of all rituals was the celebration of
the Eucharist, or Mass, in which the bread and wine offered
by the priest at the altar were believed to change into the body
and blood of Jesus Christ. Every mass was a hierophany, a
miracle linking heaven and earth, and the temporal and the
eternal, for the body and blood of Christ were not only made
present but also offered as food to be consumed. In the crud-
est possible sense, Christians could eat and digest the eternal,
incarnate God.[34] Of course, they could also adore the consecrated bread, or host, which is what most of them did.

Whether ingested or adored at a reverent distance, there
was no denying the fact that the Eucharist brought Christians face to face with eternity, as then conceived. Jesus
Christ—God himself—somehow became present, as did his
sacrifice on the cross. Every mass was a reenactment or reliving of that awful moment on Calvary, centuries ago, made
manifest anew, repeatedly, everywhere. And every atom of
the consecrated elements contained God completely. It did
not matter how minutely one could dice a consecrated host
(Latin: *hostia*, sacrificial victim), Christ himself would be
fully present in each and every piece—the very same Christ
who sat at the right hand of God the Father in heaven, literally and physically, for eternity. The same was true of the
wine. Since Christ was believed to have ascended to heaven
in his resurrected body, this meant that the Eucharist was the
most dazzling and most frequent proof of God's ability to
transcend time and space and of the church's ability to link
heaven and earth, time and eternity.[35]

Though lay communion was rare, the mass still played a
pivotal role in piety. As the most frequently celebrated rite,

Figure 3.3. *The Mass of St. Gregory* by Albrecht Dürer (1511). This painting is a concise visual summary of late medieval beliefs concerning the Eucharist and its power to transcend time and space. It depicts a sixth-century miracle known as the Mass of St. Gregory, in which Pope Gregory the Great suddenly found himself face-to-face with Jesus Christ while he was celebrating Mass. This apparition in the flesh of the bloodied and bruised Jesus—"The Man of Sorrows"— was a graphic confirmation of several beliefs at once, including the sacrificial dimension of the Mass, the real presence of Christ in the Eucharist, and the power and authority of the priestly class as intercessors with eternity.   *Source:* Hermann Knackfuss, *Dürer*, trans. Campbell Dodgson, 5th ed. (Bielefeld: Velhagen & Klasing, 1900), p. 77.

the mass brought communities together for prayer, instruction, and celebration more often than any other ritual. As an enactment of the deepest mysteries of the faith, expressed symbolically, the mass allowed the laity to experience repeatedly a synthesis of the ultimate Christian values they ostensibly shared. As the ultimate ritual in which the divine was addressed and made present, the liturgy of the mass also acquired a therapeutic value. Masses known as "votive" could be offered to ward off or correct as many ills as can befall the human race: to protect crops from hail, to be spared by plagues, to prevent evil thoughts or lust, and even to help find lost objects. Some of these specific votive masses were offered locally, others more widely.[36]

And it was not just the thousands upon tens of thousands of masses offered all over Christendom every day that linked time and eternity but also those consecrated hosts miraculously transformed at the altar. Because the church taught that Christ was made physically present in the eucharistic bread and wine, the mass itself, and the consecrated bread, especially, became the supreme *locus divinitatis*, the ultimate materialization of the divine and eternal. If each consecrated bread wafer was indeed God, then devotion to this object seemed not only right and just but mandatory. Consecrated hosts were displayed for adoration in special vessels known as monstrances, which could be set up inside the churches or taken out for processions. Consecrated hosts were believed to work wonders, especially when denigrated by skeptics, heretics, and infidels. Reports of eucharistic miracles sharply increased in the fifteenth century, as did the number of shrines built to revere the hosts, which reportedly bled, levitated, or crippled their would-be assailants.[37]

It was also during the fifteenth century that the yearly feast devoted to the Eucharist, *Corpus Christi* or *Corpus Domini*, which had been established in 1264, assumed an especially privileged place on the Christian calendar. This summer feast was observed in towns and cities with pageants, mystery plays, and grand processions that sought to include the whole community, and especially its elites. On Corpus Christi day, the focus of devotion was the consecrated host that processed through the streets, sacralizing the world outside the churches. These processions served multiple functions at once, at various levels. On a social and political level, these very carefully arranged Corpus Christi processions, in which all participants traversed the streets arranged according to their place in society, with the lowest-ranking in front and the highest at the rear, reified and sanctified the hierarchical structure of every town and city. They also reified the church's claims to authority, especially in cases where monarchs or other rulers took part. In such cases, temporal authorities displayed their submission to the eternal God as mediated by the church, admitting through symbolic gestures what they often denied in their dealings with bishops and popes.[38]

The mass also loomed large in lay piety for yet another reason. Because every mass was believed to transcend time and space and to link all Christians, past and present, to Christ's sacrifice on the cross, this liturgy also assumed a practical spiritual and social function connecting time and eternity, the living and the dead. Theologically, masses for the dead lessened the time spent in purgatory by the souls of the deceased; practically, these masses functioned on various levels to cement relations among kin and neighbors. By the fifteenth century, masses for the dead had become a key element of lay piety throughout Europe, and a constant and unavoidable link between time and eternity. This subject of obsequies for the dead will figure prominently in the next chapter. For now, we must concentrate on another dimension of the Christian cult of the dead: their veneration.

It could be argued that one of the greatest changes brought about by Christianity in the late antique period was the redefinition of relations between the living and the dead, an area of human endeavor—and also a form of commerce with social, political, and economic consequences—that is inseparable from beliefs about the afterlife. Some years ago, Peter Brown argued that the joining of heaven and earth at the graves of the dead in late antiquity had not been explored as fully as it deserved, and then proceeded to fill the void with a brilliant study of the rise of the cult of the saints.[39] As Brown demonstrated, Christians reversed the ancient practice of segregating the living and the dead. By bringing the remains of their saints and martyrs into their churches and venerating them as points of contact with heaven, Christians reified some of their most basic metaphysical and theological assumptions, reordering social relations in the process.

Among those basic metaphysical assumptions reified by the cult of the saints, the most significant was that of the interconnectedness of matter and spirit, and time and eternity—an assumption neatly summarized in St. Martin of Tours's tomb inscription, cited previously, and quoted here anew for emphasis: "Here lies Martin the bishop, of holy memory, whose soul is in the hand of God; but *he is fully here*, present and made plain in miracles of every kind"[40] (italics mine). As we have already seen in the second chapter, relics localized not only the divine but also the eternal. In the words of Victricius of Rouen, every fragment of a saint's remains, even the most minute, was "linked by a bond to the whole stretch of eternity."[41] Devotion to relics had been part of the Christian religion since its earliest days, when the remains of martyrs began to be enshrined and venerated, and the practice expanded very rapidly as soon as persecutions ended in the fourth century. Throughout the late antique and medieval periods, the cult of relics was deeply woven into the fabric of lay piety and the rhythms of everyday life. As we also saw in the previous chapter, the cult of the saints was a significant component of the medieval economy, for the resources devoted to relics and their veneration were substantial among elites and non-elites alike. Shrines and reliquaries demanded the very best and costliest materials available and often required an uncommon marshaling of resources: stone, lumber, glass, gems, and precious metals, all of the highest quality, usually assembled by the most skilled builders, artisans, and artists.[42]

One of the most detailed accounts we have of the building of a shrine is that of Abbot Suger (1081–1151), who constructed the first chapel in the gothic style, to honor the relics of St. Denis, who was entombed a few miles north of Paris.[43] As happened often in the Middle Ages, the identity of the Denis buried outside of Paris had merged with that of another saint. In this case, the mistaken identity was none other than that of Dionysius (Denis) the Areopagite. Convinced that he was honoring the Areopagite, Suger spared no expense for this project, and boasted of the cost of the materials and labor. After all, his own reading of Dionysius had convinced him of the intimate relation between temporal and eternal realities. Confident in the transparency of symbols and their ability to communicate higher, eternal realities, Suger inscribed the following on the shrine's gilded doors:

All you who seek to honor these doors,
Marvel not at the gold and expense but at the
    craftsmanship of the work.
The noble work is bright, but, being nobly bright, the work

Should brighten the minds, allowing them to travel through
  the lights
To the true light, where Christ is the true door.
The golden door defines how it is imminent in these things.
The dull mind rises to the truth through material things,
And is resurrected from its former submersion when the
  light is seen.[44]

A portal to heaven, the doors of the shrine and every single object within it led to eternity itself. Employing Neoplatonic metaphysics, Suger reasoned through his fascination with "the most expensive things":

Thus sometimes when, because of my delight in the beauty of the house of God, the multicolor loveliness of the gems has called me away from external cares, and worthy meditation, transporting me from material to immaterial things, . . . then I seem to see myself existing on some level, as it were, beyond our earthly one, neither completely in the slime of earth nor completely in the purity of Heaven. By the gift of God I can be transported in an anagogical manner from this inferior level to that superior one.[45]

The shrine for St. Denis was not just an economic and artistic marvel, but also a political one, for it was the burial place for the French monarchs, who desired to be linked to the saint for eternity. This was a fairly common practice: those in positions of authority eagerly sought points of contact with the eternal and heavenly. The vast majority of Christians could not enjoy a privilege as great as burial next to a mighty saint, but they too could gravitate toward them in other ways, through pilgrimages. Medieval Europe bristled with holy places, which were portals to eternity, just like St. Denis. Some shrines attracted local pilgrims,

Figure 3.4. Basilica of St. Denis, northern France, twelfth century. This is the first church built entirely in the Gothic style, under the direction of Abbot Suger, a monk who sought to employ the Neoplatonic mystical theology of Dionysius the Areopagite in architecture. Suger sought to build a church so magnificent, and so filled with light, art, and the finest materials, that it would naturally bring to mind the perfection of heaven and eternity.   Photograph by the author.

usually those who could not afford to travel far. Other shrines, however, such as those at Aachen, Santiago de Compostella, or Conques, drew thousands of pilgrims, all of whom supported a thriving hospitality industry along well-traveled routes as they stopped for food and lodging along their way. Rome or Jerusalem attracted even more pilgrims.[46]

And no place on earth was more highly charged with the presence of the sacred and eternal than Jerusalem and the Holy Land. Anyone who doubts the influence of concepts on human history need only consider the Crusades, those epochal adventures through which Western Europeans sought to claim direct access to the eternal. Granted, crusaders and pilgrims did not necessarily embark on their quests for purely spiritual reasons. A few pages of Geoffrey de Villehardouin's *Chronicle of the Fourth Crusade* (1204) and Geoffrey Chaucer's *Canterbury Tales* (ca. 1390) can easily dispel whatever illusions one might have about quests undertaken under the guise of piety. Pilgrims and crusaders, it seems, could display the seven vices more often than they did the seven virtues. Moreover, for every genuine relic, there seemed to be many of doubtful origin.[47] Remnants of the true cross of Christ could be found nearly everywhere; the head of John the Baptist was revered at at least seven different shrines; fragments and entire bodies of the apostles were claimed simultaneously in unlikely places. Geneva, for instance, boasted of having the brain of St. Peter, whose body was entombed in Rome (which Protestants would claim was merely a pumice stone), and the arm of St. Anthony (which Protestants would identify as "the desiccated virile member of a stag").[48] Some among the clergy and laity apparently resolved these conflicting claims by believing that God miraculously multiplied relics for the benefit of humankind, or by relying on assumption that such "pious frauds," as they were known, were a very useful and proper way of engendering genuine devotion among the simple folk. But no matter how crassly unspiritual many of the established customs, feasts, and rituals of medieval Europe might have been, the fact remains that eternity infringed on the temporal world at nearly every turn, not just as a concept but also as something of real political, social, and economic value.

One of the most salient traits of medieval piety was this keen fixation on specific earthly points which were believed to be closer to heaven and eternity. Consequently, much of religious life revolved around the processes of identifying, confirming, approaching, and venerating those special junctures between heaven and earth, and of seeking to tap the supernatural power that was believed to reside in specific loci, with the hopes of obtaining specific favors. In brief, piety was strongly inclined to localize the divine and eternal, make it tangible, and harness its power.

If space was a grid upon which sacred places could be plotted, so, too, was time itself. Another distinctive feature of medieval Christianity was the constant presence of a higher kind of time, which intersected with ordinary time. This higher time was *liminal*, that is, an entryway connecting ordinary time with eternity (Latin: *limen*, threshold). Medieval piety had a rhythmic quality—an endlessly cyclical oscillation between ordinary, undifferentiated time and sacred, recurring time, which was the conjunction of *here* and *now* with *there* and *then*.[49] The passion of Christ especially had an eternal, timeless quality to it, not just because it was made present with every celebration of the Eucharist but also because it was relived and reenacted every year, during Holy Week. The same was true of other major events in the life of Christ, his mother Mary, and all the saints. The most important feasts were Epiphany, Good Friday, Easter, Pentecost, and Christmas.

The cyclical nature of all feasts lent them an aura of eternity, both within and outside of time. Time did not have a straight, one-directional horizontal flow, as it does for many of us nowadays. Instead, time was layered on various tracks and studded with vertical doorways and all sorts of thresholds to eternity, where one could find oneself transported to higher realities and eternal moments, if one paid attention. And all of those thresholds, those special days and times, were in God's realm, in eternity, and as such they were closer to one another, year after year, than ordinary days were to one another.[50]

The shortest cycle was the week, which marked off Sunday as a sacred day, a holy time when attendance at mass was required, and all work should cease. The longer cycles were the two penitential seasons of Advent, before Christmas, and Lent, before Easter. In preparation for the reliving of the birth and death of Jesus, Christians were asked to fast and pray, because it was assumed that such high times required purification. Year in, year out, special days recalled the presence of the saints to whom communities were bound. Saints were honored on the anniversary of their deaths, according to the church calendar. Some saints' feasts, such as that of John the Baptist, were widely observed and had a universal quality to them. Other feasts were local in nature. Each community, and even each parish or guild would have its own special feasts, according to which saints were considered patrons. Feasts were marked by the celebration of special masses, processions, and public celebrations. Since communities hardly ever took their patrons off the calendar, the feasts could pile up, as new ones were added. In Germany, by the late fifteenth century, there would be 161 feast days to celebrate, all of which required some kind of self-denial. That is one-third of the entire year. Of course, as one might expect, religious feasts could often turn into riotous self-indulgent occasions on which the lines between the sacred and profane dissolved and no one gave a single thought to fasting, or to eternity. Yet, profanity aside, there is no denying the fact that the multiplication of feast days or "higher times" linked to eternity interfered with productivity.[51]

Sub specie aeternitatis: Eternity and Politics

Finally, in no other area of human endeavor did eternity infringe most persistently and rudely, or with more fractious results, than in the case of church-state relations. As early as the fourth century, when persecution ceased, church leaders found themselves disagreeing with civil authorities on various points. At bottom, most disputes were jurisdictional, over the boundaries of power claimed by church and state. From very early on, Christian bishops claimed the highest ground of all, arguing that their spiritual authority was derived from God himself, and that since they held the so-called keys of the kingdom that Christ had granted to the Apostle Peter, they had the highest responsibility of all. Viewing all of life under the light of eternity, *sub specie aeternitatis,* church elites began to argue that their *spiritual* authority, which touched on the *eternal* destiny of the human race, was far superior to the *temporal* authority of civil rulers, which only touched on life in sequential time, that dimension dismissed by Augustine and others as *merely* transitory.

As feudal society evolved in Western Europe after the collapse of the Roman Empire, this conception of the clergy's role in society became part and parcel of the very fabric of life, with the entire social order sorted into three distinct classes of people: those who prayed (the clerics), those who fought (the nobles), and those who worked (the peasantry). Consequently, eternity did more than intrude into the fabric of daily life as an unseen dimension: it actually gave shape to the social structure of the medieval West. The keys to eternity that were in the hands of the clergy may seem metaphorical to us, but to medieval Christians they were much more than that: whether they liked it or not, their society was structured in such a way as to assign those keys a value as essential as that of the swords wielded by the knights and the plows employed by the peasants.[52]

A polarity thus emerged in all discourse concerning church and state, in which the otherworldly *spiritual* and *eternal* power of the church was contrasted with the *temporal* and *mundane* authority of civil rulers. The spiritual and eternal, of course, was assumed to be that which was divine and eternally true, *per omnia saeculae saeculorum*, while the temporal or mundane was assumed to be inferior, illusory, and besotted with original sin.[53] It did not take very long for this sort of thinking to emerge. We find it fully developed, for instance, in a letter written by Pope Gelasius I to Emperor Anastasius in 494. Distinguishing between the sacred authority (*auctoritas*) of the priesthood and the royal power (*potestas*) of the emperor, Gelasius went on to say:

> Of these the responsibility of the priests is more weighty in so far as they will answer for the kings of men themselves at the divine judgement. Know . . . that although you as emperor take precedence over all mankind in dignity, nevertheless you must piously bow the neck to those who have charge of divine affairs and seek from them the means of your salvation.[54]

Clerical and papal claims to preeminence over civil authorities were further substantiated by the church's interpretation of the Fall of Adam and Eve and the transmission of a sinful nature to all of their descendants on earth. As the church elites saw it—and as Augustine argued in his *City of God*—human governments were a by-product of sin, an unfortunate necessity, given the innate violence and cruelty of human beings. Moreover, following the same logic as Augustine, church elites also argued that the true end of human beings lay beyond this world, in eternity, and that it was they alone, the clerics, who had authority over that realm. *Sub specie aeternitatis*, then, civil rulers could be proven to have an inferior authority vis-à-vis the clergy.

Numerous bishops and popes would wield eternity as a weapon against civil authorities, not just in their arguments but also through the power of excommunication, with which they damned kings and emperors to eternal torment in hell, and in the process also absolved their subjects from obedience to them, making rebellions legally possible. At times, ecclesiastics would win battles, as Pope Gregory VII did in 1077 over Emperor Henry IV, who had to beg for forgiveness, kneeling in the snow in Canossa for three days, bareheaded, outside the castle where the pope was staying.[55] Sometimes, however, brute force overpowered all clerical claims. This is what ultimately happened to Pope Gregory VII, whose victory over Emperor Henry IV was hollow: in 1081 Henry IV marched on Rome, deposed Pope Gregory, and drove him into the hands of Robert Guiscard, Duke of Normandy, who in turn forced Gregory to flee Rome. Pope Gregory died in Salerno, and his last words were, "I have loved justice and hated iniquity, therefore I die in exile."[56] Brute force also gained the upper hand in 1170, when the English archbishop Thomas à Becket was murdered at the altar by King Henry II's knights, and in 1303, when Pope Boniface VIII was captured and physically assaulted by allies of the French king Philip IV. It mattered little to Philip IV and his allies in Rome, the Colonnas, that Pope Boniface had issued a bull, *Unam Sanctam*, in which he had said:

> We must recognize the more clearly that spiritual power surpasses in dignity and in nobility any temporal power whatever, as spiritual things surpass the temporal. . . . [W]e declare, we proclaim, we define that it is absolutely necessary for salvation that every human creature be subject to the Roman Pontiff.[57]

Sometimes popes actually did win, despite their relative military weakness, and a great deal of credit must be given to their hold on eternity, as employed through the power of excommunication. One such victor was Pope Innocent III (ca. 1161–1216), who managed to outmaneuver the imperial dynasty of the Hohenstauffens.[58] Taking the *sub specie aeternitatis* perspective to dizzying heights, Pope Innocent not only survived but prevailed after saying:

> The creator of the Universe set up two great luminaries in the firmament of Heaven; the greater light to rule the day, the lesser light to rule the night. In the same way for the firmament of the Universal Church, which is spoken of as Heaven, he appointed two great dignities: the greater to bear rule over souls (these being, as it were, days), the lesser to bear rule over bodies (these being, as it were, nights). These dignities are the pontifical authority and the royal power. Furthermore, the moon derives her light from the sun, and is in truth inferior to the sun in both size and quality, in position as well as effect. In the same way, the royal power derives its dignity from the pontifical authority.[59]

Experts tend to agree that Innocent III and his successors Gregory IX (ca. 1170–1241) and Innocent IV (ca. 1185–

1254) effectively stifled the Hohenstauffens. One theory even blames these medieval popes for crippling German political sensibilities beyond repair, thus preventing the unification of Germany until the nineteenth century.[60]

Popes and bishops were not the only clerics who based their claims for preeminence on their guardianship of eternity. The entire clerical class from top to bottom brandished the same arguments, turning themselves into a people set apart who could not be taxed or tried in civil courts, and who were literally outside the civil law and immune to it.

What does this drawn-out political tug-of-war reveal about the place of eternity in medieval society? Two items stand out, as hard to ignore as the papal tiara on Innocent III's head.

First, it seems quite obvious that while eternity could be invoked by the clergy to buttress their claims to authority, plenty of lay rulers simply did not believe in the claims. This is not to say that they did not believe in eternity but rather that they did not see it exactly the same way as the high clergy did. In many cases, what the lay rulers refused to accept was the total monopoly on eternity claimed by the clergy. Disagreement was as much a part of medieval life as it is of our own. But the difference between their age and ours is that the boundaries for disagreement were narrower then, when it came to religion.

Medieval society was structured in such a way as to make the total rejection of the church extremely difficult, and the rejection of eternity nearly impossible, at least insofar as social relations were concerned. Western Christendom was divided into three classes: those who fought, those who prayed, and those who toiled, and the functioning of medieval society depended on the clerical class as much as it did on the other two, hard as that may be for us in this secular age to imagine.[61] The clergy did much more than pray: they were the gatekeepers to positions of authority, and without their blessing and support, secular offices could vanish and thrones crumble. They were also the gatekeepers to the afterlife and eternity, which may strike us as too far removed from daily life to be of any significance, but their possession of the keys to the kingdom—their power to excommunicate—had a profound effect on social relations in this world. Most monks may not have held those all-important keys, but their place in the social structure and in the economy was deemed as necessary as their prayers and their closeness to eternity, for their holiness was supposed to ensure the blessings of heaven on their neighbors.

When all is said and done, however, there is no denying that eternity could be open to interpretation. As was the case with just about all aspects of medieval religion, norms could be flexible or flash points for conflict, and exceptions to the norm could easily be found everywhere throughout Western Christendom. This helps to explain the great rupture that would come in the sixteenth century.

A second characteristic of medieval conceptions of eternity revealed by the struggle between church and state is the symbiotic relationship between thinking and social and political structures.

In the language of the clerics, "the world" they ostensibly left behind was called "secular" for a good reason: it was the world enmeshed in this age (*saeculum*), in time rather than in eternity. The distinction was not specious at all to them, or to the laity. In fact, the claim the clergy made on eternity was visible, palpable, and measurable: the clergy were indeed a class set apart, exempt from all sorts of taxes and laws, protected by their own courts of law, enriched by their substantial property holdings and the contributions the laity were obliged to make to the church's coffers.

Medieval clerics, it could be argued, were not just the gate-keepers to eternity but also its architects, engineers, ambassadors, and middlemen. They could no more do without eternity than without the rituals and symbols of the church they served: it was the very reason for their existence. This is not to say that they brandished eternity as a weapon against a repressed, unbelieving laity or that their teachings and rituals were cunningly devised to hoodwink and exploit their flocks. Not at all. Clergy and laity alike both shared in this worldview quite willingly and eagerly most of the time, though the constant presence of heretics of one sort or another proves that not everyone was ready to agree with the church on all points, all the time. Medieval eternity was a social invention as much as a theological one: it was guarded by the clergy, but freely and willingly developed, maintained, and *lived with*, constantly, as much by the laity as by the clergy. After all, the sublime cathedrals and shrines of Europe that attract hordes of tourists in our own day—these mirrors of eternity—were not built by priests alone, or monks or nuns. And the most celebrated literary masterpiece of this age, Dante's *Divine Comedy*, which is all about eternity, was not written by a priest either, or read exclusively by clerics.

By the late fifteenth century, this mindset and all of the social, political, and economic realities that reflected it seemed permanently entrenched. Eternity had overflowed so abundantly into time and space that the world seemed awash in it, yet thirsty for more. In the wink of an eye, however, everything changed. And that change would make a world of difference.

IV

Eternity Reformed

"**I** go to seek a great perhaps," said François Rabelais at the moment of his death in 1553. Or so we are told.[1] Whether he said it or not matters little: it fits the man perfectly, and also his era. It's an aphorism that sums up a great rupture in Western history, when unquestioned assumptions were successfully challenged and eternity was reconfigured.

How that "perhaps," which had been barely audible for centuries, became louder and more persistent is the subject of this chapter.

As we have seen, eternity was much more than an abstract concept back then, before Rabelais, and before the Western world became modern. Yes, without a doubt, there were those who did approach eternity as a philosophical and theological puzzle: the scholastic theologians. Eternity was precisely the kind of intellectual challenge they loved. This is also true of modern scholars. Pick up almost any book on eternity written in the twentieth century, and chances are that if it deals with the Middle Ages at all, its focus will be on scholastic disputes about eternity.[2] Fine distinctions and elaborations on prior definitions flowed copiously from their quill pens and lecterns, and heated debates were never scarce. While the Augustinian take on eternity remained very much in play— eternity as a realm that transcends time wholly and is separate from it—this did not stop the scholastics from debating other definitions, especially concerning *sempiternity*, that is, eternity as a boundless continuum, without beginning or

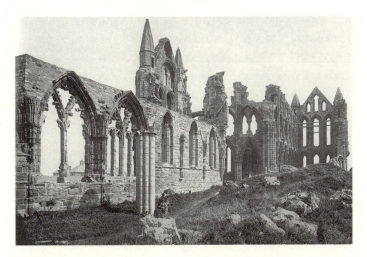

Figure 4.1. Ruins of Whitby Abbey, Yorkshire, England. Whitby Abbey was established by Benedictine monks in the seventh century, destroyed by Vikings in the ninth, and rebuilt between the eleventh to thirteenth centuries. In 1538, when King Henry VIII dissolved and confiscated all of the larger monasteries in England, the abbey and its land holdings passed into the hands of the crown. In keeping with the king's wishes and Protestant attitudes toward monasticism, the abbey was wantonly wrecked (in ca. 1540) and turned into a quarry for other buildings. As the new owners and their fellow iconoclasts throughout England soon found out, buildings erected with eternity in mind do not topple very easily. Left in place largely because of the high cost of demolition, the ruins became monuments to a vanished way of life and the collapse of the Catholic Church in England.

Shakespeare's reference to "bare ruined choirs, where late the sweet birds sang" (Sonnet 73) reveals that relics such as those of Whitby were widespread enough to be a recognizable point of reference in Elizabethan England. Constant reminders of the rejection of monasticism as totally useless, this ruin and all others like it bore silent witness not just to the expulsion of the monks, but also to the eternity they ostensibly dedicated themselves to gaining. Secularization seldom gets more vivid, or more poignant, than this. Photograph by Philip S. Evans of www.photosofchurches.com.

end. Medieval conceptions of time and eternity were not rigidly confined to a single dimension; one kind of time or one kind of eternity did not necessarily cancel out another. And, since eternity involved thinking about God, the possibilities were infinite, literally. In the long run, their discussions

---

Scholastic Distinctions

Sempiternity, the total eternity, which has neither beginning nor end, may be regarded as divisible into two eternities by any moment, as it moves along:

1. The past eternity: *aeternitas a parte ante*
2. The future eternity: *aeternitas a parte post*

One may speak of this total eternity in four ways:

a. Absolute eternity, having neither beginning nor end.
b. The two "eternities": *aeternitas a parte ante* AND *aeternitas a parte post.*
c. The past eternity; time without beginning: *aeternitas a parte ante* ONLY.
d. The future eternity; time without end: *aeternitas a parte post.*

And each of these four ways has its own point(s) of reference:

a. Pertains to God and his nonsuccessive knowledge of everything.
b. Pertains to God **before** AND **after** the creation of the universe and time/space.
c. Pertains to God **before** the creation of the universe and time/space.
d. Pertains to God AND the universe **after** creation AND **after** time/space.

arrived at greater logical clarity but did not have any practical effect, for they weren't supposed to anyway. Scholasticism was a highly technical language spoken by an expert few, a privilege, much like the rare and very expensive furs that could only be worn by the nobility. Scholastic "advances" or "findings" involved intense hairsplitting, such as distinguishing between eternity that has passed (*aeternitas a parte ante*) and eternity yet to come (*aeternitas a parte post*).

No matter how engaging or forbidding these distinctions may seem, they were really a sideshow. In essence, they cannot be linked to any substantive changes in the core concept of eternity, much less in daily life. What mattered most about eternity in the Middle Ages, especially in the later period, was the way in which eternity was woven into the fabric of everyday life, as something very real and very accessible. Eternity might have delighted the scholastic theologians as a topic, yes, but for them, as for everyone else, eternity was also something inescapable in the realm of piety and everyday life. And it would be in that realm, precisely, that eternity would implode, so to speak, the concept rupturing along all those finely tuned dichotomies, those seams that ostensibly joined the eternal to the temporal.

The initial rupture would occur along the fault line of the afterlife, that elaborate seam that joined the living and the dead. Immediately, as this seam broke apart, so did others, including those three significant ones analyzed in the first chapter: that of monasticism, which had bound one social group to eternity more intensely than others; that of mysticism, which had ostensibly allowed some individuals to experience eternity; and that of clerical claims of superiority, which had divided the body politic into two distinct spheres and two classes of elites.

So let us begin with the dead, who, until the Protestant Reformation came along, were never really dead and gone.

The Reformation of the Hereafter

Praying to the Father in heaven, or to the dead saints who thronged his celestial court, up there, above the stars, did not involve believing in some other dimension outside of space and time, or figuring out the difference between *aeternitas a parte ante* and *a parte post*. Neither did praying for the dead, most of whom would be in purgatory, that place down there, that antechamber to eternity below one's feet, between the surface of the earth and hell, which had its own peculiar time, determined by suffering and measured in thousands of years. Back then, the dead were just as demanding of one's attention as one's living relatives and neighbors, haunting not just one's memory and imagination but one's calendar, purse, and estate as well. The dead could also be immensely useful, perhaps even truer and more valuable than any kin or friend on earth, for the saints who had passed on to heaven were loyal advocates, eager to plead one's case before God's throne. And the proximity of eternity was not limited to the souls of the departed: in churches everywhere, many of the dead were buried within the sacred space, right beneath the living congregation's feet, or perhaps, as was the case with many saints, directly beneath the altars or above them.

In brief, time and space were linked directly to eternity through innumerable points of contact, through loci which were clearly marked off as sacred. Guarded by the clergy within carefully controlled spaces, eternity could not only be seen and touched, but also smelled. Philosophers and theologians may have scrupulously parsed distinctions in terminology, but as far as the rituals of medieval Christendom were concerned, there was no essential difference between eternity and heaven and hell, or between the afterlife and the eternal. Any point of contact with the divine realm—any link between the spiritual and the material—was a link with eternity. This belief was driven home repeatedly in worship, whether in the doxology, "Glory be to the Father and the Son and the Holy Spirit, *as it was in the beginning, is now, and ever shall be, amen*," or in the Creed, "and His kingdom shall have no end . . . and we look for the resurrection of the dead and the life of the world to come."

Theology and piety were linked by a common assumption: as matter is to spirit, so the temporal is to the eternal. Consequently, metaphysical syllogisms gave shape to doctrine and devotion. God is in heaven; God is eternal; heaven is eternity. God is spirit; God is eternal; the spiritual is eternal. The human soul is immortal; the human soul goes to heaven or hell after death; heaven and hell are eternal. And so on. The Eucharist was one such intense link with eternity—perhaps the most intense of all—for the ritual of the mass transcended time and space and made God himself physically present.[3] The words of Christ, repeated by the priest at consecration— "This *is* my body; this *is* my blood"—were taken literally. Belief in the real presence of Christ in the bread and wine consecrated at every mass was conjoined with belief in the sacrificial dimension of the ritual, not *in spite of* the *fact* that Christ's physical body was in heaven, as we might be tempted to think, but rather *because* of it. The divinity of Christ and his physical presence in eternity made him ubiquitous, along with his sacrifice. In other words, Christ, the Son of God, the second person of the Trinity, could be *there* and *here* at the same time, and his crucifixion could be *now* as well as *then*. This crossing of boundaries in time and space, repeated countless times every single day throughout all of Christendom, linked the living and the dead.[4]

The dead, therefore, were another intense and unavoidable point of contact. And all such loci were not mere abstractions but rather concrete linkages, with very specific social, political, and economic dimensions. Even the afterlife itself, Rabelais's "great perhaps," was made manifest by social bonds. In the Middle Ages, the extension of social bonds into the afterlife had its foes, who labored to abolish it: most notably the Cathars, Waldensians, Lollards, and Hussites, all of whom were hunted down as heretics. But most medieval Christians seemed to embrace their dead most ardently and to invest heavily in them, literally and figuratively. The evidence they left behind is overwhelming. One notorious example should suffice here. Consider, for instance, the case of Johann Tetzel and the most infamous jingle in all of Western history.

In the fall of 1517 the Dominican preacher Johann Tetzel made his way through Saxony offering indulgences, a highly prized commodity. Tickets to heaven, one could say. Entrance passes to eternal bliss that were never bought and sold outright, not technically anyway, but were obtained through charitable contributions to church-approved causes, much like the pledge rewards of tote bags, coffee-table books, and compact disks now ceaselessly hawked ad nauseam by America's public radio and television stations. Tetzel's legitimate cause was to raise funds for the building of a new basilica of St. Peter's in Rome. Exposing a yawning abyss between official theology and popular piety, and dredging up nearly every guilt-inducing, pocket-picking pitch through which he could hawk indulgences to an anxious laity, Johann Tetzel would preach the following words to many a Saxon crowd in 1517, on behalf of Pope Leo X and Archbishop Albrecht of Mainz:

All of you, run for the salvation of your souls. . . . Listen now, God and St. Peter call *you*. Consider the salvation of *your* souls and those of *your loved ones* departed. . . . Listen to the voices of *your dead relatives* and friends, beseeching *you* and saying, "Pity us, pity us. We are in dire torment from which *you* can redeem us for a pittance." Do *you* not wish to? Open *your* ears. Hear the father saying to his son, the mother to her daughter, "We bore you, nourished you, brought you up, left you our fortunes, and you are so cruel and hard that now you are not willing for so little to set us free. Will you let us lie here in flames? Will you delay our promised glory?". . . Remember *you* are able to release them, for *as soon as the coin in the coffer rings, the soul from Purgatory springs*. Will *you* not then for a quarter of a florin receive these letters of indulgence through which *you* are able to lead a divine and immortal soul into the fatherland of paradise?[5]

Of course, everyone knows—or should know—how the rest of this story unfolded. Tetzel unwittingly changed the course of history, in the most unexpected manner. Martin Luther, an Augustinian monk, took issue with Tetzel's take on salvation and challenged him to a debate on ninety-five very fine points of theology—the sort of points that scholastics routinely debated and lay people couldn't care less about. The challenge drew an angry response from Tetzel and others in the church hierarchy, which in turn caused Luther to dig in his heels. Pope Leo X dismissed it all as nothing more than a monkish squabble between Dominicans and Augustinians. But while Leo wasn't looking, Luther widened the scope of his challenge way beyond mere theology to issues that touched on raw nerves and everyday life, and Saxony and other parts of Germany quickly rallied around him. One thing led to another, and before anyone could stop it, by 1521 the Protestant Reformation was in full swing and Western Christendom was well on its way to an irreversible breakdown. And right there, at this embryonic stage of the Protestant Reformation, as densely packed as all of the matter in the universe before the Big Bang, what does one find?

The dead, and their relationship to the living, linked inextricably by the Eucharist.

One of the most profound changes brought about by the Protestant Reformation—and one of the most ignored—is that which was effected in regards to the dead. What Martin Luther began as an assault on Tetzel and indulgences would end as a wholesale revision of the relationship between the dead and the living, and between the temporal and eternal. Luther and all other Protestants would reject not only belief in indulgences and purgatory but also belief in any kind of interrelationship between the living and dead. A mere three years after he challenged Tetzel to a debate on indulgences with his ninety-five theses, Luther would be arguing that praying *for* the dead was as wrong as praying *to* the dead. To believe that those on earth could pray for the souls in purgatory or that the dead in heaven—the saints—could pray for anyone on earth was dead wrong, as the pun would have it, or even worse. "The Scriptures forbid and condemn communication with the spirits of the dead," Luther argued, citing Deuteronomy 18:10–11 ("No one shall be found among you who . . . consults ghosts or spirits, or who seeks oracles from the dead"). Moreover, Luther also demonized all of the medieval apparition tales that undergirded belief in purgatory, saying: "whatever spirits go about, making a noise, screaming, complaining, or seeking help, are truly the work of the devil."[6] Masses for the dead, then, were nothing but demonically inspired sorcery and necromancy.

For Luther, then, death was no gossamer veil through which the living and the dead remained within sight of each other but rather the thickest of final curtains. Nor was the communion of saints mentioned in the Creed to be understood as anything other than an eschatological hope about the promised resurrection and the kingdom to come. In other words, the *communio sanctorum* was an expectation, not a concrete reality. And death was the deepest abyss of all, an unbridgeable metaphysical and ontological chasm. Even before time and space were thought of as interdependent, Protestants insisted that this chasm between the living and the dead applied to both dimensions, that crossing over from *here and now* to eternity was the loneliest of one-way journeys, and that the dead could only be thought of in terms of *there and then*. Luther summed it all up in 1522, in a sermon:

> The summons of death comes to us all, and no one can die for another. Every one must fight his own battle with death by himself, alone. We can shout into each other's ears, but everyone must himself be prepared for the time of death: I will not be with you then, nor you with me.[7]

To fully understand what Luther rejected and what the Catholic Church struggled to emphasize as a response to his challenge, we must first come to terms with the place of the dead in late medieval religion.

Purgatory, the Dead, and Indulgences

The flash point of Luther's attack on Tetzel was the doctrine of purgatory and the custom of performing certain rituals to alleviate the suffering of the dead in the afterlife. What

Luther rejected as a medieval invention was actually an ancient practice. By the fourth century it was already so widespread that St. Augustine (354–430) not only accepted it without question but also promoted it.[8] By the sixth century it was also commonplace to believe that purgation, or a painful cleansing of the soul, could take place in the afterlife, and that the living on earth could alleviate the suffering of those souls.[9]

Formal theology had little to do with this notion of purgation in the hereafter. This was no carefully reasoned doctrine, such as the Trinity, but rather an odd amalgam of practical piety, ritual, and logic. The sacred scriptures had little to say about the dead, or their relation to the living, save for a few texts that speak of such things obliquely.[10] Sheer hope in the possibility of forgiveness in the afterlife, coupled with the longing for some connection with the dead, had more to do with purgatory than did biblical interpretation: it was an eschatological necessity drawn from the inevitably painful reality of grief, the certainty of moral failure in this life, and the fear of eternal damnation. As a result, then, the relation between postmortem cleansing and eternity was not given much thought, if any at all. The *where* and *when* and *how* of purgation mattered much less than the fact that something could be done about it in the *here and now*, by oneself and others. From the very start, this purgation was a corporate responsibility as well as a personal one, a way to salvation through mutual aid: you help me and I will help you.

Nebulously poised between time and eternity, purgatory gradually acquired more definite features. Eventually, the Latin Church developed a way of measuring purgatory in terms of years, even though no one ever conceived of that measure in earthly terms. By Luther's day, a very precise formula was widely accepted: one day's suffering on earth equaled a thousand years in purgatory. Indulgences—the spiritual favor Tetzel hawked—were keyed to this formula too, and measured in terms of how many thousands of years they would shave off in the afterlife. Specific acts of devotion could be granted specific numbers of years in value for the afterlife, and the accounting could get very precise. For instance, the relic collection amassed by Luther's prince, Frederick the Wise of Saxony, could earn anyone who venerated it all—on the first of November, the one day a year when the pope had decreed this was possible, at the castle church in Wittenberg—exactly 1,902,202 years and 270 days off from one's stay in purgatory.[11] It was a formula at once logical and illogical, and a measure of how unlike earthly time purgatory must be, for no one expected the earth to last that long. After all, not only did Luther and many of his contemporaries expect the end of the world imminently, they also thought that the universe itself was only about five thousand years old.

So, while purgatory was definitely temporal rather than eternal, its time ran on a vastly different clock. The dead being purged in that realm were already in eternity's vestibule, so to speak, merely undergoing a slight waiting period. Any amount of fixed time is slight when compared to eternity. Even 1,902,202 years and 270 days.

Purgatory provided a realm of spiritual activity for the dead, a realm into which the church extended and on which the living could have an impact. A key contributor to the definition of this outreach to the dead was Pope Gregory the Great (540–604), who summed up and approved what was already part and parcel of Christian belief and piety in his own day. Pope Gregory promoted the redemptive power of the Eucharist over this realm, saying: "If the sins after death be pardonable, then the sacred oblation of the holy host useth to help men's souls."[12] Here, in a nutshell, was the rationale behind saying masses for the dead. Medieval Catholics would hold firm to five basic beliefs, all of which had been stressed by Saint Gregory at the end of the sixth century.

1. That the human person is made up of two basic components: a perishable body and an immortal soul.
2. That the soul separates from the body at death and is instantly judged.
3. That the soul is instantly sent to one of three destinations: heaven, purgatory, or hell.
4. That purgatory is a temporary destination, a painful antechamber to heaven and eternal bliss where the soul is cleansed, and where it can be aided by the sacrifice of the mass offered by the living through the church.
5. That there will be a Final Judgment at the end of history, when purgatory will be abolished and all souls will be reunited with resurrected bodies for eternity, some to enjoy eternal bliss and others to endure eternal torments.

All five of these tenets were neatly summarized in the Latin adage, *salus hominis in fine consistit*, which, loosely translated, means "one's eternal fate is decided at the moment of death." Within this theological framework, each soul's eternal destiny depended on its behavior—on performing good works and avoiding sin—and also on whether or not its sins had been forgiven by the church. Furthermore, each soul's fate in the afterlife depended on its state at the moment of death, which meant that if one wanted to avoid hell, one needed to die a "good death." By far the most important element of a good death was the presence of a priest who could administer the sacraments of penance, the Eucharist, and extreme unction. Medieval Christians believed that confessing one's sins and receiving absolution, communion, and the last rites was so essential that they looked on sudden, unexpected death as one of the most awful things in the world, or worse, as a clear sign of God's wrath.

One more set of beliefs and practices loomed large in the late Middle Ages. In its official teaching, the medieval Church made it clear that while all sins were forgiven by its sacrament of penance, what one gained from priestly absolution was not a totally clean slate, but rather a commuted sentence, a reduction of eternal penalties into temporal ones. This is why the priest always imposed *penances*, so one could make *satisfaction*: prayers, fasts, pilgrimages, almsgiving, and other such good works that ostensibly made up for one's failings. If one sinned very infrequently, like the saints, then penances were manageable, and one could ostensibly go straight to heaven at death. But if one sinned with regularity, like most people, then penances could never be made up before one died. And this meant that the penances had to be completed in the afterlife. This is why ending up in purgatory was the best outcome that most Christians could hope for, and why purgatory was always so crowded.

At the highest reaches of monastic and mystical devotion, purgatory could be seen as an absolute necessity, and an evolutionary step that the souls of the dead would be eager to suffer through. On the eve of the Protestant Reformation such sentiments were clearly expressed by St. Catherine of Genoa. The way she saw it, as soon as the soul separated from the body at death, it instantly realizes that its sinfulness "cannot be removed in any other way [and] hurls itself into Purgatory." Moreover, as Catherine saw it, "in purgatory, great joy and great suffering do not exclude one another." The more a soul endures in purgatory, the closer it gets to God, and the more willingly it suffers. In fact, Catherine went as far as to propose something that ran against the grain of prevailing attitudes toward suffering in the hereafter, stating unequivocally that no soul in purgatory would wish to be released before its well-deserved torment was complete:

> Were a soul to appear in the presence of God with one hour of purgation still due, that would be to do it great harm. It would then suffer more than if it were cast into ten purgatories, for it could not endure the justice and pure goodness of God, nor would it be fitting on the part of God. That soul, aware that complete satisfaction was not as yet fully rendered to God, even if the time lacking were but the twinkling of an eye, would prefer to submit to a thousand Hells rather than so appear in God's presence.[13]

What mystics understood, however, was not exactly in line with popular piety, which was intensely focused on the negative aspects of purgatory: on its painful torments and on the need to release the souls of the dead from that suffering as quickly as possible. Even though purgatory was an entry point to eternal bliss, it was nonetheless frightful, perhaps as scary as hell itself, for the suffering depicted there was often outrageously unbearable. Even before St. Gregory's day, Christians told stories about tormented souls who visited the living to ask for suffrages and remind them of the awful reality of purgatory. One such tale that ended up in the influential *Golden Legend* sums up this myth succinctly. Silo, a scholar, asked a friend to return from the dead to let him know how things were going in the afterlife. A few days after his death, this friend showed up in Silo's study, "wearing a cape made of parchment written all over with sophisms, and woven of flames inside." When the friend explained that this cape was a punishment for his intellectual pride and his love of soft, expensive furs, and that the flames burned him constantly while the cape pressed down on him with all the weight of a huge tower, Silo responded by saying that this looked like very light punishment and that purgatory must therefore not be so awful after all. "Put out your hand and feel how light the punishment really is," said the visitor from purgatory. So, Silo held out his hand,

> and the scholar let a drop of his sweat fall on it. The drop went through Silo's hand like an arrow, causing him excruciating pain. "That's how I feel all over," the scholar said. Master Silo, alarmed by the severity of the other man's punishment, decided to abandon the world and enter the religious life.[14]

While this story focused on the pain of purgatory, many others added yet another message: that of the value of suffrages on the part of the living. Quite often, the dead appeared to beg for relief, and to remind the living of their duty toward them. Not surprisingly, then, one of the most salient characteristics of the Catholic West was the way in which its living members constantly acted as intercessors for the dead. This means that by the late Middle Ages, masses were always being offered for the dead, everywhere, at all times, on a much larger scale than ever before, with the support of a highly sophisticated theology. One significant component of this theology gave rise to yet another link between the living and the dead, and the church and the afterlife, a link that made purgatory ever closer to earth: the issuing of indulgences.

Indulgences—which we briefly touched upon a few pages ago—were a favor, or privilege granted by the church, which remitted the punishment one still owed God for sin after being absolved in the sacrament of penance. Indulgences came into widespread use in the eleventh century, in connection with the crusades, when Pope Urban II granted all warriors who would fight to regain the Holy Land a plenary indulgence; eventually, they would be extended to the souls in purgatory, whose fate became the responsibility of the living.

And, as can be seen in the text of Tetzel's sermon, by 1517 indulgences could be understood quite crassly as guaranteed passage to heaven, and their purchase an obligation. Ironically, then, indulgences gained an inverse value, as a potential sin of omission, that is, as yet another good deed one must never neglect. *The Mirror of a Sinner*, a confessional manual published around 1470, made this very clear to penitents who wished to examine their consciences: "Have you failed to offer prayers, give alms, and endow masses for departed parents? These are sins against the fourth commandment."[15] Tetzel used the guilt that indulgences could produce to his advantage, and this struck Luther as objectionable. It was not only bad theology and quackery, as he saw it, but an injustice.

But purgatory was not the only abode of the dead accessible to the living, or the only one where Protestants found much to condemn. Heaven hovered close to earth, and so did hell. Heaven was where the saints dwelt in the presence of God and where they tirelessly served as advocates at the celestial court. Hell was home not just to the damned but also to the legions of demons who roamed the earth, tirelessly attempting to ensnare the souls of the living. In official theology and popular piety, the boundaries between earth and these two other eternal realms seemed equally permeable.

Heaven was constantly accessed, not only through the sacraments of the church, and above all through the Eucharist, but also through prayer and through those extraordinary visitors who fairly often appeared on earth, favoring the living with messages and blessings of all sorts. Apparitions of Christ, the Virgin Mary, angels, and saints were not necessarily commonplace, but frequent enough. And they were constant reminders of the infinitesimally small gap between heaven and earth, and between the living and the dead. Examples abound, from all the medieval centuries. St. Gregory

the Great, for instance, saw Christ on the altar as he consecrated the bread and wine at mass; St. Bernard of Clairvaux
drank milk from Mary's breast; St. Anthony of Padua held
the infant Jesus in his arms; and St. Catherine of Siena took
Jesus as her husband in a ceremony attended by all her patron
saints and an angelic choir. A nameless nun in Florence saw
St. Peter Martyr ascending to heaven at the instant he was
murdered miles and miles away. The same St. Peter Martyr
also appeared after death to assist and cure a dying man and
to save a ship from sinking in a storm. And so on. Two of
the most popular books of the late Middle Ages, Jacobus de
Voragine's *Legenda Aurea*, or the *Golden Legend* (thirteenth
century), and Caesarius of Heisterbach's *Dialogue on Miracles* (thirteenth century), are so replete with such accounts
as to make any quantification or systematic cataloguing of
them a daunting challenge.

Praying to the saints was more than a staple of Catholic
devotion: it was part and parcel of its very structure, perhaps
also its very heart. The saints in heaven could become personal advocates, sometimes one's only true friends, and their
power was considered awesome by many. Of course, there
were doubters and skeptics, and these were often folded into
the hagiographies, as fall guys, to stoke the saints' wrath.
Mocking a saint was dangerous business, for just as they
could bless, so also could they curse. The same St. Peter Martyr who healed the lame could strike scoffers dumb, plague
them with fevers, or make their knitting yarn bleed.[16]

Hell could be close too. Nothing could be done for the
damned down there in the flames, but they were sometimes
allowed to visit the living, to warn them of their impending
doom. Such stories also abound, not just in monastic literature but also in popular devotional texts. Books such as
Caesarius of Heisterbach's *Dialogue on Miracles* also made

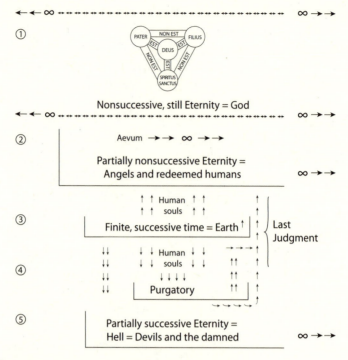

Figure 4.2. A diagram of the medieval Christian cosmos.

1. God, in his nonsuccessive still eternity, represented by the symbol of the Trinity. This eternity simply is an eternal *now* moment. Until the seventeenth century, this eternity was thought to be the highest, or empyrean heaven, above the concentric spheres that made up the universe. In this diagram, the lines pointing infinitely in both directions indicate that God has no beginning or end.

2. Aevum, or aeviternity. This is where angels and all humans who are redeemed live eternally, in God's *now* moment. It is partially nonsuccessive because angels and humans are creatures who have a beginning, unlike God who has no *before* or *after*.

3. Finite, successive time. This is the material cosmos, which begins at creation and ends with the Last Judgment. This is where humans are born and die, in sequential time. Upon dying, a few go directly to heaven, most go to purgatory, and some go to hell. This world ends at the Last Judgment.

4. Purgatory. This is a temporary dimension, which will cease to exist at the Last Judgment. Here, souls pay the penalty for their sins and are gradually cleansed. It has its own time, different from earth's. Some souls rise to heaven before the Last Judgment, some at that final time.

5. Hell. Eternal in the same way as aeviternity. Souls who go to hell never get out. This is a place of everlasting punishment, inhabited by the fallen angels (devils) and sinful, unredeemed humans.

tales of such hellish apparitions common fare in sermons, further popularizing the idea that the dead could visit the living, even from hell.

The Protestant Challenge

Jacques Le Goff has dated the birth of purgatory somewhat precisely to the twelfth century—not the idea of purgation or the practice of praying for the dead, which he admits can be found among early Christians, but purgatory as a *locus*, a distinct place in the cosmos.[17] This dating has proven controversial. In contrast, no one can argue with the very exact date that can be given to the death of purgatory: October 31, 1517, when Luther began his challenge of Tetzel's indulgence preaching.

Luther would not reject purgatory outright until around 1520, but had sealed its fate by challenging the church's soteriology, its theology of salvation. The medieval Catholic afterlife was a dimension constructed out of specific behaviors, of "works," as Luther would say. The very formula *salus hominis in fine consistit*, which placed such an emphasis on the moment of death, and the very notion of purgatory were both inconceivable without a corresponding belief in the relation between specific acts and one's status for eternity in the afterlife. By rejecting what he called "salvation by works," Luther also necessarily destroyed the medieval Catholic conception of the afterlife, and of the way in which the living and the dead relate to one another. Luther's soteriological formula may have changed only one measly letter, but that single consonant made a world of difference: *salus hominis in fide consistit* (human salvation depends on faith). No longer was it *the end* that determined one's place in the afterlife but *faith*—a faith freely given by God in *this* life, a faith in Christ's once-and-for-all sacrifice on the cross, which forgave all sins and made purgatory totally irrelevant. Cleansing in the afterlife was totally unnecessary in Lutheran soteriology.

What Luther rejected, and what he replaced it with may be summarized as follows:

Medieval Catholic Soteriology: Salus hominis in **fine** consistit

1. **Ars vivendi**: *The art of living*: How one lives determines how one will spend eternity.

2. **Non posse non peccare**: Sin is inevitable: *It is impossible not to sin.* Due to the Fall of the human race caused by Adam and Eve, all humans are stained by original sin and cannot help but offend God. But each and every sin can be forgiven, no matter how awful.

3. **Mea culpa, mea culpa, mea maxima culpa**: *It's all my fault, my well-deserved punishment.* One is totally responsible for one's actions, and therefore every sin needs to be forgiven by God. Merely one unforgiven mortal sin can land one in hell for eternity. Penalties for every sin must be paid, either in this life or the next. Unforgiven sins are paid for eternally, in hell. Forgiven sins are paid for over time, on earth or in purgatory.

4. **Extra ecclesiam nulla salus**: *No salvation outside the Church.* The only way to escape hell is to rely on the Church and its sacraments, which are the most direct source of grace. Especially the sacrament of penance. No confession, no absolution, no salvation.

5. **Caelum, Purgatorium, Infernus**: Upon dying, one is immediately judged by God, and one goes directly to heaven,

purgatory, or hell, depending on the state of one's soul. Only very few souls go directly to heaven. Most go to purgatory, but many go to hell.

6. **Ars moriendi**: *The art of dying*: One must seek help in order to die well, for one's eternal destiny depends on how one deals with one's sins at the moment of death.

7. **Ora pro nobis**: *Pray for us*. The living on earth can pray for the dead in purgatory, and the dead in heaven can pray for the living on earth. And since the sacrament of the Eucharist—the Mass—transcends time and space, it can help free souls from purgatory.

Lutheran Soteriology: Salus hominis in **fide** consistit

1. **Sola fide; sola gratia**: One is saved by *faith alone* rather than works. Faith is gained through *grace alone*, as a gift freely given by God. Nothing can be done to obtain faith.

2. **Simul justus et peccator**: *Sinful and justified, all at once*: Even with faith and grace, one will always continue to sin, but the penalty for the sins is cancelled out. Forgiveness for sins depends on faith in Christ's once-and-for-all redemptive act on the cross.

3. **Theologia crucis**: *Theology of the cross*: It is Christ alone who saves, through his death on the cross. He is the sole intercessor between heaven and earth, and the Father and the human race.

4. **Sola scriptura**: *Scripture alone*: All true Christian teachings are found only in the Bible, and purgatory is nowhere mentioned in Holy Scripture. Neither is the intercession of the saints.

5. **Docendi sunt christiani**: *Christians should be taught* that purgatory and saintly intercession are both unscriptural fictions and theological errors of the highest magnitude. Unmasking this fraud is paramount: the living cannot pray for the dead in purgatory, nor can the dead in heaven pray for the living.

The rejection of purgatory was universal among Protestants: Luther, Karlstadt, Zwingli, Bucer, Oecolampadius, Calvin, the Anglicans, and even the Radicals. All of them denounced it as a fable, a depraved invention designed by corrupt clerics to fleece the laity. On a popular level, the flow of money to the cult of the dead came to be seen as one of the surest signs of the falsehood of the Roman Catholic Church and of its exploitation of the people, giving rise to the English expression, "Purgatory pick-purse."[18] A Swiss playwright had the pope's character say in his highly satirical anti-Catholic play, *Die Totenfresser* (Those Who Feed on the Dead):

> Church offerings, weekly, monthly, and annual masses for
>   the dead
> Bring us more than enough . . .
> We also put a lot of stock in Purgatory,
> Although Scripture doesn't have much to say about it.
> The reason is that we must use every chance
> To scare the Hell out of the common folk.
> For that is what keeps the cover on our deception.[19]

The unmasking of this "deception" was one of the central messages of the Protestant Reformation, and the logic of purgatory and of the role of suffrages seems to have been a vulnerable point in Catholic theology, and perhaps the surest entry point for doubt. As one sensible Englishman from Lincoln put it:

> If there were any Purgatory and every mass that is said should deliver a soul out of Purgatory, there should be never a soul there, for there be more masses said in a day than there be bodies buried in a month.[20]

Along with the death of purgatory came also a concomitant rejection of all of the "works" or suffrages that supposedly helped to free souls from it. Gone were the masses for the dead, the prayers, anniversaries, chantries, and all else that went with these rituals for the dead. The expression "dead and gone" acquired a new meaning among all Protestants, for once dead, one was literally whisked to either heaven or hell, to realms totally beyond the reach of living humans, where, as that all-important Gospel text (Luke 16:26) put it, a "great gulf" was fixed, "so that they which would pass from hence to you cannot; neither can they pass to us, that would come from thence."

The Protestant dead, therefore, inhabited another dimension in eternity, and were totally segregated from the living. Moreover, when it came to the last vestige of their presence among the living, that of burial, the dead were subjected to physical segregation as well, for it became common among many Protestants to remove the dead from the churches and churchyards, to suburban sites where there could be no easy daily mingling of the sort that had become so commonplace throughout medieval Christendom. Spiritual apartheid and physical apartheid had come into existence, sundering almost all commerce between the living and the dead, save for the disposal of corpses.

This segregation, or apartheid, came into existence rapidly and thoroughly wherever Protestantism took root. One incident alone reveals the depth of the change. Commenting on the revision of Nuremberg's criminal code in 1521, a jurist argued that punishments could no longer be carried out against the corpses of convicted criminals, as had been customary. If a criminal died before his execution, why bother with the full sentence against him? Citing Luther in his report, this jurist opined: "after death a person is freed from all human authority, and stands in God's judgement alone."[21]

Such a change was not only momentous but also very sudden in most places that turned Protestant. The spiritual and cultural consequences of such a rapid transformation are difficult to measure and will have to be taken up in the conclusion to this chapter. The material consequences are easy enough to measure, however, and point to effects that have not been explored very carefully or thoroughly outside eighteenth-century France.[22]

The most immediate effect of the death of purgatory was the disappearance of masses for the dead and of all rituals connected to their postmortem well-being. And this was an economic revolution of sorts. Suffrages for the dead always involved money: whether it was a single mass or a perpetual chantry, some cost always had to be borne by the living, who were usually related to the deceased and had to acquiesce to seeing part of their inheritance consumed by the dead, or, to be more precise, by the clergy. Many postmortem rituals were funded in one way or another through real estate: either through rents or through outright gifts of property to the church. Over the decades and centuries, the transfer of funds and property to the church became substantial.

Though we have no comprehensive analysis of how many clerical positions were funded directly or indirectly by the cult of the dead in pre-Reformation Europe, the relatively spotty research carried out thus far suggests that the link between the dead and the clerics was indeed intense, and that the financial bond between the living and the dead also held much of the church's fabric together. In 1529, a young Protestant lawyer named Simon Fish complained to King Henry VIII that belief in purgatory had placed "more than the third part of all your Realm" in the hands of the clergy.[23] The young John Calvin, writing to his former friend Gerard Roussel—who had just accepted the bishopric of Oleron—upbraided him for taking part in a scam as large and heinous as that of growing rich off the dead.

As Calvin saw it, the annual rents that supported most of the clergy would not exist at all were it not for belief in purgatory, since such income was drawn from bequests that funded masses and prayers for the dead. Moreover, the beneficed clergy lived off the dead, and more specifically on the fiction (*"fause imagination"*) of purgatory. "It is indeed fair to say," Calvin told Roussel, "that you do not own any piece of land that has not been placed in your hands by Purgatory." Calling Roussel a "villain," "thief," and "plunderer," and comparing him to a pirate, Calvin ended their friendship by observing, "you cannot cook your food unless the fire of Purgatory is lit."[24]

Calvin was right, and even Catholic polemicists agreed on this point. Writing in the 1560s, the English cardinal William Allen acknowledged that the whole world knew that the doctrine of purgatory had "founded all Bishoprics, builded all Churches, raised all Oratories, instituted all Colleges, endowed all Schools, maintained all hospitals, set forward all works of charity and religion, of whatever sort soever they be."[25]

Of course, the most immediate effect of the abolition of the cult of the dead, wherever the Protestant Reformation took hold, was the redistribution of the property and funds that the clergy had been consuming in the name of the dead.

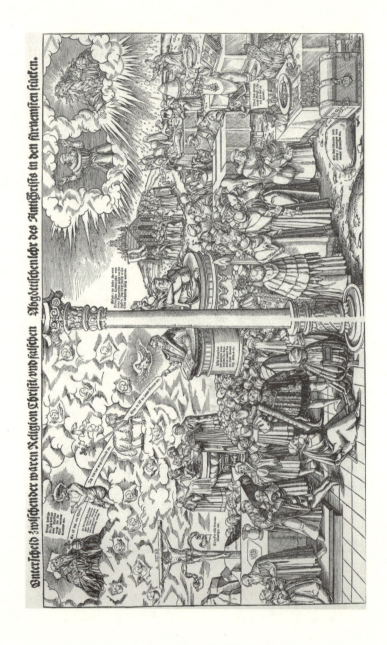

Figure 4.3. Lucas Cranach the Younger, *The Difference between the True Religion of Christ and the False Idolatry of the Antichrist* (ca. 1545). This engraving compares and contrasts Protestant and Catholic rituals to highlight the errors of Catholicism and its obsession with eternity and the dead. The "False" Church on the right stands in sharp contrast with the "True" Church of Martin Luther on the left. It is a visual indictment of all of the "erroneous" rituals of the Roman Catholic Church, most of which have something to do with greed and deception, centered on the afterlife and eternity.

Pictures were especially useful before literacy became widespread. This is an example of the ways in which Protestants used printed propaganda and of how the complex theology of Protestantism could be reduced to simple formulas.

Items to notice in the "False Church" on the right include the following: At lower left, a fat, corrupt monk preaches without a Bible as a demon blows in his ear. His congregation is composed of secular and clerical elites, distinguishable by their attire. At lower right, the pope collects money for indulgences, aided by a fat monk and a nun. In the center is a table full of fat monks; their abbot depicted as a raven in a fool's cap. At center right a priest celebrates mass for the dead, by himself, without a congregation. Above this priest a bishop blesses or exorcizes a bell with holy water. Next to the bell is a dying man, being fleeced at the last minute by Franciscans, who are selling him a cowl and sprinkling him with holy water. Above the dying man are two pilgrims on their way to a shrine. At top left, a shrine and a procession are shown. At top right, St. Francis is trying to intercede (unsuccessfully) before God the Father. God is angry, hurling fire and brimstone.

Items to notice in the "True Church" on the left include the following: At lower right, Luther is preaching from a Bible that is connected directly to God, through Jesus and the Holy Spirit. The large man bearing a cross is John-Frederick of Saxony, Luther's prince, who was imprisoned by Emperor Charles V after being defeated in battle. He symbolizes the price the state is paying for supporting the true church. In the center a baptism is under way, a sacrament mentioned in the Bible. At lower left the Eucharist is being celebrated for the congregation only (not the dead), and communion is being distributed in both species, that is, the bread and the wine. Everyone is taking communion. In the upper half, heaven contains God and angels only, and is devoid of the anger found in the heaven over the False Church.   *Source:* Max Geisberg, *The German Single-Leaf Woodcut: 1500–1550*, 4 vols. (New York: Hacker Art Books, 1974), vol. 2, p. 619.

Smaller changes, too, changed the social and economic fabric in both urban and rural areas. Recently, Eamon Duffy has detailed how the segregation of the dead to an unreachable realm changed life drastically in the small Devonshire village of Morebath.[26] The repercussions of such a change need to be studied in greater detail, especially outside England: how, exactly, was all of this wealth and property redistributed, and how did such a change affect local economies and the European economy as a whole?

The intellectual and spiritual repercussions of this reconfiguration of eternity have yet to be fully assessed, too, and this is no small matter. To reconfigure eternity in the sixteenth century was to redefine many social, political, and economic realities. Changes in belief and changes in the fabric of society went hand in hand, not in a simple cause-and-effect relation, as extreme materialists or intellectual historians might argue, but in a complex and mutually dependent relationship. Altering a mindset or a worldview entails much more than simply rearranging ideas inside people's heads: external changes are as essential for the change in thinking as the ideas are for changes in the "real" world. The reconfiguring of eternity, then, is as much a cause of change as it is a symptom of change.

Without a doubt, in the realm of the abstract, the greatest change brought about by this Protestant reconfiguration of the eternal was a change in focus: away from philosophical speculation and specificity and toward a more practical and apophatic or agnostic approach ("agnostic" in the sense of admitting that what one can know or affirm about certain subjects is severely limited). Whereas the scholastics had debated at length over the logic of eternity, and searched for greater precision on points such as the relation between God's eternity, omniscience, and providence, the Protestants now focused on the ethical, practical effect such concepts should have on the believing Christian.

Martin Luther, for one, saw no point in dwelling on the mystery of eternal bliss: "Human reason can't grasp it by speculation. With our thoughts we can't get beyond the visible and physical. No man's heart comprehends eternity. . . . What pleasure is like in eternity we can't imagine."[27] This is not to say that Luther found meditating on eternity to be useless; on the contrary, he dwelt on it in order to deconstruct medieval paradigms. More than any other Protestant reformer, Luther was given to thinking in terms of paradoxical propositions and binary dialectical oppositions that depended on each other for meaning, despite their apparent contradiction, such as faith and works, law and gospel, flesh and spirit. Consequently, Luther saw mortality and eternity as inescapable horizons, and a basic starting point for understanding human nature and the relationship between God and the human race:

> For we were not created like oxen and asses; we were created for eternity. Therefore when God speaks with us to give a promise, He is not speaking with us for the sake of temporal things only; nor does He concern Himself with the belly only. No, He wants to preserve our soul from destruction and to grant us eternal life.[28]

Luther had read Augustine's *Confessions* and was well acquainted with its discussion of time and eternity, but hardly ever found it necessary to dwell on it, or even to mention it.[29] Meditative speculation of this sort did not suit him at all. Instead, he chose to take the apophatic route—not because he found much to like in Dionysius the Areopagite but because it fit his biblicism and his somewhat nominalist understanding of the hidden God in his absolute power (*potentia absoluta*). "Christ has such length of life that it cannot be expressed," he once said. "Unless we believe it by faith, eternity is beyond expression."[30]

Such musings were rare. In fact, his reflections on eternity are fairly skimpy, overall, and focused on the subject of faith, such as this description of the role of the Eucharist: "Thus the sacrament is for us a ford, a bridge, a door, a ship, and a stretcher, by which and in which we pass from this world into eternal life. Therefore everything depends on faith."[31] Most of the relatively few passages in his writings that deal with eternity are less mystical. In fact, most of them have a very practical, ethical or pastoral bent, even from the earliest days of his career. "To think about the punishments of the wicked as lasting without end, and the equally lasting joys of the good causes the soul to be horrified and stunned in a remarkable way," he once said. "And for one who is not horrified this is a sign that he does not really think nor carefully ponder but passes through superficially and carelessly."[32]

Catholics and Their Dead

As a response to the Protestant Reformation, Catholics embraced their dead even more tightly than before, intensifying the differences between the two religious cultures that arose in the sixteenth century.

Concerning purgatory, the Council of Trent (1545–1563) decreed that indeed "there is a Purgatory, and that the souls there detained are aided by the suffrages of the faithful and chiefly by the acceptable sacrifice of the altar," Further, it also enjoined all bishops to "strive diligently to the end that the sound doctrine of Purgatory, transmitted by the Fathers and sacred councils, be believed and maintained by the faithful of Christ, and be everywhere taught and preached."[33]

Concerning the veneration of the saints in heaven, the council was equally firm in its defense of tradition, asking all bishops to

> instruct the faithful diligently in matters relating to inter-cession and invocation of the saints, the veneration of rel-ics, and the legitimate use of images, teaching them that the saints who reign together with Christ offer up their prayers to God for men, that it is good and beneficial suppliantly to invoke them and to have recourse to their prayers, assistance and support in order to obtain favors from God through His Son, Jesus Christ our Lord, who alone is our redeemer and savior.[34]

This reaffirmation of tradition was extremely successful at all levels, not so much because it was decreed from on high, by pope and council, but because it seems to have been embraced wholeheartedly throughout the Catholic world, both by elites and by common people. Of course, it helped immensely that the elites of church and state cultivated a revival of interest in the dead and the afterlife.

In Spain, arguably the most influential Catholic nation on earth at the time, a prime elite exemplar of this renewed Tridentine piety was the king himself, Philip II, who worked very hard at reifying not only his role as a Catholic monarch but also the church's power over the dead, and the bond between the living and the dead. For starters, King Philip built for himself and his successors a palace-monastery complex unlike any other on earth, the axis of which was the cult of the dead. Built between 1563 and 1596, at the cost of an entire year's worth of treasure from the New World, the immense structure of San Lorenzo del Escorial was in its day the largest building in the world. Within its perimeter, Philip crammed a palace, monastery, basilica, library, and seminary, along with 8,000 relics of the saints, the world's largest and most meticulously catalogued collection, to which were assigned tens of millions of years of indulgences. Staffed by Hieronymite monks, whose sole purpose was to pray for the king and the royal family, both living and dead, the monastery at San Lorenzo was a veritable ritual machine, where masses were offered constantly at numerous altars—except when the Hieronymite rule forced the monks to sleep—and where hundreds of monks chanted the entire psalter day after day, ceaselessly.

Not content with merely living with his monks and priests, King Philip also built his private chambers as close as possible to heaven, directly behind the main altar of the basilica, which was flanked on all sides by the 8,000 relics, and he positioned his room in such a way as to be able to see the main altar from his bed. Directly below this altar, and therefore also beneath his bed, Philip built an immense crypt for the entire Hapsburg dynasty, including his father, himself, and all his future successors to the throne. Whenever Philip stayed at the Escorial, which was as often as he possibly could, he lived and worked and slept directly over his father's corpse and the grave he himself would soon occupy, as well as the grave of his son and of all descendants not yet born.

In his will, Philip addressed so many saintly intercessors that his list of advocates matched name for name the total list of saints invoked in every will written in Madrid. He also pulled out all the stops when it came to suffrages, consigning the Hieronymite fathers to perpetual labor and laying heavy demands on priests elsewhere. Even the Escorial was not enough. First, Philip wanted masses to be said by every single

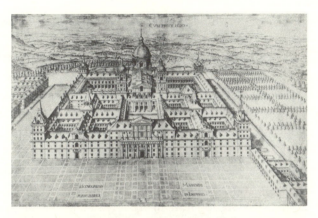

Figure 4.4. San Lorenzo del Escorial: the palace complex of King Philip II of Spain, late sixteenth century. Architects: Juan Bautista de Toledo and Juan de Herrera. When it was completed in 1584, this was the largest building in the world. It served multiple functions: as a palace, monastery, library, school, mausoleum, and reliquary. The bird's-eye view at top gives a sense of its imposing scale. The cutaway view at bottom shows the axis of church and state, sacred and secular, eternal and temporal: the section farthest to the left contains the king's chambers, which adjoin the sacristy and altar, where 8,000 relics were stored and where mass was celebrated constantly. Directly below the altar, an underground crypt (the lowest chamber in the lower left-hand corner of this diagram) served as a burial place for all the monarchs. Philip II not only attended mass while sick in bed, he also slept directly over his own grave and those of his parents and descendants. *Source*: Luis Cervera Vera, *Las estampas y el sumario de El Escorial por Juan de Herrera* (Madrid, 1954).

priest at the Escorial for nine days following his death. Then he asked for 30,000 masses to be said "as quickly as possible" by Franciscans throughout the realm, "with the greatest devotion." Not content with this, Philip also requested that a High Mass be said for his soul at the main altar of the Escorial basilica every single day until Christ's second coming, and added a special prayer for his soul to the Hieronymites' daily canonical hours. Let us not even consider how many tens of thousands of other masses he requested for his relatives, or how he dwelt on every detail of his funeral, or how he practiced dying, or how many memorial services were held throughout the realm after his death and how many hundreds of thousands of candles were used. It might make us all lose our bearings.

Lest this hallucinatory tour of the Escorial prove unimpressive, given that extravagance befits a king, let us consider that Philip and his prayer factory–cum–city of the dead were just the tip of the iceberg. What we find when we examine the wills of his subjects are thousands upon hundreds of thousands, even millions of mirrors reflecting the same sort of obsession, only at a relatively smaller scale. Taken as a whole, the masses and prayers requested by Spaniards during the time of Philip II and his successors, Philip III and Philip IV, would dwarf the efforts at the Escorial and make them seem like a mere period at the end of one sentence in Cervantes' *Don Quixote*. When the cost is finally tallied some time in the future, as I am sure it will be, chances are that the amount of money spent by the subjects of these three Philips on their souls and those of their dead could easily dwarf the amount spent by the monarchs and add up to much more than several years' worth of treasure from the New World.

Two studies carried out independently point in this direction: one by myself in Madrid, the other by Sara Nalle in Cuenca. Using very similar methods and samples—and working without knowledge of the other's efforts—Nalle and I ended up with nearly identical findings. In both Madrid and Cuenca, spending on the dead increased steadily after the decrees of the Council of Trent were put into effect in 1565. In Madrid, the inflation in mass requests was proportionately larger than in Cuenca, owing to the fact that the royal court moved there in 1561, altering the social and economic structure of the city. But the overall pattern in both places reveals an identical obsession with higher numbers, as well as with ever more elaborate funerals. The cost of this inflated interest in the afterlife, which took place parallel to an inflation in the economy, can seem astronomical and perhaps even unhealthy or insane to us. Since Nalle had complete parish records and I did not, she was able to find the prize that eluded me: the long-term cost of all of this. Tracing the bequests that funded the masses over nearly two centuries, Nalle calculated that by 1750, the church owned more than half of Cuenca's properties and nearly half of all of the surrounding land. It also employed about two-fifths of the total population.[35] Given the number of masses requested in Madrid and how much they cost, a similar profile was probably discernible in Madrid's parish records as well, and the figures would prove it, had not all of the papers been burned by the Communists in the 1930s, in an Orwellian effort to erase the past.

Though I could not trace the money in Madrid, I did stumble into a valuable insight when I posed some basic questions about my findings to the eminent economist Albert Hirschman. After helping me make sense of the relation between the inflation in the Spanish economy and the inflation in mass requests, which proved relatively easy to figure out, he said something unexpected, which cast a whole new light on my research. His observation is, at bottom, the tiny seed that eventually grew into this book: "Just think of what else they could have done with that money," said the economist. "Imagine how much more Spain could have accomplished instead!"[36]

Spoken like a good capitalist, perhaps even a Calvinist, as Max Weber might have said. We shall return to this point shortly.

Sinking money into eternity—basically spending a substantial part of their estate into eternal life insurance policies that could only be cashed in beyond this world—was not the only way that Catholics enhanced their links with the dead. All medieval paradigms were reinforced and intensified after the Council of Trent. Devotion to the saints escalated, their ranks swelled by an influx of remarkable holy men and women. Apparitions of the dead continued to be reported and represented in religious art and literature—especially apparitions that confirmed the existence of purgatory and the efficacy of prayers for the dead. Saint Teresa of Avila, for instance, was but one of hundreds of nuns who reported seeing the souls of the dead as they were sprung from purgatory. Teresa herself would also make her rounds, appearing to scores of nuns and priests after her death, even giving instructions on what should be done with her incorruptible body.[37]

In contrast, Protestants did away with apparitions, at least in theory. Though belief in ghosts continued to be part and parcel of Protestant culture, their theologians insisted that all such events were really demonic in nature and that all "ghosts" were really demonic deceptions. Chances are that the afterlife described by the ghost of Hamlet's father in Shakespeare's play brings us closer to popular beliefs than nearly anything else, and what we find him describing to a

Protestant Elizabethan audience is a perfect blend of very *wrong* un-Christian folklore and Catholic beliefs about purgatory:

> I am thy father's spirit,
> Doomed for a certain term to walk the night;
> And for the day confined to fast in fires,
> Till the foul crimes done in my days of nature
> Are burnt and purged away.[38]

It is also highly likely that Shakespeare wanted his audiences to experience the full ambivalence of the Anglican Church's teaching on ghosts, for, given the trouble that Hamlet's father causes, it is indeed quite possible that he was simply a demon.[39]

But if one looks for sharp differences rather than ambivalence, few contrasts can be starker than that between John Calvin's burial and that of Teresa of Avila. Buried in an unmarked grave outside the walls of Geneva, as per his own instructions, Calvin intentionally made himself disappear from the world of the living. After his death, no one prayed for his soul and no one prayed to him. Aside from his many texts, which continue to be read to this day, Calvin ceased to have any relations with the living. How different it was for Teresa. Continually exhumed and reburied, cut, sliced, carved, and scattered all over the world in pieces large and small, Teresa's miraculously incorruptible body became the focus of intense veneration, even to this day. Even as Machiavellian a dictator as the Fascist Francisco Franco tried to claim her hand for himself. Though some masses and prayers were offered for her, as for all souls, no matter how holy, Teresa was soon venerated as a saint and prayed to instead. Canonized in 1620, elevated to Doctor of the Church in 1970, she remains alive among Catholics in myriad ways, beyond her texts.

Monasticism as Vice

Monastics such as Teresa of Avila were close to eternity in several ways, but in two respects they were almost like the dead. First, they were ostensibly "dead" to the world and focused on heaven. In fact, their legal status was akin to the dead, insofar as many of them had to write their last will and testament before going into the monastery. Their wills in sixteenth-century Madrid differed in no respect from those of lay people on their deathbeds. Second, monastics were a lot like the saints in heaven not just because they were ostensibly beyond this world, but also because they were supposed to pray ceaselessly and act as intercessors. Their prayer, combined with their holiness, was supposed to be very effective and to benefit the church at large and especially their patrons and neighbors. In many ways, the relationship between patrons and the monasteries they funded was not very different from that between devotees and their saints in heaven, for whom they built shrines or commissioned artwork. The same was true for entire communities that supported their local monastics. With one foot in eternity, so to speak, monks claimed a very special place in the social, political, and economic structure of the West.

One of the most profound changes brought about by the Protestant Reformation was the abolition of monasticism. Suddenly, in many places, monks and nuns disappeared overnight, their properties seized by civil authorities, along with their vast collective wealth. This massive change, which involved a considerable transfer of property from the church into secular hands, was defended on theological grounds that had a very sharp pragmatic edge to them, an edge that revealed fully one of the most distinctive qualities of Protestantism: its this-worldliness and its disdain for any attempts to lay claims on eternity. Monastics were dismissed as totally useless, not just because the Protestant theology of salvation by faith alone made all of their asceticism and prayer seem like a total waste of time and effort, but also because they seemed like parasites who drained the resources of every community. As one document written by some monks who became Protestant put it:

> We should not sit around idly, waiting for baked doves to fly into our mouths. Work, yes, work is what men must do, each according to his ability, in service to his fellow man. Idleness is forbidden; there is nothing Christian in contemplation.[40]

Another monk turned Protestant, Eberlin von Günzburg, complained about the wastefulness of monasticism, arguing that the way in which "the pious laity pray" through their physical labor was far superior to the singing of the monks. In addition, Eberlin also argued that the empty praying and all of the rules forced on monks—especially the vow of celibacy—were a form of torture, "burdensome, un-Christian, and inhumane," even worse than slavery under the Turks. Among other things, he proposed that all nunneries be turned into academies for marriage, where young girls would be trained for the only kind of life suitable for a Christian woman, that of housekeeping.[41] The contrast between such worldviews and those of Bernard of Clairvaux, cited at the beginning of chapter one, could not be any starker.

Intercession no longer counted as "work" or "service" to the community because Protestants steadfastly refused to consider such a thing possible. Monks were no closer to heaven and eternity than anyone else simply because such closeness was a delusion, even an abusive fiction concocted to exploit the common people. The sole focus of life should be the here and now, not eternity. Physical labor and engagement with the concerns of this world could not only count as prayer, but could also be superior to the kind of prayer monks constantly offered up, in "idleness." In other words, Protestantism "secularized" life: it strained to argue that the *saeculum*, this age, this world, was the only realm Christians could concern themselves with. Protestantism also strained to level the hierarchy that allowed some Christians to be closer to God and eternity than others—the very hierarchy that Dionysius the Areopagite had extolled. And by ridding society of that hierarchy, and of a social order that accepted two tracks to salvation, one higher and one lower, Protestants therefore hoped to bring everyone back to earth, to the temporal realm, at the same level, far from eternity. The rejection of monasticism, which eliminated not only an entire social class but also its otherworldly claims, undergirded the secularizing tendencies of Protestantism. Centuries later, some Protestant theologians would realize this and bemoan the way in which Protestant Christianity had lost its capacity for transcending secular culture. Among those who suggested that Protestants reconsider the Reformation's rejection of monasticism was none other than the eminent twentieth-century theologian Karl Barth.[42]

Mysticism as Delusion

Needless to say, if monasticism was a waste of time and resources, so was its prime objective, contemplation of divine, eternal realities. Aside from a few radicals, such as Thomas Müntzer, who joined the peasant revolts of 1524–1525, and Melchior Hoffman, whose followers took over the city of Münster in 1534, Protestants tended to reject all claims to extraordinary mystical experiences. Müntzer, in fact, held

Luther in contempt for his worldliness and lack of mysticism. "All true pastors must have revelations," Müntzer exclaimed. But very few did, indeed. Convinced that God spoke through prophets who had been tried in the mystical furnace of spiritual self-abandonment, like himself, and sure that the end of the world was at hand, Müntzer raged against them all, calling them "diarreah-makers," "straw doctors," "scrotumlike doctors," and "donkey fart doctors of theology."[43] He saved his worst invectives for Luther, whom he called

> Doctor Liar . . . Doctor Mockery . . . Brother Soft-Life . . . the godless flesh at Wittenberg . . . Malicious black raven . . . Father pussyfoot . . . poor flatterer . . . godless one . . . overlearned scoundrel . . . arch-scoundrel . . . new pope . . . Hellhound . . . clever snake . . . sly fox . . . arch-heathen . . . arch-devil . . . crook . . . rabid, burning fox . . . ambassador of the devil. . . .[44]

Müntzer was an exception, not because of his vitriolic crassness but because he was one of the very few Protestants who thought it possible for time and eternity to intersect, not just in an imminent apocalypse but also within the souls of the faithful. The same was true of the mystically inclined radicals who tried to establish the New Jerusalem at Münster, convinced as they were of their prophetic gifts and of the approaching end of human history. But their tradition would vanish like a puff of smoke with their defeat and executions.

The overwhelming majority of Protestants rejected the possibility of mystical intimacy with the divine in this life, even in the radical Anabaptist tradition.

Although some Protestant leaders, such as Luther, had read the writings of Meister Eckhart's Rhennish disciples, Tauler and Suso, which had influenced Müntzer, the central claim made by all mystics was deemed false by most of them. Luther dismissed all who claimed intimacy with God of this sort as *schwärmer*, or maniacs. Gone was the concept of the *fünklein*, or divine spark of the soul, replaced by a very low anthropology which placed the stain of original sin at the core of the soul instead. Gone were the ecstasies, trances, and transports of contemplatives who merged with God in his eternal now moment, replaced by the flat assertion of sinfulness and finitude and estrangement from God. On this, all major Protestant Reformers could agree. And what Luther had to say, somewhat inchoately, John Calvin (1509–1564) would refine into crystal-clear doctrine. As John Calvin put it, the human soul "is not only burdened with vices, but is *utterly devoid of all good.*"[45] Taking what Luther had said about human nature to its logical conclusion, Calvin would argue that the only way human beings can be saved is by having their will totally effaced by divine grace. So, rather than having some ontological point of contact with the divine, some spark that might enable us to encounter God in his eternal realm, what we have is something so vile, it must be annihilated:

> The Lord corrects our evil will, or rather extinguishes it; he substitutes for it a good one from himself. . . . Good takes its origin from God alone. And only in the elect does one find a will inclined to good. . . . It follows, thence, that man has a right will not from himself, but that it flows from the same good pleasure by which we were chosen before the creation of the world.[46]

For Calvin, and for all those who followed his teaching, the work of salvation and regeneration was all about making humans obedient to God, rather than enabling any sort of spiritual perfection or mystical bonding with God. To obey the commandments and to worship correctly is the most we could hope for, to "express Christ," as he put it, and to "take care that God's glory shine through us . . . and not defile ourselves with the filthiness of sin."[47] Ironically, though Calvin brought eternity to bear on his theology through the doctrine of predestination (being "chosen before the creation of the world"), he denied that we could have any access to it in this life through any sort of mystical ecstasy. And this ironic twist would become one of the distinguishing marks of Protestantism, and through it, of modernity.

Secularism Triumphant

Once eternity had been dismissed from theological discourse as a distant, unreachable dimension, the claims that held together the very structure of the medieval church came tumbling down like a house of cards. If clergy were not the keepers of the keys to eternity, then what was their function? How on earth could they claim a superior status? As Protestants saw it, every claim to clerical supremacy was voided, from the gilded pope all the way down to the most ignorant and slovenly parish vicar.

Shorn of its connection to eternity—which Protestants left in God's hands entirely—the nature and function of the clerical class had to be redefined. And Protestants wasted no time in doing this, both at the highest levels of theological discourse and at the lowest levels of popular propaganda. At the most abstract level, Luther began this redefinition by speaking of "the priesthood of all believers," arguing that all Christians had an equal share in the priesthood of Christ. Other well-educated theologians followed suit. At a popular level, dozens of pamphleteers immediately aimed their sights at whatever resentment the laity must have felt toward the clergy and their claims of superiority. If, in fact, all Christians had an equal share in Christ's priesthood, why should clerics be exempt from taxes, or from the justice of civil courts? Why should bishops and popes claim a higher place than "temporal" or "secular" rulers when, in fact, absolutely everyone, including the pope, was totally outside of eternity, stuck in this "temporal" realm? As an ex-Augustinian monk put it, why should the clergy turn themselves into "sacred cows," promoting the illusion of separateness and special "spiritual right," claiming "all kinds of exemptions and privileges from Heaven"?[48] One of the leaders of the Protestant faction in Strasbourg, Wolfgang Capito, summed up his party's argument by saying that all clergy should instead be subject to the same civil obligations as the laity, instead of being "treated as gods," and that any claim to the contrary was "against God, against the love of one's neighbor, against all sense of fair play, against human nature and reason, and detrimental to the community at large."[49]

Given such sentiments, it stands to reason that Protestants also accused the Catholic clergy of subjecting the laity to all sorts of fictions and superstitions, especially through ritual. If their claim to eternity was false, then why not everything else they handled? One pamphleteer dismissed the work of the clergy as "fantasy, magic, heresy, ghosts of the Devil, and superstition."[50] Eberlin von Günzburg zeroed in on what he saw as the greatest deception of all: the clergy's claim over the dead. As Eberlin saw it, no other claim did more to exploit fear and foster "superstition." Of course, to make that argument, and to hope it would strike a responsive chord, Eberlin had to assume that his readers had already figured out that the clergy's claims on eternity was bogus, and that their sole intention was to fleece the laity:

Superstition and naiveté are so obvious among simple, trusting people, and have been carefully observed by priests. The priest is such a sly and clever fellow. He projects such apostolic authority in the confessional and from the pulpit and has so many stories and explanations about everything that pertains to the dead. Simple, naive people are no match for him, and he easily moves them to establish perpetual masses and anniversaries and to increase weekly and monthly vespers, vigils, and masses for departed souls.[51]

Protestants would not agree on how church and state should relate to one another. Luther would propose a "two-kingdom" theory in which church and state each minded their own business but in which the church was ultimately under the control of the secular powers. In Switzerland and southern Germany, Ulrich Zwingli and others would simultaneously insist on stripping the clergy of their exalted status and on making them instrumental in the running of the civil order. Some have called their approach "theocratic."[52] John Calvin and all of his followers seized on this theocratic ideal, in which the clergy, stripped of their hold on eternity, did their best to make sure that civil government was godly, and that no one in the here and now would commit themselves to anything but the present order. Ironically, as it turned out, by focusing on the transformation of the here and now rather than on the community's bonds to eternity, Calvinists turned their clergy into a formidable elite class.[53] In contrast, Protestants in the radical tradition created a semi-monastic ethic for themselves, of separation from "the world" and its wicked ways. And they would pay dearly for holding on to such an ethic, being persecuted by other Protestants and Catholics alike.[54]

But no matter how bitterly they disagreed about their interpretation of the true Christian approach to church-state relations, all Protestants could agree on one item: the clergy were not at all ontologically superior to the laity, precisely because they had no "magic" or "superstitious" key to eternity. Their role was to preach the Gospel and to make sure their flocks stayed keenly focused on their behavior in the here and now. The hereafter was beyond everyone's reach.

As the clerics were secularized, so were time and space. One of the hallmarks of the Protestant Reformation was the nearly instant abolition of sacred places and sacred times. As all Protestants saw it, regardless of their differences on other issues, the divine and eternal were not more intensely present in any special locations. Gone were shrines, pilgrimages, processions. Gone were the altars. Churches were still special places, insofar as they allowed the faithful to gather together to hear the Word of God preached by clerics who were full citizens, just like everyone else. But there was nothing inherently sacred about that physical space. A barn would be just as good, or even an open field. As Protestants also saw it, the only special day mentioned in the Bible is the Sabbath. Although Luther retained a fondness for Christmas, other Protestants did not even hang on to that. The calendar was cleared, usually in one brutal sweep. Gone were all the feasts and the fasts, gone were all public celebrations that surrounded the cult of the saints. As all places were equally good for finding God, so were all days. And six days out of the week were all equally good for devoting oneself to useful activities: no breaks in the routine except for Sunday, when in many a Protestant town one was expected to show up at church, a place that was no more or no less sacred than one's bedchamber or workshop.

Salvation had been considerably "secularized." And so had the world.

But secularization cannot and should not be ascribed to Protestants alone, much less to their theology. Not at all. In fact, it could be argued that their take on church-state relations is a reflection of much deeper social, political, cultural, and economic changes that were sweeping through Western Europe in the sixteenth century. It could also be argued that their success was due to the fact that they were responding to trends rather than creating them. In many ways, what was then known as "Christendom" was bubbling over with a renewed interest in things of this world rather than in eternity. In quite a different sphere, away from earnest reformers, we find proof of this, above all, in the work of one political theorist who ended up being equally despised by Catholics and Protestants, Niccolò Machiavelli (1469–1527).

If it is taken literally, at face value, Machiavelli's manual for rulers, *The Prince,* could be interpreted as an outright rejection of any conceptions of virtue held dear by Christians. It could also be seen as totally devoid of any interest in eternity whatsoever, and solely focused on the here and now, totally stripped of any intimations of immortality beyond those that come from seizing and holding on to earthly authority. Prevailing opinion leans toward this sort of interpretation, even though there are eloquent dissenters.[55] Given the shockingly this-worldly and cynical tone of the text, a spiritual reading of any sort takes effort. Some would say it also takes a leap of the imagination to see Machiavelli as anything but a cold-blooded materialist, but others dig deep beneath the surface of the text, for hidden spiritual nuggets.[56]

But let us step aside from these scholarly disagreements for now. Whether or not Machiavelli was a spiritual man matters little when it comes to the attitude reflected in his *Prince,* which is itself, on the surface, boldly unchristian. If nothing else, this text is a clear testimony not only of attitudes that could be held in the early sixteenth century, but also of the totally unchristian behavior of ostensibly Christian rulers. So, even if seen as an oblique critique of "the world," as monks might have said, *The Prince* still provides us with a very clear glimpse of attitudes and behavior that were part and parcel of late medieval and early modern civilization. If we focus on the text itself and take it at face value, *The Prince* has plenty to reveal about Machiavelli's and Luther's world, if not about Machiavelli himself.

In *The Prince*, Machiavelli boldly argues that the only genuine virtue in rulership is the ability to gain and maintain power, and the only genuine immortality is that which is found in monuments and histories that celebrate someone's deeds. Gone are many of the chief assumptions of Christendom, such as an unquestioning belief in the seven virtues, or in the necessity of modeling one's behavior on fixed principles that favor love of neighbor, justice, magnanimity, or faith in anything other than raw power.

Indebted as much to the Christian notion of original sin as to his own observations, Machiavelli argued that human beings were driven by selfishness and greed, and deeply prone to violence; consequently, ignorance of human nature seemed worse to him than ignorance of history. It was not through the arts of rhetoric or catechisms or observance of the seven virtues that one could attain and maintain power, he argued, but rather through the exercise of raw power, and even through cruelty, if necessary. Clergy have no place in *The Prince* save as tools of the cunning ruler. According to Machiavelli, people did not respond as well to a fine speech or a magnanimous gesture as they did to plain fear. "Is it better for a ruler to be loved or feared?" asked Machiavelli. His answer was as dispassionate as all of his advice, and every bit as calculating: fear is the better tool, he said, perhaps even a mix of love and fear, for love alone will never prevail over human wickedness.[57]

Employing historical examples, Machiavelli went on to show how the classical and Christian virtues could be seen as vices in some cases: temperance could turn into inefficiency, generosity into bankruptcy, and charity into vulnerability and collapse. Conversely, cruelty, judiciously applied could turn into a virtue higher than any other. A lot depended on "whether cruel deeds are committed well or badly."[58] Something that might count as a vice in Christian ethics, then, could really lead to safety and well-being rather than divine retribution. Eternity is nowhere to be seen, on any horizon: no heaven or hell, and no purgatory, even though he was a Florentine, just like Dante. If taken literally, Machiavelli was an unflinching realist whose advice was utterly antithetical to reigning paradigms, and as brutal as the world itself: "I believe that we are successful when our ways are suited to the times and circumstances, and unsuccessful when they are not. . . . If it were possible to change one's character to suit the times and circumstances, one would always be successful."[59]

Published posthumously in 1532, when the Protestant Reformation was already eleven years old, *The Prince* went on to elicit a wide range of responses, from emulation at one end to fear and censure at the other.[60] Though thoroughly condemned by Catholics and Protestants alike as "atheistic,"[61] Machiavelli's book would never disappear from view, a constant reminder of the gulf between the real and the ideal, or the best and the worst in human nature. One might also say it proved beyond a shadow of a doubt that eternity could be unmasked as a *mere* concept, not by railing against its existence, but simply by ignoring it altogether. No wonder, then, that the true measure of Machiavelli's place in history may lie in language rather than political thought. From the sixteenth century down to our own time, the adjective *Machiavellian* has seldom been meant as a compliment.[62]

If Machiavelli proves anything at all besides the fact that Christian idealism had become but a dream by the early 1500s, it was that his age was immensely complex, and full of contradictions. Perhaps he also proves, even more than any Protestant Reformer bent on "secularizing" the world, that belief in eternity was more ephemeral than any theologian would admit at that time, and that all changes in world view that would follow could not help but shuffle eternity ever closer to the realm of the purely imaginary and the totally dispensable.

Eternity at Twilight

What are we to make of the Protestant Reformation of eternity, then? Much, I would like to argue, but not too much. Protestants did more than simply change beliefs by doing away with purgatory, rejecting an accessible eternity, and segregating the living and the dead: they reordered their society and their economy. In the sixteenth century as in our own, to change beliefs was to change the world, or to adjust thinking to changes in the world.

Catholics had a way of interweaving the temporal and eternal and of calling the dead to mind in a very concrete way, re-figuring and re-presenting their social proximity constantly, whether through relics or masses for the dead. Among Catholics, then, the dead were not merely remembered, as was the case among Protestants, but actually *re-membered* and reintegrated into the social and economic fabric of the community.[63] Masses for the dead, like relics, served various purposes simultaneously at different levels. Masses were both currency and a commodity: as currency they purchased insurance for eternity, as commodities they could be purchased for a certain price. Either way, they had real value, the kind that translates into money, and into social bonds and obligations of all sorts, linking not just the living and the dead but all of the living who find themselves handling the postmortem affairs of their dead. Relics were both material and spiritual treasures, priceless temporal and eternal gems that demanded veneration and always exacted some kind of price, like everything else. If one was a king or prince, one could collect them by the thousands; if not, one could at least genuflect before them at church, or perhaps even be lucky enough to kiss them. Either way, they too had real value, the kind that translates into power, and into the most tangible sort of bond between heaven and earth, the temporal and eternal, and the living and the dead.

Among Protestants, what do we find in place of masses and relics? What, if anything, fills the void left by the disappearance of the dead in purgatory and heaven?

The social and cultural repercussions of this redefinition of death and the afterlife have never been the subject of much sustained study. Only very recently has it been proposed that this severing of the bond between the living and the dead should be viewed as a major change in the daily lives of Christian Europeans.[64] On a personal and social level, the shift from a communally shared responsibility for each death to a very personal and private one signified a turn toward individualism—a turn that has been identified as the key to modernity.[65] This individualistic turn was perhaps most intense for Protestants at the moment of death, and Martin Luther was well aware of it. The words of Luther quoted once before bear repeating at this point: "The summons of death comes to us all, and no one can die for another. Every one must fight his own battle with death by himself, alone."[66]

The psychological and cultural impact of this individualism has yet to be adequately analyzed by historians. Suddenly, death and the afterlife stopped being a communal experience. Barred from aiding the poor souls in purgatory, and also from praying to the saints in heaven, and from seeking the suffrages of their relatives and neighbors, Protestants now faced the divine tribunal and their eternal destiny *alone*, at the end of *this* life. Gone was the communion of saints, and gone too was the chance to earn salvation in the world to come, for eternity. *This* life and *this* world, then, became the sole focus of religion, as did the *individual* over the community and even over all of history itself. This fundamental Protestant insight was eloquently summarized in the mid-twentieth century by Rudolph Bultmann, as follows:

> *The meaning of history lies always in the present*, and when the present is conceived as the eschatological present by Christian faith the meaning in history is realised. Man who complains: "I cannot see meaning in history, and therefore my life, interwoven in history is meaningless," is to be admonished: do not look around yourself into universal history, you must look into your own personal history. Always in your present lies the meaning of history, and you cannot see it as a spectator, but only in your responsible decisions. In every moment slumbers the possibility of being the eschatological moment. You must awaken it.[67]

In *The Protestant Ethic and the Spirit of Capitalism*, Max Weber argued that Protestants gained an economic edge over Catholics because they shifted their attention away from the hereafter to the here and now, developing a piety he dubbed "this-worldly asceticism."[68] Weber also argued that the Reformation was one giant step in the long, arduous process of "the elimination of magic from the world."[69] Though he did

not focus on death rituals per se in order to defend his the-
sis, perhaps he should have, for the economic repercussions
of this individualistic, "this-worldly" and "un-magical" turn
were profound and very easy to discern and quantify. Societies that had previously invested heavily in the cult of the
dead suddenly redirected a substantial amount of money and
resources to other ends. The significance of this major difference between Protestant and Catholic cultures seems even
larger when one takes into account that the Catholic Church
responded to the Protestant rejection of purgatory by stressing the value of masses for the dead more than ever before,
and that Catholics everywhere intensified their investment
in the afterlife, at least until the eighteenth and nineteenth
centuries.

Religion is all about finding more in life than meets the
eye, and especially about intimations of immortality. The
Protestant Reformation is a key turning point in Western
history for many reasons, so anyone who singles out one or
two of the changes brought about by Protestantism is really
shortchanging history. But way up on the list, among the big-
gest of changes, we can see the dead disappearing, vanishing
into a nebulous eternity, with only two small doors on the
horizon, only large enough for one person to pass through:
one leading to heaven and the other to hell. And what lies
behind the doors can only be imagined with great caution, a
leap of faith, and a Bible in hand.

The Reformation of eternity was a significant first step toward the elevation of this world as the ultimate reality and
towards the extinction of the soul. I am not suggesting an
immediate causal relationship, but merely pointing to a clear
trajectory over several centuries. Whether or not the secularization of the West is due mainly or even solely to Protestants is not the issue. Lest we forget, Rabelais could speak

of a "great perhaps" in 1553, when Protestantism had not yet made serious inroads in France. And Machiavelli's *Prince* may have been published in 1532, but it was written before Martin Luther ever thought about taking on John Tetzel's traveling indulgence carnival. On the surface, Machiavelli seemed untroubled by the absence of eternity in all of his thinking, or by the absence of Protestants. Moreover, if we listen to the complaints of reforming clergy, we can come away with the impression that unbelief was rampant, as in this allegation from 1620: "A great number of Christians, even of Catholics, do not believe that there is an eternity in Hell and in Heaven; that is to say, they would certainly live otherwise if they truly did believe it."[70] Apparently, then, there was already some unbelief and some "secularization" at work in sixteenth-century Europe, gnawing at the status quo from within.[71] But there is no denying the fact that, on the whole, zealous Protestants did much more than Machiavelli to dismantle those social, political, and economic structures that reified eternity for early modern Western Europeans. After all, the vast majority of Italians continued offering masses for the dead for centuries, and many do so still, even in our own day. But the vast majority of Saxons and Zurichers, and Englishmen and Scots, stopped praying for their dead altogether nearly five centuries ago.

Tracing the history of a concept such as that of eternity allows us to see how ideas can indeed become concrete realities, or reflect them, and how, with the passage of time, ideas and their concrete manifestations can wax and wane, often in tandem. Many of our chief unquestioned assumptions about "reality" are social constructions. As an exile who fled a repressive, soul-crushing regime in which thought was carefully monitored and all deviations from Marxist ideology were brutally punished, I speak from experience. Anyone who ends up in North America or Western Europe after fleeing a totalitarian state where talk of "liberty" or "human rights" or "freedom of the press" is illegal will be immediately stunned by the way in which such concepts—so utterly *wrong* and inconceivable, and so costly to espouse in the place one has fled from—are accepted with total nonchalance, unquestioningly, in a society that holds them not only as "self-evident" truths but even as sacred ones.

The stark difference that ideas can make in society and the interdependence of ideological and political superstructures can be perceived most easily by those who have lived in places where thinking is carefully monitored and the meaning of key terms such as "dignity" are cunningly manipulated. When all is said and done, however, one must grudgingly admit that dignity itself is a culturally conditioned concept. To admit this at all, even grudgingly, is painful. Cultures and culturally conditioned responses are inseparable, as are the unquestioned assumptions, concepts, and structures that govern every society. This is what my own experience as an exile has taught me. That ideas are culturally conditioned does not make them any less real, or any less of a blessing or a curse.

That we sophisticates in the early twenty-first century can think of ourselves as "animals," and as closer to chimps than to God, is a culturally conditioned response: a distinctly modern or postmodern attitude that requires a Machiavellian take on the world and an acceptance of the spiritual apartheid that the Protestant Reformers began to enforce on the dead in the sixteenth century.[72] Thinking this way is our greatest blessing and our greatest curse as a culture. It's our blessing because it keeps us from blowing ourselves up on a crowded bus for the sake of some unseen paradise or from killing each other over the correct interpretation of the afterlife. It's our curse because it makes death so final, evil so banal, and life so utterly puzzling or pointless.

So we treasure those few, precious chromosomes that separate us from the chimps, or we bewail them. Knowing that we came from nothing and are headed back to nothing is quite a burden to bear, as is nakedness in any climate. We rage against the dying of the light, along with the poets, unable to really understand the eternal silence of those infinite spaces between our words.

And since we can't ask questions about ultimate concerns, we have no answers.

Welcome to modernity and to its fleeting shadow, post-modernity, into which we must now venture.

V

From Eternity to Five-Year Plans

In 1882, four years before her death, Emily Dickinson would write from her splendid isolation in Amherst, Massachusetts:

> Those—dying then,
> Knew where they went—
> They went to God's Right Hand—
> That Hand is amputated now
> And God cannot be found—[1]

Dickinson, who thought of herself as given to "Sweet Skepticism" whenever she chose not to call herself a Druid, Cynic, or Hermetic, thus expressed her awareness of living in a "now" quite different from some "then," when God and his eternity could be taken for granted. Belief had been replaced by doubt and a distrust of anything the senses cannot confirm. A mere thirty-five miles from the spot where Jonathan Edwards had delivered his infamous sermon, "Sinners in the Hands of an Angry God," one hundred forty one years earlier, Emily Dickinson could say:

> Death is a dialogue between
> The spirit and the dust.
> "Dissolve," says Death. The Spirit, "Sir,
> I have another trust."
> Death doubts it, argues from the ground.
> The Spirit turns away,
> Just laying off, for evidence,
> An overcoat of clay.[2]

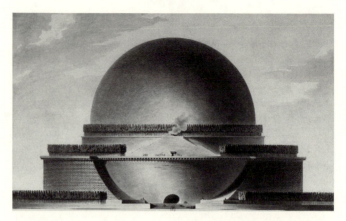

Figure 5.1. Étienne-Louis Boullée, *Cénotaphe a Newton* (1784). This design for a monument in honor of Isaac Newton is a fitting symbol for its age, and for the displacement of faith by reason and of heaven and eternity by mathematics and physics. The colossal sphere is a celebration of Newton and his discoveries, and of humanity's newfound freedom from ignorance and superstition. The geometrical purity of the structure, all planes, circles, and spheres, is intended to reflect that of the universe, which is not only perfectly intelligible but very orderly and homologous with reason itself. The gigantic scale (highlighted by the diminutive trees and human figures) reflects the Enlightenment's take on the significance of Newton's findings, and also its attitude toward eternity and immortality as something found only in the collective memory of posterity.

This hollow sphere would have been some 120 meters in diameter (nearly 400 feet, or forty stories), and would have functioned as a planetarium as well as a memorial. Its upper masonry shell was to be pierced all around to let in points of sunlight during the day, precisely arranged like the stars in the night sky, to recreate the vault of the heavens. At night, the sphere was to be illuminated within by an enormous armillary sphere at its center containing a candle-lit model of the solar system, mounted on a series of interlinked rotating rings. Though the structure was never built, this engraving was widely circulated. Architectural historians doubt that eighteenth-century technology was advanced enough for such a project.

Boullée's written paean to Newton—"Sublime spirit! Vast genius and profound! Divine being! . . . I conceived the idea of surrounding thee with thy discovery, and thus, somehow, surrounding thee with thyself."—reflects the Enlightenment's penchant for deifying the human.

Though much of her poetry is suffused with a transcen-
dental, mystical fervor, a reverent agnosticism also prevails:

> At least—to pray—is left—is left—
> Oh Jesus—in the Air—
> I know not which Thy Chamber is—
> I'm knocking everywhere—[3]

In many ways, Dickinson is one of us still, despite the fact
that she was merely modern and we are supposedly postmodern. Her "then" is also ours, as is her "now." The aim
of this chapter is to trace the evolution of the skepticism that
found voice in Dickinson, and to puzzle over some of the
ironic twists that make every "now" and every "then"—even
postmodern ones—seem as insubstantial and mystifying as
eternity itself.

Fanning the Flames of Hell

It could be argued that the flowering of doubt and skepticism
that accompanied the upheavals of the Reformation era was
fertilized by a surfeit of belief and religious zealotry and that,
paradoxically, the excesses of faith were also engendered by
an overabundance of doubt. It's an ancient conundrum, as
old as the human race: those who cast doubt on belief often deepen faith among those who believe, and those who
stridently insist on promoting their beliefs over and against
those who deny them often strengthen their unbelief, at least
immediately. Few vicious cycles can compete with the vortex engendered by faith and doubt, the ultimate yin and
yang. And few such vortices can compare with that which
spun out of control in the sixteenth and seventeenth centuries. As religious strife intensified and as skepticism became

more prevalent, rival churches seized on eternity ever more intensely, claiming sole possession of heaven and fanning the flames of hell.

Various historians have argued that Protestants and Catholics were very much alike in their obsession with hell, especially in the seventeenth century, when highly detailed meditations on the subject flourished. Apparently, many among the faithful loved the subject too, for devotional texts that focused on death and the afterlife in which hell figured prominently were a popular best-selling genre. Hellfire sermons rang out in both Protestant and Catholic churches frequently, and their warning cry was always clear: eternity could best be understood in connection to sin and hell. As one Spanish Jesuit put it, "Watch your step. Why do you mock eternity; why don't you fear the eternal death, why do you love this temporal life so much? You are on the wrong track; change your life."[4] If such warnings were not enough, graphic descriptions of hell might do the trick:

> I wish you could open a window through which you would view what happens in Hell, and see the torments inflicted on the rich who live in ease and have no compassion for the poor. Oh, if you could see how their flesh is boiled in those cauldrons and how they are baked in those inexorable flames, where every single devil will sear them with firebrands. . . . And it will be very good to imagine how those who can't stand the summer heat outside of their roomy cellars will suffer in the blaze of the eternal fire.[5]

According to some historians, books, essays, and sermons on hell proliferated in this period owing to the common processes of "confessionalization," "social disciplining," and "state building" shared by Protestants and Catholics. Scaring the hell out of people, literally, was a strategy of the early modern state: it was a way of creating a more fearful and docile citizenry, with the help of the church.[6] Whether or not this reductionist interpretation of the place of hell in early modern culture will stand the test of time remains to be seen, but it is safe to bet that hell itself will not be easily dismissed by those who study this time period.[7]

One of the most significant devotional texts of the seventeenth century was Juan Eusebio Nieremberg's *The Difference between the Temporal and the Eternal,* a treatise that was not only published repeatedly but also translated into many other languages.[8] Nieremberg's *Difference* is as intensely dualistic and ascetical in tone as the title suggests: the chief aim of this Jesuit naturalist and theologian was to instill fear and hope in his readers simultaneously: to warn them of the easy road to hell and to point them toward the steep and narrow path to heaven. As did all his predecessors and contemporaries, Nieremberg emphasizes the contrast between the temporal, passing world we inhabit and the eternal world that awaits us; its dualism is as stark as its anthropology. "Everything that is precious on earth, everything honored and esteemed, is smoke and shadow, considering its brief duration and the eternity of that fire of the life to come."[9] He also elaborates on the torments each sense will be subjected to for eternity as retribution for sin, and presses further beyond the "fire-bodies" of Ignatius Loyola's *Spiritual Exercises,* forever engulfed in flames, inside and out, to consider even greater internal suffering. The powers of the soul—will, reason, and memory—shall suffer the worst torments. The will, he warns, shall be wracked by an eternal self-abhorrence, and undying anger toward God and all of creation. It will also be eternally subjected to "insufferable sadness."[10] Adding fuel to the flames—on top of all the horrible demons he has described at length, and the physical tortures they will inflict on sinners, which he has just outlined in great detail—Nieremberg goes on to claim that one's own memory will become one of the worst and cruelest torturers (*verdugos*) in hell.

The memory will remind one constantly of what one did wrong, and of what opportunities were missed. In brief, one will blame oneself for eternity, without rest, without end. Nieremberg drove home the point with prose as overbearing as a Baroque altarpiece:

> The miserable wretch in Hell will remember with great regret how many times he could have deserved Heaven, and how he ended up deserving Hell instead, and shall say to himself: "Oh how many times I could have prayed, but wasted the time on playing instead! Now I'm paying for it! How many times I should have fasted, but gave in to my appetite! Now I'm paying for it! How many times I could have given alms, but spent the money on sin! Now I'm paying for it! How many times I was asked to forgive my enemies, but instead I took vengeance on them! Now I'm paying for it! How many times I should have been patient, but suffered grudgingly! Now I'm paying for it! How many times I could have performed acts of charity and humility, but I was cruel to my brothers! Now I'm paying for it! How many times I could have partaken of the sacraments, but instead remained unwilling to avoid occasions of sin! Now I'm paying for it!" You never lacked an opportunity to serve God, but never availed yourself of the chance; and now you're paying for it. See here, you damned wretch, how you lost Heaven by giving in to yourself and fooling around with childish things. . . . It is all your fault, and now you're paying for it.[11]

Despite its florid Chirrigueresque excess, so fossilized, this is a very modern hell, for the guilty ego torments itself forever, with no psychotherapists to consult. But this is not all. This realm of everlasting self-inflicted pain is smack in the middle of the fiery pit and the slimy stink-hole, where all of damned humanity is crammed together like grapes in a wine press. And Nieremberg makes it clear that there will never, ever, be any relief from all of this:

> That fire shall never die, as Isaiah says, nor will you ever die, so that your torments can be everlasting. After a hundred years, and after one hundred thousand million years, your torments shall be as alive and strong as on the first day.[12]

If you are depressed by now, as well you should be, then you might not want to ponder the fact that Nieremberg was just the tip of the iceberg, so to speak. Many other writers and preachers harped on these themes, ad nauseam. Most of them stoked the fires of hell in the imagination, through graphic meditations. One such writer, another Jesuit named Drexelius, or Jeremiah Drechsel (1581–1638), penned many best-sellers, including *Considerations on Eternity*, first published in 1620, and *Death, the Messenger of Eternity*, published in 1627. Drechsel's books on eternity were not philosophical or theological explorations of eternity but very pragmatic guides that aimed to improve their readers' attitude and behavior. In our own day, they might be called self-help books, though it is hard to imagine them on any bookstore shelf, much less next to the tabloids and the diet books at the supermarket checkout. Drechsel's *Considerations on Eternity*, which was reprinted and translated numerous times, is filled with the kinds of meditations that Jesuits were famous for, such as the following, which merits being quoted at length, simply because the cadence of its seemingly interminable sentences is inseparable from its message:

Suppose there is a mountain composed of minute grains of sand, as large as the whole world, or in mass and size even greater, and that only a single grain be taken from this mountain by an angel each year. How many thousands of years, and again thousands upon thousands; how many hundred thousands, nay how many thousand millions of years will have passed before the mountain would appear to diminish and decrease? . . . Let us suppose that finally the last grain of this immense mountain has actually been counted; yet eternity exceeds it by an incomparable length (and nothing is more certain), because there is no comparison, no proportion between the finite and the infinite. Eternity admits of no confines, no boundaries; therefore the damned will burn during this long, this incomprehensible term of years in perpetual flames, until a mountain of so great size . . . be transferred to another place. But the measure and limit of their torments will be so far from being ended at that time, that it can then be said: "Now eternity is just beginning; nothing has been subtracted from it, it is still entire. After a thousand years, after a hundred thousand years, there is not yet an end nor middle nor beginning of eternity, but its measure is *always*."[13]

Such meditations had a point, beyond scaring the hell out of readers. Drechsel was a Jesuit, after all, and their core training manual, the *Spiritual Exercises*, was all very much like this: meditations with a purpose. Drechsel himself delivered the message several times, just in case the reader was too dense to catch the drift of such exercises:

"Momentary is that which delights; eternal that which tortures" . . . these words, thus engraved on the heart, must then especially be pondered on and more frequently repeated, when pleasure attracts, when passion incites, when luxury entices, when the flesh is rebellious, when the spirit grows weak, when there is occasion or danger of sin.[14]

Historians who stress "social disciplining" as the main characteristic of this period might say that Drechsel was doing his best to create compliant citizens for the rising nation-states, especially when none of them had regular police forces patrolling the streets. But Drechsel might disagree with such an assessment, at least in part. What he also had in mind went beyond that level of pragmatism, or indoctrination.

> Think therefore of the ancient days, and have in mind the eternal years. Think on eternity, my friend, think, think on eternal punishments and eternal joys, and never (safely do I promise it) will you complain about any adversity. The following words will never fall from your lips: "This is too severe; this is intolerable; this is too hard." You will say that all things are tolerable and easy, and never will you be more satisfied with yourself than when you are most afflicted.[15]

So *that* was the payoff: with eternity as one's horizon, life can be tolerable, even good. In an age without anesthesia, vaccines, antibiotics, indoor plumbing, air conditioning, or toilet paper, this might have very well been the greatest self-help book on the market. And readers must have agreed, for it sold consistently well for over a century.[16]

Heaven, Reshuffled

Drechsel and Nieremberg were contemporaries of scientific and mathematical pioneers Galileo Galilei, René Descartes, Johannes Kepler, and William Harvey. Nieremberg, who outlived Drechsel by two decades, was much younger than Francis Bacon and much older than Gottfried Wilhelm Leibniz, John Locke, and Isaac Newton, but walked the earth at the same time as they.[17] Nieremberg might have lived in the seventeenth century, the so-called Age of Reason, or the time of the scientific revolution, but he nonetheless embodied older values one could call "medieval." A liminal figure, Nieremberg was both an ascetic and something of a modern scientist who spent most of his life in Madrid, teaching natural history at the Jesuits' Colegio Imperial, serving as a confessor at the royal court, and writing on subjects as diverse as botany, biology, astronomy, political theory, philosophy, history, biography, biblical exegesis, theology, and mysticism. Although he authored an extremely influential book on the flora and fauna of Asia, Africa and the New World (*Historia Naturae Peregrinae*), Nieremberg did no research of his own but simply compiled with consummate care all the detailed information sent to him by Jesuit missionaries from all corners of the globe.[18] So, while he taught science and worked as an encyclopedist, relying on others for empirical observations of nature, Nieremberg did no research of his own. Moreover, he tended to view nature as a theologian rather than as a scientist, and chose to prepare himself for eternity by shunning the material world and punishing his own body. His asceticism was not only unusual for a Jesuit but also an extreme manifestation of values that would have repelled "modern" men such as Descartes, Locke, and Newton:

> There was not a single part of his body that he failed to mortify in its own way: on his arms and thighs he wore iron cuffs and chains with sharp points; on his wrists, bristle bracelets and smaller iron chains. He would fill his shoes with hard peas and beans, which dug into his feet like nails, and

wounded him with every step he took. Around the neck he wore a cord made of bristle studded with barbed wire, and this he stretched across his chest and waist. He wore girdles and crosses on his chest and back, and on top of it all, a hair shirt that reached down to his knees.[19]

Yet at the very same time that Nieremberg was busy torturing himself, others were developing the scientific method and shifting paradigms, altering the way in which the entire cosmos was perceived. Critiques of religion, and of Christianity in particular, grew in intensity throughout the seventeenth and eighteenth century, gaining ever more ground among educated elites who trusted reason rather than faith and considered themselves "enlightened." First came the dismantling of the traditional cosmos, in which heaven and hell were not other dimensions but physical locations. In the older, traditional cosmos, earth was at the center of the universe, surrounded by seven heavenly spheres: the heaven where God and the blessed souls dwelt was the highest place of all, the empyrean or seventh heaven, eternity itself, beyond time; hell was the lowest place of all, inside at the center of the earth. Illogically, hell was also eternal, though part of the terrestrial dimension. Thanks to the astronomical discoveries of Nicholas Copernicus (1473–1543) and Galileo Galilei (1564–1642), the traditional geography of the cosmos and the afterlife was blown away, and questioning increased.

No longer the center of the universe, the earth now seemed a mere speck among many, adrift in that boundless expanse of nothingness that was once known as heaven. The existential axis mundi that made human beings the ultimate end of creation had not only shifted, it had vanished altogether, along with God's eternal realm, only to be replaced by a seemingly meaningless assemblage of gyrating objects that pointed to nothing beyond themselves. From that time forward, no one who was well educated could envision heaven or eternity itself as part of the visible universe. All that was "out there" was boundless space, flecked with lifeless orbs, all of which gyrated with mathematical precision, much like the inside of a clock. Poets such as John Donne (1572–1631) had their way of reacting to the paradigm shift:

> And new Philosophy calls all in doubt,
> The Element of fire is quite put out;
> The Sun is lost, and th'earth, and no man's wit
> Can well direct him where to look for it . . .
> 'Tis all in pieces, all coherence gone.[20]

The gifted mathematician, inventor, and philosopher Blaise Pascal (1623–1662) gave voice to this trauma in starker terms, saying, "The eternal silence of these infinite spaces fills me with dread."[21]

So it was that the heaven of old was displaced, that heaven which was one with the sky—always above, always visible—that heaven above the planets and stars, *up* to which Jesus had ascended bodily, which was occupied by God, the angels, and the saints. The Copernican revolution was not only a conceptual paradigm shift but also a spatial and dimensional one. So many of the most important prayers recited by Christians in church had this heaven in them, as a spatial point of reference. For starters, the new heaven required a wholly new understanding of these key prayers: the Gloria: "Glory to God in the *highest*"; the Sanctus: "Heaven and earth are filled with thine Glory"; the Lord's Prayer: "Our Father who art in Heaven"; the Creed: "Jesus Christ . . . who for us men and for our salvation came *down* from Heaven. . . . And he *ascended* into Heaven, and sits at the right hand of the Father."

This displaced heaven had been in our cosmic neighbor-hood, so to speak, the last of the seven concentric celestial spheres that surrounded the earth. One could literally point to it, for it was *up there*, and merely the *seventh* of a limited number of heavens. In other words, before the Copernican revolution in astronomy, heaven was a location, and there-fore also eternity: just another place, conceived of much in the same way as we now conceive of the orbits of the planets in our solar system. This older heaven thus shared a bound-ary with the physical universe and with time. At the highest of all levels, above all of the planet-carrying spheres, and above the starry firmament, the last of the spheres, God dwelt on two levels. The first of these was the empyrean or "highest Heaven," which theologians also called "God's ex-terior dwelling place," where angels and saved humans lived eternally in the presence of the Divine. In the fourteenth century, Jan van Ruysbroeck, a disciple of Meister Eckhart, described it with great certainty:

> God created the empyrean or highest Heaven as a pure and simple radiance encircling and enclosing all the Heavens and every corporeal and material thing which he ever created. It is the exterior dwelling place and kingdom of God and of his saints and is filled with glory and eternal joy. Because this Heaven is externally resplendent and free of admixture, there is within it neither movement nor change, for it is securely established in a changeless state above all things.[22]

Above this empyrean abode, the Holy Trinity dwelt in the "Heaven of Heavens," into which no creature could pass. This heaven was God himself, and therefore not the same sort of "heaven" as the others: it was more a dimension, God's eternal being, rather than a place. And it was from here that God's radiant presence illuminated and filled the

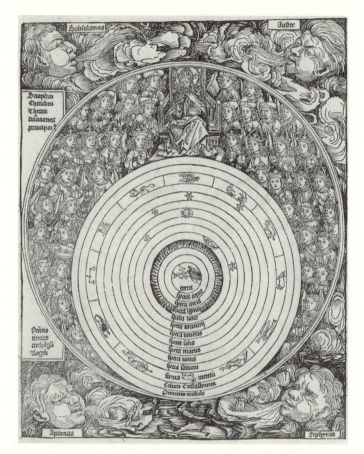

Figure 5.2. The pre-Copernican cosmos, from *The Nuremberg Chronicle* (1493). The concentric spheres of the pre-Copernican universe depict the empyrean heaven as the outermost ring, directly above the starry firmament and the constellations, full of God and the redeemed.

abode of the blessed, which was the telos or ultimate destination of human beings.[23]

The telescope made this old heaven vanish like a puff of smoke. Banished from physics, heaven went into exile in metaphysics, a location that Immanuel Kant (1724–1804) would soon unmask as an imaginary island. And since nearly all of the educated elites would agree with Kant on this point, metaphysics, too, vanished like another puff of smoke. It stands to reason, then, that as this older heaven vanished, efforts would be made to reify it, make it visible, and immortalize it. And what better place to do this than inside churches?

Beginning in the sixteenth century, Catholics began to see eternity depicted in their churches, usually in such a way as to give the impression that ceilings or domes were opening up to heaven itself. Employing the painting technique known as *trompe-l'oeil* (French for "trick the eye"), artists such as Antonio da Correggio, Andrea Pozzo, and Franz Joseph Spiegler skillfully created the illusion that the tall vaulted ceilings and massive domes of churches were not really there at all. Every one of these ceiling paintings is filled with bodies, both angelic and human, which are suspended in midair, moving sinuously toward a focal point in the upper reaches of heaven itself. The movement of all of these bodies is carefully orchestrated, much like some celestial dance—a spectacle that became a staple of church decoration for three centuries, as evidenced by three examples.

Correggio's *Assumption of the Virgin* in the Cathedral of Parma (1526–1530), one of the earliest of these attempts to depict eternity in such a way, turns a dome into an upwardly spiraling vortex of clouds, saints, and angels who throng around the Virgin Mary as she ascends toward the golden light of the empyrean heaven, her bare legs kicking most ungraciously.

Figure 5.3. Antonio da Correggio, *Assumption of the Virgin* (1526–1530). This fresco, on the dome of the Cathedral of Parma, is an example of the tromp-l'oeil style, which through an illusion of visible eternity invites the viewer to contemplate eternity.

Of Pozzo's numerous illusionist ceilings, his *The World-wide Mission of the Society of Jesus,* in the Jesuit church of Sant'Ignazio in Rome (1694), is the most impressive. It shows St. Ignatius Loyola, the founder of the Jesuit order, ascending into the empyrean heaven, beckoned by a cross-carrying Christ who floats above him, bathed in the golden light of eternity. As in all such paintings, the upward sweep of the composition is as much an attempt to depict the negation of gravity as of time and space.

Figure 5.4. Andrea Pozzo, *The Worldwide Mission of the Society of Jesus* (1694).

Figure 5.5. Dominicus Zimmerman's depiction of heaven, Wies, Bavaria (1754). Photo ©
Bryan Lacey, Rixel Studios Photography.

The heaven depicted by Dominicus Zimmerman in the pilgrimage church of Wies in Bavaria (1754) is very complex. Zimmerman, a contemporary of aggressive Enlightenment atheists such as Julien Offray de La Mettrie and Paul-Heinrich Dietrich, Baron d'Holbach, gave the Last Judgment a very modern turn by bringing all who would enter that church into the picture, and by depicting eternity behind closed doors. Up above, Christ sits on a rainbow, judging the human race. But the blessed and the damned—normally depicted in great detail—are nowhere to be seen. Only a few angels and saints are depicted, along with the cross, which Jesus himself points to, emphatically, as the symbol of salvation. At one end of the ceiling, Zimmerman depicts the empty throne of Jesus, bedecked in regal Bavarian splendor, and at the other end a door, over which is curled none other than the ancient symbol for eternity, the Ouroboros, the serpent devouring its own tail. The message encoded in the ceiling is very clear: those being judged by Jesus Christ are none other than those who are standing beneath the ceiling fresco, for whom time has not yet run out. The Final Judgment is still off in the future and eternity still waits behind closed doors. Those who are to be judged still have time to earn either eternal bliss or eternal damnation, concealed behind the door. The theatricality of it all is overwhelming. And it is also as modern as the disbelief it seeks to deny.

By dissolving the boundary between the church building itself and heaven through illusionist techniques, these artists did more than make a powerful statement about the spatial relation between heaven and earth, which was then being challenged: they also made visible the metaphysical truth claims of the Catholic Church that were under attack by Protestants and skeptics, "proving" to the eye of worshipers that the church in which they found themselves was indeed the gateway to heaven and eternal bliss. Add to this the fact that such imagery would be considered idolatrous and blasphemous by Protestants, and what you have is a perfect summation of modern Catholic propaganda, eerily prescient of our own age, in which the medium itself is often the message.

Anyone who has ever stood under one of these hallucinatory ceilings has to admit that they are most impressive, even overpowering. The mastery with which the optical illusion is rendered in many cases can leave one wondering what sort of shift in perspective they represent, not just visually but also in terms of worldview, for they seem to be trying to convince a bit too hard while winking at the same time, so to speak, as if fully conscious of the fact that trickery is involved. One could say that these ceilings are very modern, perhaps the very epitome of modernity on multiple levels, for in addition to being exemplars of a technique that reflects very sophisticated advances in mathematics, of the same sort as those that displaced the old heaven, they also hover, literally, over the line between belief and doubt, very knowingly asking everyone to suspend disbelief—a disbelief that is as real as the paint on the ceiling and as post-medieval as the mathematical calculations that render the eye helpless in the face of illusion, forcing it to make a leap of faith.[24]

Doubt à la Mode

Speaking of such leaps, and the doubts that engender them: if the new invention of the telescope and new mathematical calculations could prove that the Bible and all the churches were mistaken about the visible universe, why not also doubt their reliability about things unseen, such as eternity, and the hereafter? Among the first to take issue with Christian notions of an eternal afterlife were thinkers heavily influenced by the new science, contemporaries of Nieremberg, such as John Locke, John Toland, and Isaac Newton in the British Isles, Pierre Bayle in France, and Gottfried Wilhelm Leibniz in Germany. Arguing that reason alone should govern all thinking, and that reason always trumps revelation, many began to deny the existence of hell, principally because the idea of a just and merciful God tormenting his creatures for eternity seemed thoroughly contradictory and unreasonable. Though many of these early critics of hell thought that it was a useful teaching for the simpler folk, who might become even more immoral without the fear of eternal punishment, some nonetheless began to deny hell openly and aggressively.[25]

Denying hell and the afterlife was also one step closer to denying the existence of the soul, eternity itself, and even the existence of God. It is no surprise, then, that by the mid-eighteenth century, full-fledged atheists were not too hard to find, at least among the educated elites.[26] In 1747, for instance, Julien Offroy de la Mettrie published a treatise titled *L'homme machine* (Man the Machine), in which he argued that it was impossible to prove through reason the existence of anything beyond the material universe, and that eternity, God, and the soul were irrational concepts. We human beings are nothing more than our bodies, he argued, and nothing more than an organic apparatus, sprung from the earth, like mushrooms or worms. The same is true of the entire universe, which is devoid of spirit and is merely one vast time-bound machine. After mid-century, atheism became à la mode in the brightest circles of the "enlightened," as did hostility toward Christianity and religion in general.[27] For instance, in 1761 Paul Heinrich Dietrich, the Baron D'Holbach, a good friend of Benjamin Franklin, published *Christianity Unveiled*, a book in which he denounced Christianity as contrary to reason and nature. In 1770 he issued an even more popular attack, *The System of Nature*, in which he not only denied the existence of God but denounced the Judeo-Christian concept of a bloodthirsty, capricious, and vengeful deity as the source of humankind's worst ills. Writing in 1794, the American revolutionary Thomas Paine summarized an entire century of anti-Christian polemic:

> Of all the systems of religion that ever were invented, there is none more unedifying to man, more repugnant to reason, and more contradictory in itself, than this thing called Christianity. Too absurd for belief, too impossible to convince, and too inconsistent for practice, it renders the heart torpid, or produces only atheists and fanatics. As an engine of power, it serves the purpose of despotism; and as a means of wealth, the avarice of priests; but so far as respects the good of man in general, it leads to nothing here or hereafter.[28]

Committed to replacing religion with rational "enlightment," men like Paine found themselves facing the age-old question of how societies can motivate their members to act ethically without any notion of reward or punishment in an eternal afterlife. Without the fear of hell, what is there besides brute force to prevent wrongdoing? The great *philosophe* Voltaire (1694–1778) was skeptical enough of reason to say that "If God did not exist, it would be necessary for men to invent him."[29] Governments, he concluded, always needed God and hell: "I do not believe that there is in the world a mayor or any official power . . . who does not realize that it is necessary to put a god into their mouths to serve as a bit and bridle."[30] Voltaire's friend Denis Diderot (1713–1784), editor of the venerable *Encyclopedia*, was less cynical, and more representative of the optimism shared by many Enlightenment thinkers. For Diderot, reason itself seemed enough. "Philosophy makes men more honorable than sufficient or efficacious grace," he argued. Seeing no need for God or hell, he replaced them with a vague yet powerful entity:

> Posterity is for the philosopher what the next world is for the religious man . . . O posterity, o holy and sacred support of the oppressed and the unhappy, you who are just, you who are incorruptible, you who will revenge the good man and unmask the hypocrite, consoling and certain ideal, do not abandon me.[31]

Reducing eternity to the collective memory of posterity proved harder than the philosophes expected, however. Painfully aware of the lack of commensurate symmetry between the promise of an embodied personal immortality and that of an impersonal disembodied one, many contemporaries of Diderot and D'Holbach lamented over what had been lost, often through clenched teeth. As one French essayist put it:

> The new order of things . . . no longer sees anything great in all that is bounded by space and time. The duration of Empires and the succession of ages appear to it but as instants. The widest Kingdoms to its eyes are but as atoms, and it sees the earth reduced to a point where it loses itself in the infinite space that surrounds it . . . it perceives all the absurdity and the nothingness of that chimerical immortality which had been its idol.[32]

Needless to say, as such views gained an ever larger following, particularly in Western Europe and the Americas, centuries-old attitudes toward death and eternity began to change at a relatively quick pace.

Death, Barely Tamed

One of the most significant changes brought about by the Enlightenment throughout the Western world, including North and South America, was the increasing secularization of death. An early sign of this development was the detachment of cemeteries from churches. Partly for reasons of public health, but also partly because of secularizing pressures, burials began a gradual migration from the vaults beneath churches or churchyards to lots no longer adjacent to the churches, and eventually to much larger areas outside cities and towns.[33] By the time Thomas Paine wrote his *Age of Reason,* the migration of the cemeteries to neutral space was well under way, and so was the development of the nonreligious funeral. A century later, the process was irreversible almost everywhere in the Christian world.

Another change that can be measured in last wills and testaments is the gradual decline and disappearance of any mention of the soul in these legal documents. In Protestant societies where it had become illegal to offer masses for the dead, the change is more subtle, but in Catholic societies, where masses for the dead dwindle and disappear, the shift in attitudes is so immense and abrupt that some scholars view it as conclusive proof of the "de-Christianization" of Europe.[34]

As secularization increased, so did Christian fervor. In Europe and the Americas, the age of Enlightenment and revolutions was also a period marked by renewed, intense devotion to the beliefs that were being challenged. One need only turn to the many apparitions and divine messages that Catholics embraced as genuine during this period, which gave rise to immensely popular devotions, such as that to the Sacred Hearts of Jesus and Mary (seventeenth and eighteenth centuries) and the Miraculous Medal (nineteenth century). One of these devotions, the wearing of the scapular of Our Lady of Mount Carmel, better known as the Brown Scapular, had to do with eternity. According to pious tradition dating back to the thirteenth century, the Virgin Mary had promised in an apparition that anyone who died while wearing this small piece of cloth around the neck would not "suffer everlasting fire." In other words, simply wearing this scapular could earn even the worst sinner an entrance into purgatory rather than hell—a promise undoubtedly anchored in the ancient Catholic belief that monastic garb could guarantee salvation, since the scapular was a small replica of the outermost part of the monastic habit. In the middle of the seventeenth century, thanks to the efforts of the Carmelite Order, devotion to this scapular blossomed throughout the Catholic world, and the lure of its promises regarding eternity became so attractive that between 1650 and 1900, fourteen other scapulars associated with other religious orders and confraternities would be approved by Rome, each related to some apparition and some large promise.[35] At the very same time, throughout the world, many Catholics continued to be buried in monastic habits, purchased from religious orders for the express purpose of dressing the corpse.

Among Protestants, there was plenty of fervor too, and some of it very traditionalist. In the United States, evangelical revivalism swept several regions in the so-called Great Awakening of the 1730s and 1740s, and the long-smoldering Second Great Awakening of the 1790s through the 1840s. But not all of this fervor was traditionalist. The "Burned Over District," in central and western New York, produced a welter of new sects and churches, including the apocalyptic Millerites (precursors of the Jehovah's Witnesses), and the Latter-Day Saints, more commonly known as the Mormons. Among the Mormons especially, eternity would play a key role in their theology and piety. In Germany, Pietism led to a

religious revival that transcended political and national bor-
ders. Eventually, this renewed fervor would give rise to even
grander revivals, as charismatic preachers took the Christian
message to the world at large, beyond church walls. In Great
Britain, Methodism stirred the collective soul of the newly
minted proletariat, driven into dreary smoke-clogged cities
from their rural homes by the Industrial Revolution.

And wherever Methodism had no impact, then it might
have been the eloquent, imprecise poetry of Romanticism,
best exemplified by William Blake, that could best assuage
the existential dread engendered by the loss of eternity. In
much of Blake's poetry, one can detect a lament for a vanished horizon. In *Jerusalem*, he expressed the bleakest despair
over the narrow ambit proposed by the new world-view,
along the same vein as Pascal:

O what is Life and what is Man? O what is Death? Wherefore
Are you, my Children, natives in the Grave to where I go?
Or are you born to feed the hungry ravenings of Destruction,
To be the sport of Accident, to waste in Wrath and Love a weary
Life, in brooding cares and anxious labours, that prove but chaff?[36]

In the same poem, Blake also railed against the materialistic
legacy of the Enlightenment, the new science, and the Industrial Revolution as a brutish, senseless constricting of human
potential:

I turn my eyes to the Schools and Universities of Europe,
And there behold the Loom of Locke, whose Woof rages dire,
Wash'd by the Water-wheels of Newton: black the cloth
In heavy wreaths folds over every Nation: cruel Works
Of many Wheels I view, wheel without wheel, with cogs tyrannic,
Moving by compulsion each other; not as those in Eden, which,
Wheel within wheel, in freedom revolve, in harmony and peace.[37]

Blake was not alone in railing against the rising tide of materialism and the loss of eternity. Some, like the German poet Johann Wolfgang von Goethe, turned dogmatic, appealing to nature itself rather than to any sacred scriptures: "Man should believe in immortality; he has a right to this belief; it corresponds with the wants of his nature."[38] Or, as he also put it: "Everyone carries the proof of his own immortality within himself,"[39] But now that doubt was firmly entrenched, all such affirmations of transcendence and eternity ran the risk of sounding hollow, especially if they did not acknowledge the metaphysical vacuum in which they were adrift. Percy Bysshe Shelley, among others, gave voice to this new existential angst:

> The One remains, the many change and pass;
> Heaven's light forever shines, Earth's shadows
> fly;
> Life, like a dome of many-colored glass,
> Stains the white radiance of Eternity.[40]

In North America, the Great Awakening would take place alongside the Enlightenment, and the Second Great Awakening alongside the Industrial Revolution. Belief in eternity, heaven, and hell did not vanish but rather intensified among the thousands who flocked to the sermons of Jonathan Edwards (1703–1758), John Wesley (1703–1791), and George Whitefield (1714–1770), or sang the transcendent hymns of Charles Wesley (1707–1778). Keeping in mind that Jonathan Edwards was a well-educated Yale graduate, Princeton's third president, and a contemporary of hell-deniers like D'Holbach, Voltaire, Diderot, Franklin, and Paine, one can only be amazed at the dissonant challenge offered by his sermon, "Sinners in the Hands of an Angry God," which terrified many who heard it in 1741, in western Massachusetts, leading them to fits of despair and sudden conversions:

> The God that holds you over the pit of Hell, much as one holds a spider, or some loathsome insect over the fire, abhors you, and is dreadfully provoked: his wrath towards you burns like fire; he looks upon you as worthy of nothing else, but to be cast into the fire. . . . It is nothing but his hand that holds you from falling into the fire every moment . . . Yea, there is nothing else that is to be given as a reason why you do not this very moment drop down into Hell. . . . O sinner! Consider the fearful danger you are in: it is a great furnace of wrath, a wide and bottomless pit, full of the fire of wrath, that you are held over in the hand of that God, whose wrath is provoked and incensed as much against you, as against many of the damned in Hell. You hang by a slender thread, with the flames of divine wrath flashing about it, and ready every moment to singe it, and burn it asunder.[41]

Great revivals could not stop secularizing trends from increasing in the nineteenth century, however, as industrialization and urbanization changed much of the Christian world in the northern hemisphere. On an intellectual and spiritual level, doubt and unbelief intensified in the nineteenth century, not just among the intelligentsia but also among the new working class, and especially among those who embraced socialist and materialist ideology, which tended to view all religion as a means of oppression by the elite, and to accept—uncritically—Karl Marx's proposition that "the criticism of religion is the basis of all criticism."[42]

On a very basic practical level, the funeral, the rite of passage to eternity, quickly lost much of its sacred character. Burying the dead became a business like any other, as the handling of the dead became the province of professional morticians, who gradually took over many of the tasks previously handled by families and their clergy, which bound all members of earthly society to eternity, and to one another.

At the very same time, as cemeteries moved beyond the crowded cities, their landscaping evolved in new directions, reifying new, this-worldly, materialistic attitudes that eclipsed eternity and changed the urban landscape along with the relationship between the dead and the living. Unfettered by space limitations, great necropolises sprang up all over the Christian world, where individuals and families of the rising bourgeoisie now had the chance to erect the kinds of memorials that had once been reserved for nobility and royalty. In great cities such as Paris, the dead suddenly had their own suburbs, replete with mausoleums great and small, festooned with sculptures, crosses, obelisks, epitaphs, and plaques, all in a park-like setting: an enduring image and symbol of the world of the living, where the social hierarchy was reified most permanently in stone. In death as in life, the poor ended up in the equivalent of slums, segregated from the paying clientele, often in mass graves or unmarked plots. Most of the urban areas of Europe and the Americas are still dotted with these necropolises, which were swallowed up by expanding cities and are now overcrowded and also right smack in the middle of densely congested areas, cordoned off behind imposing walls and fences. Smaller cities and towns also followed suit, and by the end of the nineteenth century, the world where most Christians lived was one in which the dead and the living were segregated, and in which the remote cemetery became the focal point of all piety for the dead.[43]

Disbelief, Briefly Suspended

Beautiful cemeteries were not the only place to commune with the dead, however. As secularization intensified and traditional Christianity lost its once dominant place in Western culture, ancient occult beliefs and practices began to resurface in the nineteenth century, under new guises, as if to fill the vacuum created by unbelief. And as eternity became ever more ambiguous a concept, ghosts began to reappear with a vengeance, and so did people who believed they could communicate with the dead. A free-wheeling movement known as "spiritualism" quickly won many adherents in the Western world. At bottom, spiritualism was a great resurgence of belief in the existence of the soul and in its immortality, for all "spiritualists" believed or hoped that the spirits of the dead lingered on earth and that they could communicate with the living. Ghosts and hauntings had long been part of popular culture, even though Protestant and Catholic clergy alike had tried to suppress such beliefs. Ghosts had never ceased to exist—nor could they stop talking, or complaining about grudges and unfinished business, it seems. But beginning in the mid-nineteenth century, reports of ghosts and haunted places began to proliferate, as did so-called experts, or "mediums," who claimed that they had special knowledge or powers that allowed them to speak to the dead and relay their messages to the living.

All of this was far from well articulated, much less a strident affirmation of eternity. In fact, it could be argued that the earth-bound ghosts of spiritualism were as much a denial of eternity as an affirmation of it, for the dimension in which they dwelt seemed but a mere extension of earthly life, reluctantly in sync with it. As befits any popular movement in a period of rapid change, spiritualism was thus symptomatic of the upheaval at work on Western societies: imprecise, and even illogical, at once an affirmation and a denial of eternity. Among the spiritualist beliefs and practices that took root in the nineteenth century, none was more common than that of the séance, a gathering at which mediums would question the dead and seek replies from them. Mediums could claim all sorts of special powers that had once been the preserve of medieval mystics or of witches and demoniacs, that is, those who were in touch with the spiritual dimension: telepathy, clairvoyance, levitation. Some claimed they could make objects materialize out of thin air or, more commonly, that they could heal the sick.[44] After the invention of photography, other "experts" appeared on the scene who claimed to be able to photograph ghosts, ostensibly giving them scientific credibility. Spiritualism cut across class lines and circled the globe: its appeal seemed universal and as boundless as the public's credulity. None other than Sir Arthur Conan Doyle, the creator of the hyperlogical detective Sherlock Holmes, was a firm believer in spiritualism, and toured the world, speaking to sell-out crowds, showing them photographs of ghosts. A lasting survival of the spiritualist craze can be found in almost any toy store nowadays: the Ouija board, a game once taken very seriously by spiritualists in which two people act as mediums, deciphering messages from dead. Spiritualism would peak in popularity in the 1920s and 1930s as millions of distraught families sought to cope with the loss of their young men between 1914 and 1918, in the Great War.[45]

An outgrowth of spiritualism that flourished in the late nineteenth century was theosophy, a movement founded by Helena Blavatsky in the 1870s. Under her leadership the Theosophical Society disseminated a combination of spiritualism, ancient Indian philosophy, gnostic teachings, and several other occult beliefs and practices. Eternity was one of the chief obsessions of theosophy, as was belief in reincarnation and in the illusory nature of time and space. As Blavatsky put it, "Time is only an illusion produced by the succession of our states of consciousness as we travel through eternal duration, and it does not exist where no consciousness exists in which the illusion can be produced; but 'lies asleep.' "[46] By reintroducing belief in reincarnation to the West and by claiming to provide access to memories of past lives, theosophists had some impact on Christians. As in the case of spiritualism, the fact that all of the mainline churches condemned theosophy did not deter all Christians from believing in some of its teachings, especially in reincarnation and the remembering of successive lives in the "eternal duration."[47]

Into the Great Dark Void

Ghosts, recycled lives, and suburban cemeteries were not the only by-products of the death of eternity. That loss also gave rise to an existential dread so pervasive that it could be taken for granted by all within Western culture. And this dread is the ether in which we still live and move and have our being; it is as inescapable and as necessary as the air we breathe. One might add that this dread—this awareness of existence as wholly ephemeral, perhaps even illusory—is the very essence of postmodernity. If existence itself is meaningless, why should meaning itself matter? Poetry, rather than philosophy, theology, or science, becomes the only certainty, along with death:

> But at the total emptiness for ever,
> The sure extinction that we travel to
> And shall be lost in always. Not to be here,

Not to be anywhere,
And soon, nothing more terrible, nothing more true.
This is a special way of being afraid
No trick dispels. . . .
And so it stays just on the edge of vision,
A small, unfocused blur, a standing chill. . . .
Being brave
Lets no one off the grave.
Death is no different whined at than withstood.[48]

While there is no denying that belief in eternity has not yet vanished altogether, or belief in universal Truth with a capital "T," as proven every day by Muslim suicide martyrs, among others, there is also no denying that all who continue to believe do so with an aching awareness of the doubt that permeates their world and still reigns supreme among the Western cultural elites, for whom metaphysical and epistemological agnosticism remain the sole unquestionable assumption. Even Stephen Hawking, perhaps the best-known scientist in the world, is willing not only to acknowledge but also to bemoan our collective lack of certainty.

Why does the universe go to all the bother of existing? . . . Up to now, most scientists have been too occupied with the development of new theories that describe what the universe is to ask why. On the other hand, the people whose business it is to ask why, the philosophers, have not been able to keep up with the advance of scientific theories. . . . In the nineteenth and twentieth centuries, science became too technical and mathematical for the philosophers, or anyone else, except a few specialists. Philosophers reduced the scope of their inquiries so much that Wittgenstein, the most famous philosopher of the twentieth century, said, "The sole remaining task for philosophy is the analysis of language."

What a comedown from the great tradition of philosophy from Aristotle to Kant![49]

If the man regarded in popular culture as the smartest scientist of all, quoting the man he regards as the most famous philosopher, complains about the epistemological uncertainty that surrounds us all, then that uncertainty must certainly be the most unquestionable of assumptions, as indicated by his exclamation point, and also the one that closes this sentence!

But just as the Enlightenment philosophes merely replaced one belief system with another, exchanging the notion of revealed truth for that of the power of human reason, so have we postmodern elites exchanged one certainty for another, no matter how much we might insist that the only certainty is uncertainty as we rail against any hegemonic discourse or epistemological conceits. From the most zealous to the most jaded, the architects and guardians of our collective mentality agree on one thing: we are all captive to terminal temporality. Eternity is out of the question, simply because it cannot be squared with reason or sensory input. Eternity is the most certain of uncertainties. At least eternity for us human beings. The stuff of which the universe is made may be eternal—and it may not—but *we* most certainly are not. It matters little that *we* may be the finest stuff in the universe, maybe even the consciousness of the universe itself. Each and every one of us is as much a candidate for extinction as every trilobite and dinosaur or all our forebears and descendants. It matters little whether one is a genius or a dimwit, righteous or depraved. All of us are the offspring of nothingness. It may be painful to admit it, our sages seem to say, but terminal temporality is our common lot: nonexistence trumps existence, as far as every individual is concerned. And perhaps the entire cosmos as well. The dark abyss of nothingness that preceded our birth is no different, perhaps, from that which preceded the Big Bang. And the same goes for the abyss that will follow our insignificantly brief burst of being and that which will eventually follow the Big Crunch or the Big Freeze, or whatever comes at the end. That unfathomable stygian abyss, the Great Dark Void, is the only eternity we can know for certain. As it is, we barely exist, we insignificant specks who are sandwiched by a yawning nothingness. And we're not alone: the same goes for the whole universe.

Ironically, this eternal abyss of nothingness that we postmoderns have to contend with is not all that different, conceptually, from those abysses that Baroque preachers and writers loved to evoke, in order to frighten the hell out of their audiences. The ascetic Father Nieremberg, wrapped in his hair shirts and barbed wire, wanted his readers to see each sin as an abyss of injustice, an abyss beyond measure. His conception of eternal justice was as severe as it was beyond imagining. For him, divine justice could only be satisfied by eternal torments, and this eternity was inconceivable. Even if all the oceans were to be drained and filled with the finest sand, he proposed, and one bird were to remove a single grain every hundred years until all the grains were gone, God would still not be satisfied with the punishment inflicted for a single mortal sin committed by any human.[50] As every grain of sand in Nieremberg's metaphor is nothing—when measured against eternity itself and God's sense of justice—so is every human life in our postmodern cosmos a "nothing" against the infinite, eternal horizon of nonbeing that totally engulfs it.

Vladimir Nabokov knew how to express his rage over the postmodern version of this Baroque meditation very eloquently, with a mixture of élan and despair, and also a grudging envy for those who still had not awakened from their premodern stupor. Still, no amount of eloquence can hide his bristling anguish, which is an echo of our own:

> The cradle rocks above an abyss, and common sense tells us that our existence is but a brief crack of light between two eternities of darkness. . . . I rebel against this state of affairs. I feel the urge to take my rebellion outside and picket nature. Over and over again, my mind has made colossal efforts to distinguish the faintest of personal glimmers in the impersonal darkness on both sides of my life. That this darkness is caused merely by the walls of time separating me and my bruised fists from the free world of timelessness is a belief I gladly share with the most gaudily painted savage. I have journeyed back in thought . . . to remote regions where I groped for some secret outlet only to discover that the prison of time is spherical and without exits. Short of suicide, I have tried everything.[51]

Nabokov's angst is not postmodern, strictly speaking. Mere "moderns" also shared in it, perhaps just as intensely. And they offered a stoical balm. Early in the nineteenth century, the English essayist William Hazlitt offered up a meditation quite similar to Nabokov's, the centerpiece of which was the insight that "The love of life . . . is an habitual attachment, not an abstract principle."

> There was a time when we were not: this gives us no concern—why then should it trouble us that a time will come when we shall cease to be? . . . To die is only to be as we were before we were born; yet no one feels any remorse, or regret, or repugnance, in contemplating this last idea. It is rather a relief and disburthening of the mind: it seems to have been holiday-time with us then. . . . It is certain that there is noth-

ing in the idea of a pre-existent state that excites our longing like the prospect of a posthumous existence.[52]

About one century later, Sigmund Freud puzzled over the effect of terminal temporality, or, as he called it, "transience," on individuals and on Western culture as a whole. Having taken a walk with a young poet on a splendid day when nature was at its resplendent best, Freud was intrigued by the fact that his companion "was disturbed by the thought that all this beauty was fated to extinction." All that this poet "would otherwise have loved and admired seemed to him to be shorn of its worth by the transience which was its doom." Ever the analyst, Freud discerned that the ubiquitous shadow of decay and non-being that envelops all beauty on earth can give rise to two very different impulses in the human mind. One leads to "aching despondency"—the young poet's reaction. The other, he averred, "leads to rebellion against the fact asserted," to thinking that "somehow or other this loveliness must be able to persist and to escape all the powers of destruction." Freud's own reaction to this insight was as clinical as it was philosophical. "This demand for immortality," he proposed, was mere a mere projection of our deepest wishes, a desperate attempt by the human mind to alter reality. While the desire for immortality was very real, Freud admitted, immortality itself was not. Unlike the Christian Platonist St. Anselm of Canterbury, who could have argued that immortality must exist if we can conceive of it, Freud, the modern scientist, argued just the opposite. What the young poet was feeling was nothing more than "rebellion against mourning." The idea of immortality, he pressed, "is a product of our wishes too unmistakable to lay claim to reality." Then he added, more as philosopher than physician: "What is painful may none the less be true."

Unable to dispute the fact that all things are transient, even the most perfect and beautiful, Freud conceived of a therapeutic balm packaged in full *wissenschaftlich* guise that required as much of a leap of faith and logic as St. Anselm's ontological argument for the existence of God. Disputing the poet's "pessimistic" view, Freud the scientist proffered the following formula:

> The transience of what is beautiful does not involve any loss in its worth. On the contrary, an increase! Transience value is scarcity value in time. Limitation in the possibility of an enjoyment raises the value of the enjoyment.[53]

The fact that the young poet was not at all cheered by Freud's very *wissenschaftlich* formula did not alter the great doctor's diagnosis. Identifying the poet's pessimism as "rebellion against mourning" seemed sufficient, and arriving at a theorem that proved that existential angst was itself a good thing seemed a step forward to Freud. In many ways his materialistic approach, which turned pain into a hedonistic bonus, hard-wired in humans by nature itself, was but a variation on a theme that had been sounded since the seventeenth century.

Centuries earlier Blaise Pascal, a devout Catholic, had confronted the great dark void with a similar bravado, and with a formula that required a leap of faith, but with a metaphysical rather than a physical turn of mind. "Man is only a reed, the weakest in nature, but he is a thinking reed," said Pascal. And thinking made all the difference: that fact alone made humans superior to the nothingness that engulfed them.

> The whole universe need not take up arms to crush him; a vapor, a drop of water, is enough to kill him. But if the whole universe were to crush him, man would still be nobler than

what killed him, for he knows he is dying and the advantage that the universe has over him. The universe knows nothing of this. All our dignity, then, consists in thought. It is from this that we must raise ourselves, and not from space and duration, which we could not fill.[54]

Pleasure was beyond the scope of Pascal's radar. For him, it was the mere principle of consciousness itself that carried the day. Whether or not this offered comfort to anyone other than philosophers did not concern Pascal: his *Pensées* were written for a skeptical intellectual audience, and this key argument was but one in a long chain leading to the conclusion that the intellect alone cannot suffice and that a leap of faith is the only way to cope with life's inevitable pain. "The heart has its reasons, which reason does not know."[55]

Pascal's argument, though religious in essence, was detached enough from theological claims to endure. Generations of intellectuals found modest comfort in his assertions and sought to improve upon them. More than two centuries later, when advances in science had made the universe seem much more complex and bewildering than Pascal's, one could find the pioneering mathematician and physicist Henri Poincaré saying,

> Strange contradiction for those who believe in time. Geologic history shows us that life is only a short episode between two eternities of death, and that, even in this episode, conscious thought has lasted and will last only a moment. Thought is only a gleam in the midst of a long night. But it is this gleam which is everything.[56]

But the gleam itself did not seem enough for everyone. For many, a life which springs from nothing and returns to nothing seemed too much like a mere shadow: insubstantial, meaningless, no matter what. Yet at the end of the nineteenth century and beginning of the twentieth, the Christian notion of eternity seemed equally unappealing to Western intellectual elites, and as ridiculous as the pre-Copernican cosmos. In its place, a welter of opinions held sway, most of them of a negative sort, laced heavily with *apatheia,* or stoical resignation. Among the more intriguing alternative views, Nietzsche's theory of the eternal return holds a place of honor, not only because it harked back to ancient Indian religion and was ambiguously poised between myth and philosophy but also because it approximated some of the most recent scientific theories about the physical universe.[57]

Much like Machiavelli, that other gadfly, Nietzsche has a way of polarizing his readers; some would like to take him literally, some not so literally, and others not seriously at all. The differences of opinion are extreme, due to Nietzsche's provocative style, which is full of bold and outrageous proposals, some of which are more suggestive than dogmatic. First-time readers usually respond by asking, "Is he serious?" Some find it difficult to say yes, but many over the years have appreciated his genius, in varying ways. Those influenced by Nietzsche range very broadly, perhaps more so than for any other thinker: at one extreme end, Nietzsche seemed very appealing to many liberal avant-garde artists in continental Europe who saw themselves as the leading edge of a systematic assault on an oppressive status quo; at the other extreme end, he was lionized and often quoted out of context by fascists, especially Nazis, who used some of his more extreme statements to justify claims of racial superiority, wars of aggression, and world domination. Nietzsche loved to challenge all of Europe's unquestioned assumptions, especially those that rested on Christian values.[58] If nothing else, he can be seen as a representative of the darkest, angriest impulses of his age. And when it came to eternity, Nietzsche was at his boldest and most mischievous, not just in terms of what he proposed but also in how ambivalently he framed it.[59]

If taken as an ontological doctrine rather than as a thought experiment, Nietzsche's idea of the eternal return suggests the probability that "everything recurs as we once experienced it, and that the recurrence itself recurs ad infinitum." This episodic sempiternal eternity, which is but a series of infinite reflections, admits no change, assigning boundless significance to every single instant. Nietzsche, as always, taunted his readers:

> What, if some day or night a demon were to steal after you into your loneliest loneliness and say to you: "This life as you now live it and have lived it, you will have to live once more and innumerable times more. . . . The eternal hourglass of existence is turned upside down again and again, and you with it, speck of dust!" Would you not throw yourself down and gnash your teeth and curse the demon who spoke thus? Or have you once experienced a tremendous moment when you would have answered him: "You are a god and never have I heard anything more divine." If this thought gained possession of you, it would change you as you are, or crush you.[60]

In the late twentieth century, novelist Milan Kundera would take this suggestion at face value and declare it as unbearably oppressive:

> If every second of our lives recurs an infinite number of times, we are nailed to eternity as Jesus Christ was nailed to the cross. It is a terrifying prospect. In the world of eternal return the weight of unbearable responsibility lies heavy

on every move we make. That is why Nietzsche called the idea of eternal return the heaviest of burdens [*das schwerste Gewicht*].[61]

In many ways Nietzsche's eternal return—if taken literally—is as frightening as Nieremberg's hell, where every sin becomes an eternal festering pustule. As Kundera puts it, eternal return makes every event, every instant "a solid mass, protuberant, its inanity irreparable." Every evil becomes eternal, as does every joy. Terrible events, such as the French Revolution, become harder to romanticize in the light of the eternal return. "There is an infinite difference between a Robespierre who occurs only once in history," argues Kundera, "and a Robespierre who eternally returns, chopping off French heads." Without eternal return, however, every evil is ephemeral, less condemnable; and every joy meaningless. This extenuating circumstance prevents us from passing judgment on anything or anyone, and frees us from worrying about the difference between good and evil. For how can anything transient be condemned, even the worst of atrocities? And how can we help but view everything ephemeral with a twinge of nostalgia? "In the sunset of dissolution," adds Kundera, "everything is illuminated by the aura of nostalgia, even the guillotine."[62]

The ethical implications of believing or not believing in any sort of eternity are thrown into high relief by Kundera's reading of Nietzsche. Eternity weighs down every moment, giving it a significance beyond itself, with truly infinite repercussions. Eternity, therefore, demands that one carefully weigh one's choices and that one invest each and every moment with infinite significance. But what about transience or terminal temporality? Like Voltaire and his contemporaries, one is forced to ask what value any act or event could possibly have if it is totally transient, and what motivation anyone might have for worrying about right and wrong.

As Freud argued that there are only two possible responses to transience, despondency or rebellion, I would like to propose that in our own day and age, in those societies that have jettisoned eternity in the formerly Christian world, two basic responses to transience took hold. Both are forms of rebellion rather than despondency and both are extreme expressions of materialism: one is individualistic to the core, the other collectivist, and they have led to the creation of very different societies. One such type of society aims to seize the day, literally and figuratively, by proposing that it is every individual's right to seek self-fulfillment and make the most out of every moment; the other tends to value the state, which is often misleadingly called "the people," and aims to seize time itself, in large chunks rather than days, for it is not the daily gratification of the individual that matters in such societies, but the gradual corporate fulfillment of grand designs, over specific spans of time, some short, some long. Both are obsessed with production and consumption, but in different ways. One rebels against terminal temporality by offering the individual limitless opportunities to consume, eat, drink, and play; the other rebels by forging five-year plans or empires that will last a thousand years. The twentieth century produced extreme examples of both types of rampantly materialistic societies, and of states and empires, and atrocities that made the guillotine look like a silly toy. Examples of both types of materialism still survive, although the collectivist societies are now much fewer in number than they were twenty years ago, and some have become strange hybrids where individualism and collectivism blend into one another and consumerism flourishes under the watch of repressive oligarchies, some moderate and others severe.

Capitalist consumerism and totalitarian collectivism denounce one another constantly, to no one's surprise. On the whole, however, relatively few moral and spiritual reformers have launched assaults on both. One notable exception was Pope John Paul II, who repeatedly condemned all types of materialistic societies as equally wrong, unjust, and dangerous, much to the chagrin of those who need to pigeonhole public figures as either *liberal* or *conservative, right* or *left.* John Paul saw modern materialism as perilous for the whole earth, in environmental terms, and for every individual too, in a spiritual sense. And, as he saw it, modern materialism was in large measure a response to the narrowed horizon of terminal temporality. Without eternity as a horizon, John Paul argued, the evanescent present acquires greater significance and the moral compass is lost. Even worse, the transience of existence itself thwarts all attempts at fulfillment. This frustration sets up a vicious cycle in which consumption and grand schemes escalate and ethics take a back seat. Echoing Jesus repeatedly, John Paul assailed all materialism, reminding the world that bread alone will never be sufficient, and that gaining the whole world and losing one's soul is a bad deal.[63]

Here we need to pause and ask a very basic question: Is it all really as simple as this? Should one place so much significance or attribute so much causality to a mere concept? Were the two world wars of the twentieth century a result of eternity's demise in Western societies? Could belief in eternity have prevented the horrors of the Holocaust or the gulag, or Hummer dealerships or the Neiman Marcus Christmas catalogue? Is it really impossible to believe in eternity and sport a bumper sticker that reads "He who dies with the most toys wins," or to set up an extermination camp? Moreover, an even more basic question needs to be raised:

Should one assume that the world as a whole has lost sight of eternity?

What about those who still believe in eternity? In a personal eternity, I mean, not in cosmic terms? One does not have to look very far to find people who are willing to exchange their present temporality for eternal life: belief in eternal rewards is, after all, a significant weapon wielded by the other side in the "War on Terror" that followed the suicidal holocaust of September 11, 2001. Suicide bombers are everywhere, it seems, and they remain incomprehensible to most Americans and Europeans. But what shocks and disturbs Westerners about these self-professed martyrs is not their belief in the afterlife, but their belief in the righteousness of killing and maiming civilians at random.

Belief in an eternal afterlife seems to be thriving in North America. The latest poll by the Pew Forum on Religion and Public Life[64] revealed the following:

- Ninety-two percent believe in God.
- Seventy-four percent believe in life after death.
- Fifty percent are absolutely certain about afterlife; nineteen percent are fairly certain.
- Seventy-four percent believe in heaven and eternal reward.
- Fifty-nine percent believe in hell and eternal punishment.

The results of this Pew poll are very similar to those of other recent polls. A national poll taken by CBS News in 2005 reported the following statistics about the United States:

- Seventy-eight percent believe in eternal life after death.
- Forty-eight percent believe in ghosts, and twenty-two percent claim to have seen a ghost.
- Ninety percent of those who attend religious services regularly believe in an afterlife.

• Seventy percent of those who rarely or never attend services believe in an afterlife too.

Even more surprising, most Americans were willing to admit that their beliefs do not need scientific confirmation. When asked, "Will science ever prove than an afterlife exists?" eighty-seven percent answered no.[65] A Harris poll taken in 2003 also revealed that thirty-one percent of Americans believe in astrology and thirty-seven percent in reincarnation, and that these two beliefs can be held by people who consider themselves Christian.[66] An ABC NEWS/Beliefnet poll taken in 2001 revealed that forty-three percent of Americans believe that their pets have an eternal afterlife too, even though a Gallup poll taken that same year revealed that ninety-six percent enjoy being carnivores. Unfortunately, the poll failed to ask whether or not Americans believe that the animals they slaughter and eat are also destined for the very same eternity as humans and pets.[67] How is such belief possible, in the twenty-first century, in one of the most technologically advanced societies on Earth? Is eternal life a necessary "fact" of the sort aptly described by Raymond Chandler—"There are things that are facts, in a statistical sense, on paper, on a tape recorder, in evidence. And there are things that are facts because they have to be facts, because nothing makes any sense otherwise"?[68]

What about an ethical dimension in eternity: heaven versus hell? What do pollsters tell us? In 1997 a majority of Gallup poll respondents—seventy-two percent—professed belief in the existence of an eternal heaven, while only fifty-six percent acknowledged belief in hell. By 2003, however, beliefs appear to have changed somewhat dramatically. A Harris poll taken that year recorded belief in heaven at eighty-two percent and belief in hell at sixty-nine percent. In a 2004 poll by ABC

TABLE 5.1
Belief in the Afterlife: Recent Polls in the United States

	Gallup (1997)	Harris (2003)	ABC (2004)	Pew (2008)
Heaven	72%	82%	81%	74%
Hell	56%	69%	70%	59%

News, belief in heaven stood nearly unchanged at eighty-one percent, and belief in hell had inched up to seventy percent.[69] A comparison of all of these polls reveals a fairly steady level of belief in eternity (see table 5.1).

What can we make of these figures? Why should belief in an eternal ethical reckoning have spiked so dramatically in 2003–4 in the United States? We historians would immediately question the accuracy of the data, or of the samples, or of the methods employed. Everyone knows polls are never one hundred percent accurate, but some polls are worse than others. If these polls are correct, however, something dramatic must have come to pass. Could it have been the terrorist attacks of September 11, 2001? All those lives, lost instantly, in a culture that is unaccustomed to large-scale catastrophes, but seems to thrive on images of these disasters? All those *innocent* lives taken so *unjustly* by a handful of *evil* men? All those images of airplanes, fireballs, smoke, plummeting bodies, and wholesale ruin, broadcast repeatedly, day and night, for weeks on end? Surely, among the many questions raised by the minor apocalypse of September 11, those dealing with the injustice of the act must rank high on the list. And, surely, thinking about proper rewards for the victims and punishments for their killers could easily lead to thinking about some realm other than Afghanistan or Iraq, beyond earth, where genuine justice wins out. But, then, how is

204 ~ Chapter 5

one to interpret the decline in hell-believers in the Pew poll of 2008? Are Americans unable to hold grudges for very long, or are the polls simply inaccurate?

As a historian, I'm simply making observations about recent patterns, trying to make sense out of them. I'm not making any predictions, or issuing any warnings about what may lie in store for us if belief in eternity breaks out of the private realm into the public sphere in the West. My own inclination is to think that such a reversal is not likely to happen any time soon, if ever.

For now, any way you look at it, polls show that eternity is not dead in the West, after all, or at least in North America. This brings us face to face with two of the most intractable problems in the history of religion: not only how ideas and social realities relate to one another, but also how it is that the beliefs of the elites relate to those of the non-elite majority and the culture at large. How do beliefs affect any society, and what difference do they make?

In the case of the United States, few would challenge the assertion that our laws and our day-to-day existence are determined by belief in the equality of all humans. It's such a basic premise it can pass for an incontestable truth. "We hold these truths to be self-evident, that all men are created equal," and so on: although social and economic inequalities and bigotry still abound, and the premise itself is interpreted differently today by the political elites than it was in 1776, 1860, or even 1960, the fact remains that the principle itself— a mere abstraction—has not only determined the course of American history but has affected all Americans, high and low. Very much the same thing can be said about France, with its commitment to the principles of *liberté, égalité, fraternité*. In contrast, the role of the concept of eternity is much more difficult to assess. Much like stealth aircraft, it fails to show up on radar, precisely because in America and France, as in most of the industrialized democratic nations, it is not an essential belief, like equality, or an essential component of political discourse. A private rather than public belief, eternity lies hidden from view, in minds and hearts. How it affects the lives of individuals is much harder to discern, even with polls, for the separation of church and state keeps it out of view. Some surely doubt that such abstract beliefs have any effect at all.

What remains beyond dispute is the fact that in the United States and almost every other nation that could be called "Western"—the direct cultural descendants of medieval Christendom—this divorce between belief and political life is directly related to the death of eternity. Simple formulas may fail to capture this relation between beliefs and social and political structures, for it is very complex, and circular. As belief in eternity declined among the intellectual elite, it began to vanish from political life, and as it vanished from that sphere, it became more of a private "belief" than a "self-evident truth," or unquestionable assumption. People may have continued to believe in an eternal afterlife, or heaven and hell, but they did so in a social and political atmosphere that made such belief totally optional and irrelevant to the public sphere. Throw in the fact that the rise of modern science was part of the process, and that the truths discerned by the scientists became the only unquestionable assumptions of Western culture, and the result is an eternity that still exists, but only invisibly, as a private wish of sorts, not much different from belief in unicorns, extraterrestrials, or astrology. The thirty-one percent of Americans who believe in astrology and the thirty-seven percent who believe in reincarnation, then, along with whatever percentage believe in unicorns, Bigfoot, and abductions by alien beings from outer space, may assemble to share their beliefs, but do not in any discernible way affect the culture at large.

Or do they? In both America and Europe, believers continue to order their lives with eternity as their ultimate horizon, even if their societies are constructed on the seemingly self-evident truth of terminal temporality. And some of these believers have grown restless, and flexed their political muscle. In America, in particular, the stirring of these believers has led to debates about the unquestionable assumptions that govern the land, and to a clash of belief systems better known as "the culture war." For many among the cultural elite, civilization hangs in the balance as this "war" pits blind medieval obscurantism against common-sense, empirically derived, unquestionable truth. For those who question the unquestionable, it is not just civilization that hangs in the balance but the eternal destiny of the human race, and the issue of eternal justice. Few on either side see past their own rhetoric to realize that the concept of eternity undergirds the whole dispute, but every now and then a perceptive observer in the news media gets to the heart of the problem. Among these rare few, David Klinghoffer has spoken most eloquently, while pondering the fact that so many of the culture warriors in the religious camp tend to believe in hell:

> The deepest question at stake in the culture war is not abortion or Hell, nor evolutionism or homosexuality, but rather this: Does the universe operate on the principle of randomness, or under the rule of transcendent Providence? Only in a random universe can the wicked get away with their wickedness.[70]

Hell is a most unpleasant belief, and not at all some self-evident truth, Klinghoffer admits, but hell is nonetheless the sort of fact that forces itself on you for lack of an alternative. Since the God of Jews, Christians, and Muslims is supposed to be a just and merciful deity, and since goodness is not always rewarded in this world and the wicked often get off scot-free, or even die in very pleasant surroundings, how, then, is true justice ever served?

Philosophers and theologians have long puzzled over the logic of evil: how can a good God ever allow for bad things to happen to his creation? This issue is known as *theodicy*. At its core, theodicy is the problem of problems for modern and postmodern believers, especially since Darwin's theory of evolution displaced the ancient Jewish myth of the Garden of Eden, which placed the blame for all suffering on Adam and Eve: how can one reconcile a good creator God with the pain and evil that envelops the earthly existence of humans and all creatures? If nature has always been "red in tooth and claw," every bough smeared with blood, where is God's goodness? Darwin's theory of evolution, and of the survival of the fittest changed Christian discourse, not so much because it took causality from God and gave it to nature (since nature itself could be attributed to God), or because it implied that humans were not a "special" creation (theologians could easily enough insert a divinely steered "special" moment in the evolution of hominids), but because it made God the author and cause of untold suffering: pain, illness, death, venom, claws, thorns, birth defects, were all part of his design from the very beginning. And predation seemed the worst of God's designs. Earlier Christians had puzzled over the incongruity of the lion and the lamb but could always attribute cruelty in nature to the Fall, which changed everything. Darwin made it much harder for everyone to see the world through that palliative lens ever again. Fittingly, it was in poetry that meditations on theodicy anticipated Darwin's heavy blow. Merely by observing nature itself, Tennyson was able to beat Darwin to the punch, referring to nature as "red in tooth and claw," turning what would be Darwin's greatest insight into sublime verse ten years before the publication of *The Origin of the Species*:

> Thou madest Life in man and brute;
>   Thou madest Death; and lo, thy foot
> Is on the skull which thou hast made.
>   Thou wilt not leave us in the dust:
>   Thou madest man, he knows not why,
> He thinks he was not made to die;
> And thou hast made him: thou art just . . .
> Are God and Nature then at strife,
>   That Nature lends such evil dreams? . . .
> No more? A monster then, a dream,
>   A discord. Dragons of the prime,
>   That tare each other in their slime. . . .
> O life as futile, then, as frail!
> O for thy voice to soothe and bless!
>   What hope of answer, or redress?
> Behind the veil, behind the veil.[71]

All the striving, loving, suffering, all the injustice cannot make sense without some eternal reckoning. No eternity behind the veil, no just God, for belief in God becomes impossibly difficult without eternal rewards and punishments. As Klinghoffer was bright enough to see: "For certain people who reject the idea of Hell, that's exactly the point."[72] And for culture warriors, proving that such logic is flawed is their call to action, for their world view is at stake, and the alternative one seems too frightful. As they see it, a temporally terminal world where very flawed humans, not God, determine what is right or wrong—a world devoid of God and eternity—is a pointlessly cruel and wasteful world. We know exactly what Freud would have to say to all of them, but that does not solve the problem. It only helps us understand it better.

Physics and Metaphysics, Redux

Oddly enough, as the so-called culture war rages, some scientists are now coming up with theories that come close to some of the ancient insights into time and eternity that modern science displaced long ago. The parallels are striking, even eerie.

Some of these theories need to be taken into consideration, even if their complexity is far beyond the capacities of any layman to fully understand them. The reason for this is very simple: poets aside, astrophysicists are now the only people in our culture who take eternity seriously. Having assumed the mantle formerly worn by philosophers and theologians, those experts of old who have spent the last century avoiding this subject as if it were the plague, what they have to say has existential implications, especially because all of these theories are based on empirical observation rather than mere logic or speculation. All of these new eternities are testable. In other words, scientists may now disagree on what sort of eternity actually exists, but some day one of them may actually figure out the real thing.

The good news from the scientists is that the universe probably *is* eternal, in some way. The bad news is that it probably doesn't include you or me.

We've already touched on some of these theories about the eventual fate of the universe, at the very beginning of this book: eternal inflation and dissipation, leading to "cold death," or a Big Freeze; eternal expansion and entropy leading to "heat death," or a Big Whimper; a total collapse leading to self-immolation, or a Big Crunch. Some of these theories predict an eternal past and future; some are an eternal wasteland of a future; some an eternity of stars and galaxies forever; some an eternal cycle of creation and destruction, or Big Yo-Yo. But none of these eternities include you and me, necessarily, or even contingently. These are eternities in which our consciousness and our ever-so-fragile existence play no role whatsoever.

These theories are concerned with the universe, not with us, not even with the geniuses who can analyze data, theorize, and speculate about an eternity that doesn't necessarily include them.

Of course, as a historian, there are serious limits to what I can say about astrophysics and cosmology, or good news and bad news, so I will focus more on the existential and metaphysical repercussions of these theories than on the science behind them. My situation is probably not much different from yours (unless you happen to be an astrophysicist): I have to rely on distillations and summaries of the latest scientific literature, often in publications that are aimed at lay readers. As a novice and amateur, I acknowledge that the experts have an unassailable monopoly on the highest sort of knowledge, and that whatever I have to say about their subject is not at all based on scientific research, but simply on reading about such research. I also need to admit that even when I think I've understood the general contours of most of these recent cosmological theories, I can't test them out, so to speak, for there is no way I can duplicate the research and calculations, or judge the conclusions.

So, I will simply report on the physics, and reserve my analysis for the metaphysics, which, as I see it, is the Big Problem.

First, when it comes to physics, there is the phenomenon of time to consider. Western thinkers have always found it impossible to speak about eternity without reference to time, since all talk about eternity in the Western tradition has been anthropocentric, focused on how we can claim eternity for ourselves, even though all we know is time. So, it's our enmeshment in time that is a problem: not whether the physical universe itself is eternal, but why it is that we appear and disappear in time so abruptly. In other words, eternity has been an existential, metaphysical problem for most of Western history, then, rather than a scientific one. So, even though scientists may not relate experiments on small time intervals with the subject of cosmic eternity, the connection is definitely there, metaphysically, for those who care about human eternity.[73]

Lately, some remarkable discoveries have been made by physicists armed with sophisticated equipment that should be of great interest to those who think about time philosophically, in relation to eternity. Some of the most recent findings would have greatly pleased St. Augustine, who was obsessed with the idea that time was far too ephemeral to be real. His thinking on this issue was shaped in part by the Bible and partly by Neoplatonic metaphysics. Since "now" could never be pinpointed with accuracy, he argued, but rather flowed constantly as a stream or a forward-moving arrow from "before" into "after," the only real "now" is God's eternal now moment, beyond time itself.[74] This was Augustine's insight, based solely on logic, not physics.

Well, lo and behold: some current speculative physics theories propose that time emerges from a more fundamental, timeless reality.[75] And recent experiments by Ferenc Krausz at the Max Planck Institute of Quantum Optics in Garching, Germany, have shown "that time may not exist at the most fundamental level of physical reality." Using ultraviolet laser pulses to track the quantum leaps of electrons within atoms, Krausz works at the edge of known physics, in a realm where incredibly tiny slivers of seconds drag by like eons and distances and intervals become so minuscule that the very concepts of time and space start to break down. The events he observes last for about 100 attoseconds, or 100 quintillionths of a second. What is an attosecond? Words fail, but analogies give us a hint: 100 attoseconds is to one second as a second is to 300 million years. In this infinitesimal dimension, Krausz has come close to the outer limits, and determined that the smallest unit of time that has any physical meaning is less than a trillionth of a trillionth of an attosecond. But beyond that, what? How about some fraction a quintillion times smaller than that? "Tempus incognito," some experts tell us; at this level, the classical notion of time becomes invalid. "The meaning of time has become terribly problematic in contemporary physics," says Simon Saunders, a philosopher of physics at Oxford. "The situation is so uncomfortable that by far the best thing to do is declare oneself an agnostic." At least for now.[76]

Agnostic. Imagine that. Science, agnostic about time, a measure essential to music and national economies, the meter by which many in the world earn their pay and their parking tickets.

But not all scientists who study time are agnostics.

Julian Barbour, for one, shuns agnosticism, arguing that "instants of time" are real in themselves, but do not belong to "something that flows relentlessly forward." According to Barbour, the apparent passage of time and the linear direction of motion may turn out to be nothing but illusions, a matter of perspective. If we could somehow stand outside the universe, he proposes, we would be able to see it as static.

And if he is right, eventually, "we shall come to see that time does not exist."[77] Much like Eckhart's Godhead in its eternal Now-ness, Barbour's universe is eternal insofar as it contains all of the individual "now" moments that we incorrectly perceive as a forward-moving arrow. Behind the illusion we perceive, he argues, there is a sempiternal universe, of the sort experienced by Kurt Vonnegut's character Billy Pilgrim, along with all the inhabitants of the planet Tralfamador, in *Slaughterhouse Five*:

> The Tralfamadorians can look at all the different moments the way we can look at a stretch of the Rocky Mountains, for instance. They can see how permanent all the moments are, and they can look at any moment that interests them. It is just an illusion we have here on earth that one moment follows another one, like beads on a string, and that once one moment is gone it is gone forever. . . . All time is all time. It does not change. It does not lend itself to warnings or explanations. It simply is. Take it moment by moment and you will find that we are all, as I've said before, bugs in amber.[78]

In other words, as a scholastic theologian might have said: it's sempiternity, or every now moment always surrounded by *aeternitas a parte ante* and *aeternitas a parte post*. Barbour's denial of time, therefore, is an unexpected scientific affirmation of one sort of eternity previously considered by scholastic philosophers and theologians, and a great writer from Indiana.

Another non-agnostic scientist who refuses to accept that time is a forward-moving arrow is Sean Caroll, who proposes that long *before* our Big Bang (all "befores" being relative, of course), in the "super-far past" there could have been other Big Bangs in which the so-called arrow of time ran backward rather than forward. The universe has always existed and always will as an infinitely complex pulsating matrix of interconnected universes with some in which time moves "forward" and others in which it moves "backward."[79]

Then there are also some scientists who are putting forward hypotheses that seek to conflate physics and metaphysics. One of these, Max Tegmark, a Swedish cosmologist who lives and works in the United States, has gone way out on a limb. According to one published interview aimed at nonspecialists, Tegmark is "harking back to the ancient Greeks with the oldest of the old questions: What is real?" His conclusions are as daring as his central question, and they bring us back to where we started, so many pages ago. As Tegmark sees it, we live in a "multiverse": several parallel universes that exist at multiple levels of space and time. Not exactly easy to comprehend, much less explain, this so-called mathematical universe hypothesis, in which integers and their relations to each other exist outside of time, builds on and expands quantum physics and cosmology.

As one might expect, some publications aimed at nonspecialists have tried to sensationalize Tegmark and his theories, even saying that his "crackpot ideas" are dismissed by some of his colleagues. Tegmark, however, is widely respected and far from a crackpot. The ultimate existential payoff of his attempt to fuse physics and metaphysics is this: go far enough out in this infinite multiverse "and you will find another Earth with another version of yourself." So, as Tegmark sees it, eternity and infinitude converge: we exist forever, always, in multiple selves. This is not some cyclical reality he is proposing, no eternal or infinite return, but an infinity and eternity of parallel selves: "You are made up of quantum particles," he says, "so if they can be in two places at once, so can you."

Well, I'll be damned, literally. That's all I can say. This seems like hell to me, maybe even worse than Nieremberg's over-crowded, slimy stinkhole of a hell.

Tegmark thinks that he is "not even asking you to believe in anything weird."[80] Such is the epistemological gulf that separates the expert and the layperson. "Weird" is one of those adjectives that cause trouble, simply because they have no fixed meaning. All I can say as a layperson about such a theory is this: I don't know about you, but I will probably remain ambivalent about my other selves *forever*, even if I feel boundless empathy for all of the mistakes they/we have made, or even if they/I can tell me/us where all those lost socks have gone. And I'm pretty sure that *they* will feel the same way about me. Or should I say about *us*? This is one eternity that would include *me* and *you*, or many of *me* and *you*, but I'm not sure this is comforting at all, or fair at all to both of us, or to anyone else.

In the meantime, while we contemplate Tegmark's multi-verse and wait for some conveyance that can take us out far enough to meet at least one of our *Doppelgängers*, or bring them to us, we can all take infinite comfort, or umbrage, at the thought that Nietzsche and *The Upanishads* and the Sto-ics may have hit the nail on the head concerning eternal re-turns. Well, sort of.

Very recently, Paul Steinhardt of Princeton University and Neil Turok of Cambridge University, two of the world's foremost theoretical cosmologists, have argued that the Big Bang we have all come to know and love as the ultimate *In Principio*, along with the approaching Big Crunch we all have been told to expect as the end of all ends, are merely but one cycle in an eternal meta-cycle of endless expansions and con-tractions, each lasting about a trillion years or so.[81] As they see it, the universe has always pulsed and will forever do so between Big Bang and Big Crunch, eternally, with a steady rhythm, like the ultimate heart, or conga drum: it evolves from hot and dense to cold and empty in each cycle, only to be replenished with new matter and energy as it transitions from crunch to bang. This theory of a cyclical universe proposed by Steinhardt and Turok is incredibly complex, of course, and comprehensible only to a very small number of experts, involving as it does the claim that our three-dimensional universe is part of a ten-dimensional "brane" and that the eternal cycles of expansion and contraction are caused by collisions between our cosmic brane and a neighboring one.[82]

Moving once again from the scientific to the existential, it is easy to empathize with Blaise Pascal, who was frightened to death by the seemingly empty vastness that some of his contemporaries had discovered in the physical universe. These new scientific theories of eternity provide all sorts of new possibilities for eternity, but all of them, while intellectually stimulating, only deepen our existential quandary as human beings. While it is one thing to marvel at the rhythmic pulse of an eternal universe, it is quite another to ponder our fate in it, both personally and collectively. If we try to inject ourselves into these multiverses, there seems to be no place for us. In a cyclical cosmos, are our selves repeatedly annihilated, infinitely dissipated and dissolved, or magnified and multiplied? Are our selves there at all, save for this insultingly brief slice of time we are now using up? What good is it if there are infinite, eternal *me*'s and I'm not conscious of that, now or ever? We're back to the question of the tree in the forest, only this time the question doesn't seem badly put: If there are infinite versions of me and I'm not aware of this at all, do I exist at all? I can't help but agree with Pascal:

"All our dignity, then, consists in thought. It is from this that we must raise ourselves, and not from space and duration, which we could not fill."[83]

Dignity meant something different in seventeenth-century France than it does in this day and age, anywhere on earth, so I can't be sure that Pascal and I see eye to eye on its meaning. For one thing, in his day and age, dignity involved wearing a wig in public and bathing as infrequently as possible. But it seems to me that what Pascal meant in this instance by "our dignity" is our capacity to transcend the ultimate insult: the fact that we are morally and ontologically superior to the physical universe, even more wondrous than the sum of it all, simply because we are conscious and can think, and discern how our killer universe works. That, in and of itself, is such a marvel—for us—that it makes our extinction seem all the more unfair, and our plight all the more noble, and tragic. Consciousness, then, is our ultimate refuge in the face of extinction. Cold comfort, indeed. Too cold for me, and not much comfort at all, if any.

I don't know about you, but I'm outraged by a universe that exists eternally, but only allows me a tiny scrap of time. I get angry thinking about the rhythmic, eternal multiverse, or the ever-expanding universe, which remind me of nothing but vicious killers. I am reminded of Pascal's description of the human condition:

> Imagine a number of men in chains, all condemned to death, where some are slaughtered each day in the sight of the others, and those who remain see their own condition in that of their fellows and, looking at each other with grief and without hope, wait for their turn.[84]

Impertinent questions issue from me that have nothing to do with the science behind these theories of eternity, but everything to do with the insult and injustice being heaped upon all of us by such a universe. Much like a condemned man who hurls insults at the firing squad that is about to kill him, I shout out my questions.

First of all, why did scientists working on string theory choose the word "brane" at all? Yes, I understand the etymology, and the history of the word's usage, and every brane's kinship to the *brane* in mem*brane*, but why wasn't anyone floored by fact that *brane* and *brain* can be mistaken for one another in English? Why should *branes* run the risk of being mistaken for that thinking organ in the human body responsible for assigning names to things, sorting out homonyms, and making sense of the universe? The irony embedded in this pun of a name is too great, as is its Nietzschean suggestiveness. What if the branes are brains? Why rule out consciousness at the largest level? But forget consciousness: what about these branes, physically? Beyond them, what? Infinite branes and universes, or just a few? Are we out there in that neighboring brane, too? Or in some other brane? Or are we stuck in this one, to be reconstructed and deconstructed, atom by exact atom, in every next cycle, to re-live this same exact life we have always lived over and over, precisely the same way, suffering through traffic jam after recurring traffic jam on the Garden State Parkway in Hohokus, for ever and ever, without air conditioning, and no memory whatsoever of a single previous instance of the same aeonian events, blinking on and off in the cosmic pulse, forever, like one dim light bulb on a Christmas tree, the day *after* Christmas? Will not even one déjà-vu experience be for real? And doesn't an endless cycle of Big Bangs beg the question of origins, anyway?

Are we that far from asking what God was doing before he created the world? We all know what Augustine would say, but that doesn't help explain anything.

It only helps us to gain perspective on our own attitudes, and to ask ourselves: should we praise Nietzsche or curse him for coming so damn close to this scientific theory without a telescope of any kind, or even a primitive slide rule, and with migraines to overcome, to boot?

When all is said and done eternity is hard to imagine, yet so much easier to conceive of than to grasp.

VI

Not Here, Not Now, Not Ever

What reason do atheists have to say that one cannot rise from the dead? Which is more difficult, to be born or to rise again? That what has never been should be, or that what has been should be again? Is it more difficult to come into existence than to return to it? Habit makes the one seem easy to us; lack of habit makes the other impossible: a vulgar way of judging![1]

Quite an argument, one must admit. But one has to wonder: if Pascal had actually lived long enough to turn the fragments we now know as the *Pensées* into a coherent book, would he have made a greater impact on unbelievers and skeptics? Or are the *Pensées* more formidable in their fragmentary form, strung together as individual gems, like beads on a rosary or .50 caliber bullets on an ammo belt?

Certainly, we won't ever know for sure, for Pascal ran out of time before he could collect his *Thoughts*, and everything is guesswork when one asks the what-if question. In such cases, uncertainty is the most certain thing.

As is also the case with eternity nowadays. And also with "nothing," as it pertains to us.

Ponder this: some hard-line corporealists argue that our consciousness resides entirely in our brain, and that when our cerebral cortex stops functioning, consciousness sputters and dies, along with the rest of the body. End of story. Nobel laureate Francis Crick has gone as far as to say that we are "nothing but a pack of neurons." Some corporealists are so keen on this idea, however, that it irks them to see anyone making too much of the "nothing" that follows death. As they see it, "nothingness" is not some condition that we enter at death, for if our consciousness vanishes at the moment that our brain turns into an inert object, no different from a stone or a cantaloupe, then "nothing" is nothing, not a positive quality, like "blackness." This is precisely why, according to some, the following statement is insufficient and misleading: "When we die, what's next is nothing; death is an abyss, a black hole, the end of experience; it is eternal nothingness, the permanent extinction of being."[2] Nothing, it seems, is too much for corporeal fundamentalists.

This leads to a question: if all thinking can be explained in purely physical terms, then what difference is there between consciousness and a headache? None? If so, then, what can one say about thought itself? If not, then what can one say about the difference? In arguing for the total certainty of corporealism, logic itself inserts a hint of uncertainty. Hard-line corporealists can't help but fall into a vicious circle concerning consciousness, a circle that calls to mind the Ouroboros, an ancient symbol for eternity. The irony of this is not lost on physicist Stephen Barr:

> The concept "neuron" itself, in fact, is on this account nothing other than a certain pattern of neurons firing in the brain. Is there not something here to make us vaguely uneasy? Is not the snake of scientific theory eating its own tail—or rather its own head? . . . We should listen to great scientific minds because they are great scientific minds. However, when they begin to tell us that they really have no minds at all, we are entitled to ignore them.[3]

Given the uncertainty of which we are so certain concerning eternity, perhaps only a post-postmodern turn can save us from being overwhelmed by our impending doom, our terminal temporality. Philosophy offers all sorts of alternatives, but little consolation. Analytic, anyone? Or would you prefer Continental? Which brand? Phenomenology? Positivism? Existentialism? Nihilism? How about a custom blend, a potpourri? Perhaps a dab of deontological ethics? A pinch of deconstruction? Bits of Martin Heidegger and his *Dasein*, or *Being-There*? Oh, but *Dasein* must be embraced absolutely, you say. Well, then, how about *Sein zum Tode*, or *being-unto-death*?[4] Or any of the other 100 new complex words Heidegger coined, all ending in -*sein*, or *being*, which won him acclaim as a genius, despite the fact that he was a card-carrying Nazi?[5] Cold comfort, I am sorry to say: something that might work for the brave, the few, the exceptionally abstracted.

Maybe prayer will do the trick? Or art, or music, or poetry, or farming? Yoga? Tattooing? Vandalism? Recycling? Maybe all of these? Or some combination thereof? Maybe none of them?

Much has been lost and much continues to be lost as certainty dwindles, on a personal and social level. Much has been gained too, and continues to be gained. It's a mixed blessing. Men who do not expect to cavort forever in some eternal paradise with eternal virgins in exchange for some horrific self-immolation that kills thousands in the name of the Almighty tend not to fly aircraft filled with passengers into tall, crowded buildings. But then, again, men who believe that they will suffer eternal torment for failing to love their neighbor usually shy away from doing that sort of thing too. Normally they also avoid building extermination camps where human beings can be turned into ashes and soap very quickly, by the hundreds of thousands, or millions, with

industrial efficiency—something that Martin Heidegger as-
sented to, openly and shamefully, as he thrilled deep thinkers
everywhere with his *Da-sein* and his *Ent-wurf* and his *Un-zu-
hause,* and other similarly turgid neologisms.

Belief is funny, that way. You never know what to expect
from it. Or from lack of belief, either.

One of the most brilliant cinematographers of the twentieth century, Luis Buñuel, tried to sum up his life and make
sense of what might await him at death, as that moment ap-
proached. An avowed atheist, he concluded that "when all
is said and done, there's nothing, nothing but decay and the
sweetish smell of eternity." And then he sketched one final
scene, a meditation on the hell that might await him, and
him alone, as befits a postmodern *auteur* who was probably
forced to read Nieremberg as a schoolboy, in Spain:

> Sometimes, just to amuse myself, I conjure up old images of
> Hell. Of course, in these modern times, the flames and the
> pitchforks have disappeared; and Hell is now only a simple
> absence of divine light. I see myself floating in a boundless
> darkness, my body still intact for the final resurrection, but
> suddenly another body bumps into mine. It's a Thai who
> died two thousand years ago falling out of a coconut tree.
> He floats off into the infernal obscurity and millions of years
> go by, until I feel another body. This time, it's one of Napo-
> leon's camp followers. And so it goes, over and over again,
> as I let myself be swept along for a moment in the harrowing
> shadows of this post-modern Hell.[6]

In the face of utter extinction, or eternal ennui, our artists
keep us amused, and occasionally offer a glimpse of something that looks like a truth, at least as far as we can tell,
just for us. We dare not think it might actually be a metaphysical truth of the universal sort Plato and St. Augustine

assumed existed, or of the sacred sort that led celibate Father Maximillian Kolbe to trade places at Auschwitz with Francis Gajowniczek, a married man with young children, knowing for certain that those Nazis meant to starve him to death, and that it would take three harrowing weeks for that death to ensue. Everyone there knew it took at least three weeks, because those Nazis kept doing it, over and over again, like psychotic disciples of Nietzsche who couldn't understand what repetition meant to him, picking prisoners at random and locking them up without any food or water, just so they could prove that they, the master race, were in control of Auschwitz and the entire world for the next millennium or so, and perhaps *forever*.

Naive old Plato believed truth, goodness, and beauty were one and the same, and so have his disciples. This is why they tend to pick fights with anyone who says that there is no arguing over taste, even though they've been a dying breed for a long time. Say "*de gustibus non disputandum*" to one of them and you might end up with a black eye, or a snide retort ringing in your ears. Humorist S. J. Perelman was no Platonist, but he nonetheless nailed it when he quipped, "de gustibus ain't what dey used to be."[7] We are now repeatedly told by the thinking class that truth, too, is strictly in the eye of the beholder, along with beauty and goodness, unless it happens to be a truth confirmed as such by a scientist or their political party. Yet, despite all disclaimers, there are still many on earth who believe in Truth with a capital T in a metaphysical sense, and some, unfortunately, who think that It is neatly encapsulated in some superior thoughts of their own, or some Book that they alone can interpret correctly. And sometimes they hanker for blood with an insatiable thirst, these rude folk who usually believe in eternity, just like Father Kolbe, though in a totally wrong way, because they overlook beauty and goodness. And they overlook love, and the golden rule, above all.

What a terrible thought.

"Eternity is a terrible thought. I mean, where's it going to end?" says one of the characters in Tom Stoppard's *Rosencranz and Guildenstern Are Dead*. It matters little whether the line belongs to Rosencranz, Guildenstern, Hamlet, or Yorick's skull. It's so clever a line, it makes no difference which character gets to blurt it out.[8] But is there anything beyond its disingenuous ingenuity? One could argue that the pun is so hypnotically cunning, like some etching by M. C. Escher, that it erases the line between certainty and uncertainty and brings you face-to-face with complexities beyond your mind. One could also argue that in our day and age, whenever we are able to tuck away our fears, all we are left with when it comes to this topic is the chance to ponder the ineffable while we keep our eye firmly fixed solely on the here and now, vaporific as that is, and decide whether or not we want to attach ourselves to anything we can touch, see, hear, smell, and taste, which, like us, may be slated for extinction at any moment.

But who can live without attachment to anything or anyone? Monks have been failing at that for centuries. I once knew a monk who was very attached to "his" books and "his" stereo equipment, and another one who liked "his" girlfriend an awful lot. And I once lived near a lake in Minnesota with a sign that read, "No trespassing: Monastic beach." I wish I'd photographed that sign, for many think I'm making up the story. Perhaps it's still there, awaiting the *parousia*, and the Final Judgment, when Christ will have to rule on whether or not that sign proves some sort of failure.

I don't know. I await eternity in suspense as my fellow travelers in time shout, all around me: "not here, not now, not ever; forget about it." ·

Eternity is no longer a thought for many, much less a real possibility, or something worth awaiting. At worst it is a cruel hoax encoded in our chromosomes, for some totally random, unfathomable reason, or, by the mysterious design of evolution, simply to keep us from killing ourselves and feeding our children to the wolves. At best, eternity is a feeling. The bridge between the evanescent here and now and the eternal is often but an emotion away, but is either end of the bridge more "real" than the other? Only poets seem to know for sure, innately. Take the young Arthur Rimbaud, for instance, who could say,

> It's been found again.
> What?—Eternity.
> It's the sea mingled
> with the sun . . .
>
> No hope, ever,
> No enlightenment,
> Science and patience reveal,
> Torment is certain.[9]

And if suffering is the sole certain outcome in this personal eternity, then maybe it's everyone's fault, not just one's own. Rimbaud seems to have stumbled on this insight, after ingesting a powerful drug and giving himself a bad trip, as those at Woodstock would say. Mocking Descartes and Christ at the same time, he could moan, along with Richard Dawkins, Christopher Hitchens, and all the new atheists: "I believe I am in Hell, therefore I am. This is the catechism at work. I am the slave of my baptism. You, my parents, have ruined my life, and your own."[10]

Bummer, man.

Unfortunately, poets, philosophers, and novelists—shy, quirky, retiring folk, given over to introspection and the occasional drinking binge rather than world domination—are not the only members of society who have feelings of eternity, or are affected by conceptions of it. Everyone is affected, whether they know it or not, like it or not. Feelings, concepts, beliefs, love, and the price of oil are equally real, and sometimes equally inconvenient. As inconvenient as the self-evident truth of terminal temporality, and the "I" who cannot fathom any "now" other than one that always eludes its grasp.

As inconvenient and as incongruous as a five-year plan in a worker's paradise, or a sign that reads "No trespassing: Monastic beach."

And *I*, an incurable chronophobiac, *I* prefer to sum up eternity somewhat brusquely, as one always must, with words left behind by William Blake. After all, when you are dealing with eternity, it's only right to let a dead man have the last word.

> He who binds to himself a joy
> Does the winged life destroy
> But he who kisses the joy as it flies
> Lives in eternity's sun rise.[11]

Appendix

~

Common Conceptions of Eternity

1. TIME WITHOUT A BEGINNING OR AN END, OR *SEMPITERNITY*

The total eternity, which has neither beginning nor end, may be regarded as divided by any moment into two eternities: the past eternity (*aeternitas a parte ante*) and the future eternity (*aeternitas a parte post*).

One may speak of this eternity in four ways:

a. Absolute eternity, having neither beginning nor end.
b. The two "eternities": *aeternitas a parte ante* AND *aeternitas a parte post.*
c. The past eternity, time without beginning: *aeternitas a parte ante* ONLY.
d. The future eternity, time without end: *aeternitas a parte post.*

In Christian thought:

a. Pertains to God and his nonsuccessive knowledge of everything.
b. Pertains to God *before* AND *after* creation of the universe and time/space.
c. Pertains to God *before* the creation of the universe and time/space.
d. Pertains to God AND the universe *after* creation AND redemption.

One version of b is Kurt Vonnegut, *Slaughterhouse Five* (New York, Dial Press, 1995), extending the Christian God's knowledge to creatures on the planet Tralfamador.

The Tralfamadorians can look at all the different moments the way we can look at a stretch of the Rocky Mountains, for instance. They can see how permanent all the moments are, and they can look at any moment that interests them. It is just an illusion we have here on earth that one moment follows another one, like beads on a string, and that once one moment is gone it is gone forever. (p. 34)

All time is all time. It does not change. It does not lend itself to warnings or explanations. It simply is. Take it moment by moment and you will find that we are all, as I've said before, bugs in amber. (p. 109)

2. A STATE THAT TRANSCENDS TIME

a. And is wholly separate from time.
b. And includes time within it.

One version of b is St. Augustine of Hippo, *Confessions* (Oxford: Oxford University Press, 1991).

It is not in time that You [God] precede times. Otherwise You would not precede all times. In the sublimity of an eternity which is always in the present, You are before all things past and transcend all things future, because they are still to come. (XI, xiii p. 230)

You [God] are before the beginning of the ages, and prior to everything that can be said to be "before." . . . In You the present day has no ending, and yet in You it has its end. . . . Because "Your years do not fail" (Ps.101.28), Your years are one Today . . . And all tomorrow and hereafter, and indeed all yesterday and further back, You will make a Today, You have made a Today. (I, vi, pp. 7–8)

3. A STATE THAT INCLUDES TIME BUT PRECEDES AND EXCEEDS IT

Psalm 90:2–4: Before the mountains were born, the earth and the world brought forth, from eternity to eternity You are God. A thousand years in Your sight are but as yesterday when it is past, and as a watch in the night.

4. PLATONIC ETERNITY: THE INTELLIGIBLE REALM (OBSOLETE, BUT INFLUENTIAL)

Eternal principles, which have immutable existence. Souls are eternal, but shuttle back and forth (reincarnation/metempsychosis/transmigration) from the eternal intelligible realm and material world of time/space.

5. RELATION TO INFINITY

Eternity is often linked to the concept of *infinity*, and shares some of the same meanings, or is confused with it.

Most common association:
eternity = time
infinity = space AND time

SOME DEFINITIONS

Infinity (*Oxford English Dictionary*):

1. The quality or attribute of being infinite or having no limit; boundlessness, illimitableness (especially as an attribute of deity).
2. Something that is infinite; infinite extent, amount, duration, etc.; a boundless space or expanse; an endless or unlimited time.
3. Math: Infinite quantity.

4. Geometry: Infinite distance, or that portion or region of space which is infinitely distant.

5. Swimming and Leisure: An outdoor swimming pool designed to give the impression that it lacks an edge or edges and merges into the surrounding landscape.

Eternity (*Oxford English Dictionary*):

1. The quality, condition, or fact of being eternal; eternalness; eternal existence.

2. Infinite time, which has no beginning or end; sempiternity.

3. In expressed or implied contrast with time.

   a. Metaphysics: Timelessness; existence with reference to which the relation of succession has no application.

   b. Eschatology: Opposed to "time" in its restricted sense of duration measured by the succession of physical phenomena. Hence, the condition into which the soul enters at death; the future life.

Notes

CHAPTER 1 BIG BANG, BIG SLEEP, BIG PROBLEM

1. Pierre Chaunu, *La mémoire de l'éternité* (Paris: Éditions Robert Laffont, 1975), p. 97: "La mort de l'homme est un scandale, elle est le scandale par excellence, tou ce qui tend à diminuer ce scandale est dérisoire, est un opium du peuple. . . . La mort . . . est l'inadmissible. La mort d'un homme, l'anéantissement d'une mémoire ne peut être compensé par l'existence du cosmos et la poursuite de la vie. La mort de Mozart, malgré l'ouvre conservée, est un mal absolu."

2. Vladimir Nabokov, *Speak, Memory* (New York: Grosset and Dunlap, 1951), p. 1.

3. Jeanne Calment, with Michel Allard, Victor Lebre, and Jean-Marie Robine, *Jeanne Calment: From Van Gogh's Time to Ours: 122 Extraordinary Years* (New York: W. H. Freeman, 1998), p. 37.

4. For recent surveys of this vast subject, see Ian Tattersall, *The World from Beginnings to 4000 BCE* (Oxford: Oxford University Press, 2008), and Jonathan Kingdon, *Lowly Origin: Where, When, and Why Our Ancestors First Stood Up* (Princeton, NJ: Princeton University Press, 2003).

5. See R. Dale Guthrie, *The Nature of Paleolithic Art* (Chicago: University of Chicago Press, 2005), and David Lewis-Williams, *The Mind in the Cave: Consciousness and the Origins of Art* (London: Thames & Hudson, 2002).

6. Some doubt the authenticity of this remark. See Paul Bahn, "A Lot of Bull? Pablo Picasso and Ice Age Cave Art," *Munibe. Antropología y arqueología* 57, no. 3 (2005–6), pp. 217–23.

7. Thomas Hobbes, *Leviathan* (Indianapolis: Hackett, 1994), chap. 13.9, p. 72.

8. Charles Dickens, *A Tale of Two Cities* (New York: Penguin, 2003), p. 5.

9. See *La cultura del morire nelle società preistoriche e protostoriche italiane: Studio interdisciplinare*, ed. Fabio Martini (Florence: Istituto italiano di preistoria e protostoria, 2006).

10. Miguel de Unamuno, *The Tragic Sense of Life*, trans. J. E. Crawford Flitch (London: Macmillan, 1921), p. 71.

11. See Jesse Bering and David Bjorklund, "The Natural Emergence of Reasoning about the Afterlife as a Developmental Regularity," *Developmental Psychology* 40 (2004), pp. 217–33.

12. Dylan Thomas, "Do Not Go Gentle into That Good Night," in *The Poems of Dylan Thomas*, ed. Daniel Jones (New York: New Directions, 2003), p. 239.

13. Augustine, Sermon 344.4. Cited by Peter Brown, *The Cult of the Saints: Its Rise and Function in Latin Christianity* (Chicago: University of Chicago Press, 1981), p. 77.

14. Blaise Pascal, *Pensées*, trans. A. J. Krailsheimer (New York: Penguin Classics, 1995), p. 66.

15. Henry Vaughan, "The World," in *English Poetry, 1170–1892* (London: Ginn & Co., 1907), p. 200.

16. Bertrand Russell, "A Free Man's Worship," in *Contemplation and Action, 1902–14*; vol. 12 of *The Collected Papers of Bertrand Russell*, ed. Richard Rempel, Andrew Brink, and Margaret Moran (London: Allen and Unwin, 1985), pp. 67, 72.

17. See Donald Kelley, *The Beginning of Ideology* (Cambridge: Cambridge University Press, 1981).

18. See Michel Vovelle, *Ideologies and Mentalities*, trans. Eamon O'Flaherty (Cambridge: Polity/Basil Blackwell, 1990).

19. See Donald M. MacRaild and Avram Taylor, *Social Theory and Social History* (New York: Palgrave Macmillan, 2004).

20. Charles Taylor, *A Secular Age* (Cambridge: Belknap Press, 2007), pp. 171–76.

21. A description can be found at http://www.livedtheology.org/index.html: "The Project on Lived Theology is a research community. . . . Our goal is to understand the way theological commitments shape the social patterns and practices of everyday life."

22. See *Lived Religion in America: Towards a History of Practice*, ed. David D. Hall (Princeton, NJ: Princeton University Press, 1997), and *Lived Religion: Conceptual, Empirical and Practical-Theological Approaches*, ed. Heinz Streib, Astrid Dinter, and Kerstin Soderblom (Leiden: Brill, 2008).

23. Taylor, *A Secular Age*, p. 212.

24. Father Juan de Talavera Salazar, Archivo Historico de Protocolos, Madrid, 586.790. See Carlos Eire, *From Madrid to Purgatory* (New York: Cambridge University Press, 1995), pp. 193–94.

25. For the classic definition of "paradigm shift," see Thomas Kühn, *The Structure of Scientific Revolutions* (Chicago: University of Chicago Press, 1962).

26. For a good guide, see Charles Caes, *Beyond Time: Ideas of the Great Philosophers on Eternal Existence and Immortality* (Lanham, MD: University Press of America, 1985).

27. Augustine of Hippo, *Confessions*, XI.12, trans. Henry Chadwick (New York: Penguin, 1991), p. 229.

28. Jesse Bering, "The End? Why So Many of Us Think Our Minds Continue On After We Die," *Scientific American Mind* 19, no. 5 (October–November 2008), p. 36.

29. Albert Einstein, in *The Yale Book of Quotations*, ed. Fred Shapiro (New Haven, CT: Yale University Press, 2006), p. 230.

Chapter 2 eternity conceived

1. Letter 64.1–2, *Sancti Bernardi Opera*, ed. Jean Leclercq, Constant Talbot, and Henri-Marie Rochais (Rome: Éditiones Cistercienses), vol. 7, pp. 32–33. English translation by Wim Werbaal, "Timeless Time: Dramatical Eternity in the Monastery under Bernard of Clairvaux," in *Time and Eternity: The Medieval Discourse*, ed. G. Jaritz and Gerson Moreno-Riaño (Turnhout: Brepols, 2003), p. 233.

2. *The Epic of Gilgamesh: A New Translation, Analogues, Criticism*, trans. and ed. Benjamin R. Foster (New York: W. W. Norton, 2001).

3. See John H. Taylor, *Death and the Afterlife in Ancient Egypt* (Chicago: University of Chicago Press, 2001).

4. See Yuri Stoyanov, *The Other God: Dualist Religions from Antiquity to the Cathar Heresy* (New Haven, CT: Yale University Press, 2000), pp. 1–123.

5. Deuteronomy 4:24: "For Yahweh, thy God is a consuming fire, even a jealous God."

6. Zechariah 10:2: "For the idols have spoken vanity, and the diviners have seen a lie, and have told false dreams."

7. See Jacob Neusner, *Judaism and Zoroastrianism at the Dusk of Late Antiquity* (Atlanta: Scholars Press, 1993).

8. Exodus 20:4.

9. For more on the evolution of the Hebrew God, see Jack Miles, *God: A Biography* (New York: Vintage, 1996).

10. Psalm 100:5.

11. Psalm 90:2–4.

12. See Jon D. Levenson, *Resurrection and the Restoration of Israel: The Ultimate Victory of the God of Life* (New Haven, CT: Yale University Press, 2006), and Jon D. Levenson and Kevin J. Madigan, *Resurrection: The Power of God for Christians and Jews* (New Haven: Yale University Press, 2008). See also Claudia Setzer, *Resurrection of the Body in Early Judaism and Early Christianity* (Boston: Brill, 2004).

13. "Quid ergo Athenis et Hierosolymis?," Tertullian, *De Praescriptionibus Adversus Haereticos*, chap. 7, J.-P. Migne, ed., *Patrologiae cursus completus, Series Latina*, 221 vols. (Paris 1844–64), vol. 2, col. 20 B. English translation by P. Holmes, *The Ante-Nicene Fathers*, ed. A. Roberts and J. Donaldson (Edinburgh: T. & T. Clark, 1870), vol. 15, p. 9.

14. Gospel of John, 1.1–14.

15. *Stoicorum veterum fragmenta*, ed. H. V. Arnim, II, 190, quoted by Rudolf Bultmann, *The Presence of Eternity: History and Eschatology*, The Gifford Lectures, 1955 (New York: Harper and Brothers, 1957), p. 24.

16. Augustine, *City of God*, XII, 13.

17. Plato, *Republic*, bk. 7. English translation by G.M.A. Grube and C.D.C. Reeve, *Plato: Complete Works*, ed. John M. Cooper (Cambridge: Hackett, 1997), p. 1135.

18. Ibid., p. 1145.

19. Plato, *Phaedo, Complete Works*, p. 57.

20. Plato, *Phaedo, Complete Works*, p. 71.

21. See Andrew Smith, *Philosophy in Late Antiquity* (New York: Routledge, 2004).

22. See the classic study by Charles Bigg, *The Christian Platonists of Alexandria: The 1886 Bampton Lectures* (Oxford: Clarendon, 1968), and Henry Chadwick, *Early Christian Thought and the Classical Tradition* (New York: Oxford University Press, 1966). See also Alfons Fürst, *Christentum als Intellektuellen-Religion: Die Anfänge des Christentums in Alexandria* (Stuttgart: Verlag Katholisches Bibelwork, 2007).

23. Luke 23:43.

24. 2 Corinthians 5:1.

25. Luke 16:20–25.

26. Revelation 21:1–4.

27. Romans 8:22.

28. τοὺς αἰῶνας τῶν αἰώνων. Paul inserts this prayer into his letters. In Romans 16:27: "through Jesus Christ be glory *forever and ever*. Amen." In

1 Timothy 1:17: "Now unto the King eternal, immortal, invisible, the only wise God, be honour and glory *forever and ever.* Amen."

29. See Bultmann, *The Presence of Eternity,* p. 51.

30. "The Martyrdom of Polycarp," trans. Cyril Richardson, in *Early Christian Fathers* (New York: Touchstone, 1996), p. 156.

31. Ignatius of Antioch, "Letter to the Romans," trans. Cyril Richardson, in *Early Christian Fathers* (New York: Touchstone, 1996), pp. 104–6.

32. Virginia Heffernan, "Sweeping the Clouds Away," *New York Times Magazine,* November 18, 2007.

33. "Semen est sanguis Christianorum," Tertullian, *Apologeticus adversus gentes pro christianis,* in *Patrologiae cursus completus, Series Latina,* ed. J.P. Migne, 221 vols. (Paris 1844–64). vol. 1, col. 535A. English translation by S. Thelwall, in *Ante-Nicene Fathers,* vol. 3, ed. Allan Menzies (Edinburgh: T. & T. Clark, 1866–72; repr. Grand Rapids, MI: Eerdmans, 1978–81).

34. E. Le Blant, *Les inscriptions chrétiennes de la Gaule* (Paris, 1856), I: 240, cited by Brown, *The Cult of the Saints,* p. 3.

35. Numerous totally secular travel guides are available in English. See, e.g., David Gitlitz and Linda Kay Davidson, *The Pilgrimage Road to Santiago: The Complete Cultural Handbook* (New York: St. Martin's Press, 2000).

36. Two excellent biographies are Jean Daniélou, *Origen,* trans. Walter Mitchell (New York: Sheed and Ward, 1955), and Henri Crouzel, *Origen,* trans. A. S. Worrall (Edinburgh: T. & T. Clark, 1989).

37. See Harold Cherniss, *The Platonism of Gregory of Nyssa* (Berkeley and Los Angeles: University of California Press, 1930).

38. *Aion* = age or aeon; *chronos* = quantitative time, as in "What time is it?"; *kairos* = qualitative time, as in "this is the right time to repent"; *diastema* = extension.

39. For an overview, see Morwenna Ludlow, *Gregory of Nyssa: Ancient and (Post)Modern* (New York: Oxford University Press, 2007).

40. See Paul Plass, "Transcendent Time and Eternity in Gregory of Nyssa," *Vigiliae Christianae* 34, no. 2 (June 1980), pp. 180–92.

41. See Rowan Williams, *Arius: Heresy and Tradition* (London: Darton, Longman and Todd, 1987).

42. Gregory of Nyssa, "On the Deity of the Son," ed. J.-P. Migne, *Patrologiae cursus completus accurante J.-P. Migne. Series graeca* (Paris: P. Geuthner, 1928–45), vol. 46, col. 557B, quoted by Timothy Ware, *The Orthodox Church* (New York: Penguin, 1964), p. 35.

238 ⌣ Notes to Chapter 3

43. For an overview, see John Binns, *An Introduction to the Christian Orthodox Churches* (New York: Cambridge University Press, 2002), and Deno J. Geanakoplos, *A Short History of the Ecumenical Patriarchate of Constantinople*, 2nd ed. (Brookline, MA: Holy Cross Orthodox Press, 1990).

44. For an overview, see Peter Brown, *Augustine of Hippo* (Berkeley and Los Angeles: University of California Press, 1967); Eugene Teselle, *Augustine* (Nashville: Abingdon, 2006); James J. O'Donnell, *Augustine: A New Biography* (New York: Ecco, 2005); and John J. O'Meara, *Understanding Augustine* (Dublin: Four Courts Press, 1997).

45. Augustine, *Confessions*, XI, xiii, trans. Henry Chadwick (New York: Oxford University Press, 1991), p. 230. All citations refer to this edition.

46. Augustine, *Confessions*, I, vi, pp. 7–8

47. See Jaroslav Pelikan, *The Mystery of Continuity: Time and History, Memory and Eternity in the Thought of Saint Augustine* (Charlottesville: University Press of Virginia, 1986).

48. Augustine, *Confessions*, XI, xxii, p. 236.

49. Ibid., ii, p. 222.

50. Ibid., xiv, p. 230.

51. Ibid., xv, p. 232.

52. Ibid., xviii, p. 233.

53. Ibid., xvi, p. 233.

54. Ibid., xiii, p. 230.

55. Augustine, *Confessions*, I., i, p. 3.

56. Augustine, *Sermon* 344. 4. Cited by Brown, *The Cult of the Saints*, p. 77.

57. See Robert A. Markus, *Saeculum History and Society in the Theology of St. Augustine*, rev. ed. (New York: Cambridge University Press, 1988).

58. "Aeternitas igitur est interminabilis vitae tota simul et perfecta possessio." Boethius, *Consolatio Philosophiae*, bk. 5, chap. 6, ed. James O'Donnell (Bryn Mawr, PA: Thomas Library, Bryn Mawr College, 1990). English translation by Victor Watts, *The Consolation of Philosophy* (London: Penguin, 1969), p. 132.

CHAPTER 3 ETERNITY OVERFLOWING

1. *Rule of St. Benedict*, prologue, 43–44, trans. Timothy Fry, O.S.B. (Collegeville, MN: Liturgical Press, 1980), p. 18.

2. See Guy Halsall, *Barbarian Migrations and the Roman West, 376–568* (New York: Cambridge University Press, 2007); Walter Goffart, *Barbarian Tides: The Migration Age and the Later Roman Empire* (Philadelphia: University of Pennsylvania Press, 2006); and Hugh Elton, *Warfare in Roman Europe, AD 350–425* (New York: Oxford University Press, 1996).

3. See Ramsay MacMullen, *Christianity and Paganism in the Fourth to Eighth Centuries* (New Haven, CT: Yale University Press, 1997).

4. See Jacques Le Goff, *The Birth of Europe*, trans. Janet Lloyd (Oxford: Blackwell, 2005), esp. chaps. 1–4.

5. See Judith Herrin, *Byzantium: The Surprising Life of a Medieval Empire* (Princeton, NJ: Princeton University Press, 2008).

6. See Andrew Louth, *Greek East and Latin West: The Church, AD 681–1071* (Crestwood, NY: St. Vladimir's Seminary Press, 2007).

7. For surveys, see Peter King, *Western Monasticism* (Kalamazoo, MI: Cistercian Publications, 1999), and David Knowles, *Christian Monasticism* (London: Weidenfeld & Nicolson, 1969).

8. Cited by Jean Leclercq, *The Love of Learning and the Desire for God* (New York: Fordham University Press, 1974), p. 4.

9. Cited by Leclercq, *Love of Learning*, p. 6.

10. Augustine, *Confessions*, XI, xxxix, p. 244.

11. Cited by Leclercq, *Love of Learning*, p. 67.

12. See Benedicta Ward, *Signs and Wonders: Saints, Miracles and Prayers from the 4th Century to the 14th* (Brookfield, VT: Ashgate, 1992) and idem, *Miracles and the Medieval Mind* (Philadelphia: University of Pennsylvania Press, 1982).

13. Wim Verbaal, "Timeless Time: Dramatical Eternity in the Monastery under Bernard of Clairvaux," in Jaritz and Moreno-Riaño, *Time and Eternity*, pp. 238–39.

14. *Sanctae Mechtildis Virginis ordi Sancti Benedictii Liber Specialis Gratiae* (Paris: Oudin, 1877), 1, 12, pp. 37–40.

15. See Andrew Louth, *Denys the Areopagite* (London: Chapman, 1989), and idem, *The Origins of the Christian Mystical Tradition: From Plato to Denys* (Oxford: Oxford University Press, 2007).

16. See William K. Riordan, *Divine Light: The Theology of Denys the Areopagite* (San Francisco: Ignatius Press, 2008).

17. *On Mystical Theology*, chap. 2, *Pseudo Dionysius: The Complete Works*, trans. Colm Luibheid, ed. Paul Rorem (New York: Paulist Press, 1987), p. 138.

18. *On Mystical Theology,* chap. 5, *Pseudo Dionysius: The Complete Works,* p. 141.

19. See Riordan, *Divine Light;* Eric D. Perl, *Theophany: The Neoplatonic Philosophy of Dionysius the Areopagite* (Albany: State University of New York Press, 2007). See also the introductory essays by Jaroslav Pelikan and Jean LeClercq in *Pseudo Dionysius: The Complete Works,* pp. 11–32.

20. See Raoul Vaneigem, *The Movement of the Free Spirit,* trans. Randall Cherry and Ian Patterson (New York: Zone Books, 1994), and Robert Lerner, *The Heresy of the Free Spirit in the Later Middle Ages* (Berkeley and Los Angeles: University of California Press, 1972).

21. For an overview, see Bernard McGinn, *The Mystical Thought of Meister Eckhart* (New York: Crossroad, 2001), and Oliver Davies, *Meister Eckhart: Mystical Theologian* (London: SPCK, 1991).

22. See Jeanne Ancelet-Hustache, *Master Eckhart and the Rhineland Mystics,* trans. Hilda Graef (New York: Harper Torchbooks, 1957).

23. See Carlos Eire, "Early Modern Catholic Piety in Translation," in *Cultural Translation in Early Modern Europe,* ed. Peter Burke and R. Po-chia Hsia (Cambridge: Cambridge University Press, 2007), pp. 83–100.

24. See Steven Ozment, *Mysticism and Dissent* (New Haven, CT: Yale University Press, 1973).

25. *Meister Eckhart: A Modern Translation,* by Raymond Blakney (New York: Harper and Row, 1941), p. 212.

26. Ibid., p. 213.

27. Ibid., p. 214.

28. Ibid., p. 215.

29. Ibid., p. 212.

30. Ibid., p. 214.

31. Ibid., p. 231.

32. See Gordon Leff, *Heresy in the Later Middle Ages* (New York: Barnes & Noble, 1967).

33. For the later history of this tradition, see John Van Engen, *Sisters and Brothers of the Common Life: The Devotio Moderna and the World of the Later Middle Ages* (Philadelphia: University of Pennsylvania Press, 2008).

34. See Charles Journet, *The Mass: The Presence of the Sacrifice of the Cross,* trans. Victor Szczurek (South Bend, IN: St. Augustine's Press, 2008), and Enrico Mazza, *The Celebration of the Eucharist: The Origin of the Rite and the Development of Its Interpretation,* trans. Matthew J. O'Connell (Collegeville, MN: Liturgical Press, 1999).

35. See Geoffrey Wainwright, *Eucharist and Eschatology* (New York: Oxford University Press, 1981), and David Gregg, *Anamnesis in the Eucharist* (Bramcote: Grove Books, 1976).

36. See Carlos Eire, *From Madrid to Purgatory* (New York: Cambridge University Press, 1995), pp. 210–31.

37. See Caroline Walker Bynum, *Wonderful Blood: Theology and Practice in Late Medieval Northern Germany and Beyond* (Philadelphia: University of Pennsylvania Press, 2007).

38. See Miri Rubin, *Corpus Christi: The Eucharist in Late Medieval Culture* (New York: Cambridge University Press, 1991).

39. Brown, *The Cult of the Saints*, p. 1

40. Cited by Brown, *The Cult of the Saints*, p. 4.

41. Victricius of Rouen, *De laude sanctorum*, 11, in *Patrologiae cursus completus, Series Latina*, ed. J.-P. Migne, 221 vols. (Paris, 1844–64), vol. 20, col. 454 B.

42. See G.J.C. Snoek, *Medieval Piety from Relics to the Eucharist* (Leiden: Brill, 1995), and Marie-Madeleine Gauthier, *Highways of the Faith: Relics and Reliquaries from Jerusalem to Compostela*, trans. J. A. Underwood (London: Alpine Fine Arts Collection, 1986).

43. See Lindy Grant, *Abbot Suger of St.-Denis: Church and State in Early Twelfth-Century France* (New York: Longman, 1998), and Georges Duby, *The Age of the Cathedrals*, trans. Eleanor Levieux and Barbara Thompson (Chicago: University of Chicago Press, 1981).

44. *Abbot Suger on the Abbey Church of St.-Denis and Its Art Treasures*, 2nd ed., ed. and trans. Erwin Panofsky (Princeton, NJ: Princeton University Press, 1979), chap. 27, pp. 46–49.

45. Ibid., chap. 32, pp. 62–65.

46. See Jonathan Sumption, *The Age of Pilgrimage: The Medieval Journey to God* (Mahwah, NJ: Hidden Spring, 2003), and idem, *Pilgrimage: An Image of Mediaeval Religion* (Totowa, NJ: Rowman and Littlefield, 1975).

47. See Patrick J. Geary, *Furta sacra: Thefts of Relics in the Central Middle Ages*, rev. ed. (Princeton, NJ: Princeton University Press, 1990).

48. The sixteenth-century reformer, John Calvin, would devote an entire treatise to cataloguing and exposing the dubious relics venerated in his own day: See his "Inventory of Relics," in John Calvin, *Tracts and Treatises*, trans. Henry Bevridge (Grand Rapids, MN: Eerdmans), vol. 1, pp. 331–74.

49. See Jacques Le Goff, *Time, Work & Culture in the Middle Ages*, trans. Arthur Goldhammer (Chicago: University of Chicago Press, 1980).

50. See Taylor, *A Secular Age*, pp. 54–61.

51. See Edward Muir, *Ritual in Early Modern Europe* (New York: Cambridge University Press, 1997), pp. 55–80.

52. See Georges Duby, *The Three Orders: Feudal Society Imagined*, trans. Arthur Goldhammer (Chicago: University of Chicago Press, 1980).

53. See J. M. Cameron, *Images of Authority: A Consideration of the Concepts of "Regnum" and "Sacerdotium"* (New Haven, CT: Yale University Press, 1966), and A. L. Smith, *Church and State in the Middle Ages* (Oxford: Clarendon Press, 1913).

54. Cited by Brian Tierney, *The Crisis of Church and State 1050–1300* (Englewood Cliffs, NJ: Prentice Hall, 1964), pp. 13–14.

55. See Maureen C. Miller, *Power and the Holy in the Age of the Investiture Conflict* (Boston: Bedford/St. Martin's Press, 2005), and Gerd Tellenbach, *Church, State, and Christian Society at the Time of the Investiture Contest*, trans. R. F. Bennett (Oxford: B. Blackwell, 1940).

56. Cited by Horst Fuhrmann, *Germany in the High Middle Ages, c. 1050–1200*, trans. Timothy Reuter (New York: Cambridge University Press, 1986), p. 68.

57. Cited by Brian Tierney, *The Crisis of Church and State 1050–1300* (Englewood Cliffs, NJ: Prentice Hall, 1964), p. 189.

58. See Jane Sayers, *Innocent III: Leader of Europe* (New York: Longman, 1994), and Helene Tillmann, *Pope Innocent III*, trans. Walter Sax (New York: North-Holland, 1980).

59. Henry Bettenson, *Documents of the Christian Church* (Oxford: Oxford University Press, 1963), pp. 157–58.

60. Steven Ozment, *The Age of Reform, 1250–1550* (New Haven, CT: Yale University Press, 1980), p. 144; Geoffrey Barraclough, *The Origins of Modern Germany* (New York: Capricorn, 1963), pp. 207–13; 231–33. See also Bernhard Schimmelpfennig, *Könige und Fürsten, Kaiser und Papst nach dem Wormser Konkordat* (Munich: R. Oldenbourg, 1996).

61. See Georges Duby, *The Three Orders: Feudal Society Imagined*, trans. Arthur Goldhammer (Chicago: University of Chicago Press, 1980).

CHAPTER 4 ETERNITY REFORMED

1. Cited in D. J. Enright, *The Oxford Book of Death* (Oxford: Oxford University Press, 1987), p. 330.

2. See Frank Herbert Brabant, *Time and Eternity in Christian Thought* (New York: Longmans, 1937); Charles J. Caes, *Beyond Time* (Lanham,

MD: University Press of America, 1985); Richard C. Dales, *Medieval Discussions of the Eternity of the World* (Leiden: E. J. Brill, 1990); Rory Fox, *Time and Eternity in Mid-Thirteenth-Century Thought* (New York: Oxford University Press, 2006); Jaritz and Moreno-Riaño, *Time and Eternity*; and Alan G. Padgett, *God, Eternity and the Nature of Time* (New York: St. Martin's Press, 1992).

3. A word on words: *Eucharist* is derived from the Greek, "thanksgiving." It refers to two things simultaneously: to the ritual in which bread and wine are consecrated, and to the consecrated elements themselves. One can therefore speak of celebrating the Eucharist (performing the ritual) and of venerating or receiving the Eucharist (dealing with the bread and wine). The ritual of the Eucharist is also called *the mass*. This word is derived from the final words spoken by the priest in Latin at the end of the ritual: "*ite missa est*," which mean "go, it's over" or "you're dis*miss*ed."

4. See Robert Barron, *Eucharist* (Maryknoll: Orbis, 2008); Ann W. Astell, *Eating Beauty: The Eucharist and the Spiritual Arts of the Middle Ages* (Ithaca, NY: Cornell University Press, 2006); Andrew J. Gerakas, *The Origin and Development of the Holy Eucharist, East and West* (New York: Alba House, 2006); and Henri Cardinal de Lubac, *Corpus Mysticum: The Eucharist and the Church in the Middle Ages*, trans. G. Simmonds, R. Price, and C. Stephens (London: SCM, 2006).

5. Translated by Roland Bainton, in *Here I Stand: A Life of Martin Luther* (New York: Abingdon-Cokesbury Press, 1950), p. 78.

6. Martin Luther, "On the Misuse of the Mass" (1521), in *Luther's Works*, ed. Jaroslav Pelikan et al. (Philadelphia: Muhlenberg Press,1955–86), vol. 36, p. 191. Hereafter LW.

7. LW 51:70.

8. *Confessions*, 9.28; 9.36

9. *Dialogues*, bk. 4, chap. 39. As Gregory the Great (540–604) put it: "In such state as a man departeth out of this life, in the same he is presented in judgment before God. But yet we must believe that before the day of judgment there is a Purgatory fire for certain small sins."

10. Sacrifices and prayers for the dead are mentioned in 2 Maccabees 12:43–46; sin that cannot be forgiven "neither in this world, nor in the world to come" is mentioned in Matthew 12:32; fire that "shall try every man's work" is mentioned by St. Paul in 1 Corinthians 3:11–15.

11. Bainton, *Here I Stand*, p. 71.

12. *Dialogues*, bk. 4, chap. 55.

13. Catherine of Genoa, *Purgation and Purgatory, The Spiritual Dialogue*, trans. Serge Hughes (New York: Paulist Press, 1979), pp. 77, 82, 83.

14. Jacob Voragine, *The Golden Legend*, trans. William Granger Ryan (Princeton, NJ: Princeton University Press, 1993), vol. 2, p. 283.

15. *Der Spiegel des Sünders*, trans. Steven Ozment, *The Reformation in the Cities* (New Haven, CT: Yale University Press, 1975), pp. 24–25. Ozment provides another guilt-inducing passage from a devotional manual on p. 30.

16. For a full account of St. Peter Martyr's many postmortem miracles, see Jacobus de Voragine, *The Golden Legend*, trans. William Granger Ryan (Princeton, NJ: Princeton University Press, 1993), vol. 1, pp. 262–66.

17. Jacques Le Goff, *La naissance du Purgatoire* (Paris: Gallimard, 1981); *The Birth of Purgatory*, trans. Arthur Goldhammer (Chicago: University of Chicago Press, 1984).

18. See Peter Marshall, *Beliefs and the Dead in Reformation England* (Oxford: Oxford University Press, 2002), p. 56, n. 44.

19. Nicholas Manuel, *Die Totenfresser* (1523), trans. Steven Ozment, in *The Reformation in the Cities* (New Haven, CT: Yale University Press, 1975), pp. 112–13.

20. Marshall, *Beliefs and the Dead*, p. 60, citing "Foxe, iv, 584."

21. Quoted by Craig M. Koslofsky in *The Reformation of the Dead: Death and Ritual in Early Modern Germany, 1450–1700* (New York: St. Martin's Press, 2000), pp. 38–39.

22. The model for all such research was established by French historians, especially Michel Vovelle, in *Piété baroque et déchristianisation en Provence au XVIIIe siècle: Les attitudes devant la mort d'après les clauses des testaments* (Paris: Plon, 1973).

23. Simon Fish, "A Supplication for the Beggars," cited by Stephen Greenblatt, *Hamlet in Purgatory* (Princeton, NJ: Princeton University Press, 2002), p. 11.

24. Calvini Opera, 5. 304–5. See my article: "Antisacerdotalism and the Young Calvin," in: *Anticlericalism in Late Medieval and Early Modern Europe*, ed. Peter Dykema and Heiko Oberman (Leiden: E. J. Brill, 1993), pp. 583–603.

25. Cardinal William Allen, *A Defense and Declaration of the Catholike Churches Doctrine, touching Purgatory* (Antwerp, 1566), fol. 215v. Cited by Greenblatt, *Hamlet in Purgatory*, p. 33.

26. Eamon Duffy, *The Voices of Morebath: Reformation and Rebellion in an English Village* (New Haven, CT: Yale University Press, 2001).

27. *Table Talk*, LW 54, p. 326. On another occasion Luther said: "Oh, how I pondered over what eternal life is like and what its joys may be! Although I'm sure that it has been given to us by Christ and that it is ours even now because we have faith, it won't be made known to us until hereafter. It isn't given to us here to know what that creation of the next world is like." *Table Talk*, LW 54, p. 297.

28. *Commentary on Genesis*, 17.17, LW 3.

29. One of the few places is his *Commentary on Hebrews*, 1.5, LW 12: "For we are temporal, or more exactly, a small piece of time. For what we were has departed, and what will be, we are still lacking. So we possess nothing of time except something momentary, what is present."

30. *Commentary on Isaiah*, 53.8, LW 17.

31. *The Blessed Sacrament of the Holy and True Body of Christ*, LW 35, p. 65.

32. *Commentary on the Psalms* 77.6, LW 11.

33. Council of Trent, Decree Concerning Purgatory.

34. Council of Trent, On the Invocation, Veneration, and Relics of Saints, and on Sacred Images.

35. Eire, *From Madrid to Purgatory*, esp. 168–231; Sara Nalle, *God in La Mancha: Religious Reform and the People of Cuenca, 1500–1650* (Baltimore: Johns Hopkins University Press, 1992), pp. 175, 188, 202–5.

36. Conversation with Albert O. Hirschman, Institute for Advanced Study, Princeton, NJ, spring 1993.

37. See Eire, *From Madrid to Purgatory*, bk. 3.

38. William Shakespeare, *Hamlet*, I. v. 9–13.

39. See Greenblatt, *Hamlet in Purgatory*, esp. pp. 1–101.

40. *Grund und Ursach auss Göttlichen Rechten, Warumb Prior und Convent in Sant. Annen Closter zu Augsburg ihren Standt verandert haben 1526* (Kempten, 1611), pp. C3a; C2b; E3b. Quoted by Steven Ozment, *The Reformation in the Cities* (New Haven, CT: Yale University Press, 1975), p. 89.

41. Eberlin von Günzburg, "Von dem langen verdrüssigen Geschrei, das die geistlichen Münch, Pfaffen und Nunnen die sieben Tage Zeit heissen," in *Sämtliche Schriften*, ed. Ludwig Enders, 3 vols. (Halle: Niemeyer, 1896–1902), vol. 1, pp. 40–41, and "Ein Vermanung aller Christen das sie sich erbarmen über die Klosterfrawen," *Sämtliche Schriften*, vol. 1, pp. 25–27.

42. See François Biot, *The Rise of Protestant Monasticism*, trans. W. J. Kerrigan (Baltimore: Helicon, 1963), pp. 144–51.

43. *The Prague Protest*, trans. Michael Baylor, in *The Radical Reformation* (Cambridge: Cambridge University Press, 1991), pp. 4–9.

44. Thomas Müntzer, "A highly provoked defense and answer to the spiritless, soft-living flesh at Wittenberg who has most lamentably befouled pitiable Christianity in a perverted way by his theft of holy Scripture," in Baylor, *Radical Reformation*, pp. 74–94.

45. *Institutes of the Christian Religion*, II.3.2, trans. Ford Lewis Battles, 2 vols. (Philadelphia: Westminster, 1960), vol. 1, p. 292.

46. *Institutes of the Christian Religion*, II.3.7–8. Battles translation, vol. 1, pp. 299–300.

47. *Institutes of the Christian Religion*, III.6.1–5. Battles translation, vol. 1, pp. 684–89.

48. Wenceslaus Link, Ozment, *The Reformation in the Cities*, p. 87.

49. Ibid., p. 87.

50. Ibid., p. 83.

51. Ibid., pp. 95–96.

52. Robert Walton, *Zwingli's Theocracy* (Toronto: University of Toronto Press, 1967).

53. See William G. Naphy, *Calvin and the Consolidation of the Genevan Reformation* (Louisville: Westminster John Knox Press, 2003), and Philip Benedict, *Christ's Churches, Purely Reformed: A Social History of Calvinism* (New Haven, CT: Yale University Press, 2001).

54. See Gary K. Waite, *Eradicating the Devil's Minions: Anabaptists and Witches in Reformation Europe, 1525–1600* (Toronto: University of Toronto Press, 2007), and Brad Gregory, *Salvation at Stake: Christian Martyrdom in Early Modern Europe* (Cambridge, MA: Harvard University Press, 1990), chap. 6.

55. For a nonliteral interpretation, see Sebastian de Grazia, *Machiavelli in Hell* (Princeton, NJ: Princeton University Press, 1989).

56. Cary J. Nederman sums it up: "Surely there is no political theorist about whom scholarly opinion is more divided than Niccolò Machiavelli. The subject of intense and continuous examination almost from the time of his death, Machiavelli has become if anything more enigmatic with the passage of time and the proliferation of interpretations." See her article "Amazing Grace: Fortune, God, and Free Will in Machiavelli's Thought," *Journal of the History of Ideas* 60, no. 4 (October 1999), pp. 617–38.

57. Niccolò Machiavelli, *The Prince*, ed. Quentin Skinner and Russell Price (Cambridge: Cambridge University Press, 1988), chap. 17, pp. 58–61.

58. *The Prince*, chap. 8, p. 33 (Skinner ed.).

59. Ibid., chap. 25, pp. 85–86.

60. See J.G.A. Pocock, *The Machiavellian Moment: Florentine Political Thought and the Atlantic Republican Tradition*, 2nd ed. (Princeton, NJ: Princeton University Press, 2003), and Robert Bireley, *The Counter-Reformation Prince: Anti-Machiavellianism or Catholic Statecraft in Early Modern Europe* (Chapel Hill: University of North Carolina Press, 1990).

61. Summed up in the title of an anonymous English work, *The Atheisticall Polititian or A briefe discourse concerning Ni. Machiavell* (London, 1642).

62. See Sydney Anglo, *Machiavelli—The First Century: Studies in Enthusiasm, Hostility, and Irrelevance* (Oxford: Oxford University Press, 2005).

63. See Peter Marshall's observations on the idioms of memory in *Beliefs and the Dead*, p. 18.

64. Craig M. Koslofsky, *The Reformation of the Dead: Death and Ritual in Early Modern Germany, 1450–1700* (New York: Palgrave Macmillan, 2000); Susan C. Karant-Nunn, *The Reformation of Ritual: An Interpretation of Early Modern Germany* (London: Routledge, 1997); Edward Muir, *Ritual in Early Modern Europe* (Cambridge: Cambridge University Press, 1997).

65. Philipe Ariès, *The Hour of Our Death* (New York: Knopf, 1981), esp. pp. 605–8; John Bossy, *Christianity in the West, 1400–1700* (New York: Oxford University Press, 1985).

66. "First Invocavit Sermon," LW 51, p. 70.

67. Bultmann, *The Presence of Eternity*, p. 155. Italics are Bultmann's.

68. Max Weber, *The Protestant Ethic and the Spirit of Capitalism* (1924), trans. Talcott Parsons (New York: Russell and Russell, 1958), p. 120.

69. Weber, *Protestant Ethic*, p. 105.

70. Jeremias Drexelius, S.J., *Considerations on Eternity*, trans. Sister Marie José Byrne (New York: Frederick Pustet, 1920), p. 162.

71. See Stuart Schwartz, *All Can Be Saved: Religious Tolerance and Salvation in the Iberian Atlantic World* (New Haven, CT: Yale University Press, 2008), and Lucien Febvre, *The Problem of Unbelief in the Sixteenth Century: The Religion of Rabelais*, trans. Beatrice Gottlieb (Cambridge, MA: Harvard University Press, 1982).

72. A worldview invoked by British actress Sienna Miller, when faced with questions about her failed, adultery-plagued marriage: "I don't know, monogamy is a weird thing for me. It's an overrated virtue, because, let's face it, we're f---ing animals." Jenny Eliscu, "Hot Actress: Sienna Miller," *Rolling Stone*, October 6, 2006.

CHAPTER 5 FROM ETERNITY TO FIVE-YEAR PLANS

1. Emily Dickinson, *The Complete Poems*, ed. Thomas H. Johnson (Boston: Little, Brown, 1960), no. 1551.

2. Ibid., no. 976.

3. Ibid., no. 502.

4. Juan Eusebio Nieremberg, *De la diferencia entre lo temporal y lo eterno: Crisol de desengaños con la memoria de la eternidad, postrimerias humanas y principales misterios divinos*, in *Obras escogidas del R. P. Juan Eusebio Nieremberg*, ed. Eduardo Zepeda-Henríquez, 2 vols. (Madrid: Atlas, 1957), vol. 2, p. 223.

5. Diego Murillo, *Discursos predicados sobre todos los evangelios* (Zaragoza, 1611). Cited in Ana Martínez Arancón, *Geografía de la Eternidad* (Madrid: Tecnos, 1987), p. 79.

6. Jean Delumeau, *Sin and Fear: The Emergence of a Western Guilt Culture, 13th–18th Centuries*; trans. Eric Nicholson (New York, 1990); Piero Camporesi, *The Fear of Hell: Images of Damnation and Salvation in Early Modern Europe*; trans. Lucinda Byatt (University Park: University Press of Pennsylvania, 1991).

7. Carlos Eire, "The Good Side of Hell: Infernal Meditations in Early Modern Spain," *Historical Reflections/Reflexions Historiques* 26, no. 2 (Summer 2000): 285–310.

8. I have used the Spanish text in the *Biblioteca de Autores Españoles: Obras Escogidas del Reverendo Padre Juan Eusebio Nieremberg*, ed. Eduardo Zepeda-Henríquez, 2 vols. (Madrid, 1957), vol. 2.

9. Ibid., p. 227.

10. Ibid., p. 218.

11. Ibid., pp. 219–20.

12. Ibid., p. 223.

13. Drexelius, *Considerations on Eternity*, pp. 70–71.

14. Ibid., p. 104.

15. Ibid., p. 193.

16. The original 1620 issue went through nine editions. In addition, it was translated into German, Polish, French, Italian, and English. In English alone, the translations span four centuries: Cambridge, 1632; Oxford, 1661; London, 1710 and 1844; and New York, 1920.

17. In order of birth: Nicolaus Copernicus (1473–1543), Francis Bacon (1561–1626), Galileo Galilei (1564–1642), Johannes Kepler (1571–1630),

William Harvey (1578–1657), Jeremiah Drechsel (1581–1638), J. E. Nieremberg (1595–1658), René Descartes (1596–1650), Blaise Pascal (1623–1662), John Locke (1632–1704), Isaac Newton (1643–1727), G. W. Leibniz (1646–1716).

18. *Historia naturae, maxime peregrinae, libris XVI* (Antwerp, 1635).

19. Alonso Andrade, *Varones Ilustres de la Compañía de Jesús* (Bilbao, 1891), vol. 8, p. 752.

20. John Donne, "An Anatomy of the World" (1611), in *The Major Works*, ed. John Carey (Oxford: Oxford University Press, 2000), p. 212.

21. "Le silence éternel de ces espaces infinis m'effraie." Pascal, *Pensées* (Krailsheimer trans.), p. 66.

22. John van Ruysbroeck, *Spiritual Espousals*, 2:50, in *The Spiritual Espousals and Other Works*, trans. James Wiseman (New York: Paulist Press, 1985), p. 111.

23. See Colleen McDannell and Bernhard Lang, *Heaven: A History*, 2nd ed. (New Haven, CT: Yale University Press, 2001), esp. pp. 80–88.

24. See Evonne Levy, *Propaganda and the Jesuit Baroque* (Berkeley and Los Angeles: University of California Press, 2004).

25. D. P. Walker, *The Decline of Hell: Seventeenth-Century Discussions of Eternal Torment* (Chicago: University of Chicago Press, 1964); Alan Kors, *Atheism in France, 1650–1729* (Princeton, NJ: Princeton University Press, 1990).

26. John McManners, *Death and the Enlightenment: Changing Attitudes to Death among Christians and Unbelievers in Eighteenth-Century France* (Oxford: Oxford University Press, 1981).

27. Louis Dupré, *The Enlightenment and the Intellectual Foundations of Modern Culture* (New Haven, CT: Yale University Press, 2004); Peter Gay, *The Enlightenment: An Interpretation* (New York: Knopf, 1968).

28. Thomas Paine, *The Age of Reason: Being an Investigation of True and Fabulous Theology* (1794), pt. 2, chap. 3. Edited by Daniel Edwin Wheeler, *The Life and Writings of Thomas Paine: Containing a Biography by Thomas Clio Rickman* (New York: Vincent Parke and Co., 1908), pp. 274–75.

29. Cited by Jonathan Israel, *Enlightenment Contested: Philosophy, Modernity, and the Emancipation of Man, 1670–1752* (Oxford: Oxford University Press, 2006), p. 364.

30. Cited by Theodore Besterman, *Voltaire* (New York: Harcourt, Brace & World, 1969), p. 223.

31. Cited by Paul Johnson, *A History of Christianity* (New York: Touchstone, 1979), pp. 350 ff.

32. Cited by Robert Palmer, "Posterity and the Hereafter in Eighteenth-Century French Thought," *The Journal of Modern History* 9, no. 2 (June 1937), p. 166.

33. Vanessa Harding, *The Dead and the Living in Paris and London, 1500–1670* (Cambridge: Cambridge University Press, 2002); Craig Koslofsky, *The Reformation of the Dead* (Oxford: Oxford University Press, 2000).

34. Michel Vovelle, *Piété baroque et dechristianisation en Provence au XVIIIe siècle* (Paris: Plon, 1973). See also McManners, *Death and the Enlightenment.*

35. *The Red Scapular of Our Lord's Passion and of the Sacred Hearts of Jesus and Mary* (Emmittsburg, MD: St. Joseph's, 1850); Michael Müller, *The Devotion of the Holy Rosary and the Five Scapulars* (St. Louis, 1885).

36. *The Poetry and Prose of William Blake*, ed. David Erdman (New York: Doubleday, 1965), p. 167.

37. Ibid., p. 157.

38. *Conversations of Goethe with Johann Peter Eckermann*, trans. J. K. Moorhead (Cambridge, MA: Da Capo Press, 1998), p. 287.

39. Johann Wolfgang von Goethe, *Goethe, the Story of a Man: Being the Life of Johann Wolfgang Goethe as Told in His Own Words and the Words of His Contemporaries*, ed. and trans. Ludwig Lewisohn (New York: Farrar, Straus, 1949), p. 353.

40. Percy Bysshe Shelley, *Adonais: An Elegy on the Death of John Keats* LII [1821] (London: The Shelley Society, 1886), p. 24.

41. Jonathan Edwards, "Sinners in the Hands of an Angry God" (1741), in *A Jonathan Edwards Reader*, ed. John E. Smith, Harry S. Stout, and Kenneth P. Minkema (New Haven, CT: Yale University Press, 1995), pp. 89–104.

42. Karl Marx, *A Contribution to the Critique of Hegel's Philosophy of Right* (introduction, 1843–1844), in *The Yale Book of Quotations* (New Haven, CT: Yale University Press, 2006), p. 498.

43. Ariès, *Hour of Our Death*, pp. 506–56.

44. Ronald Pearsall, *Table-Rappers: The Victorians and the Occult* (Stroud: Sutton, 2004).

45. Sir Arthur Conan Doyle et al., *The Case for Spirit Photography* (London: Hutchinson and Co., 1922); Sophie Schmidt, "Conan Doyle: A Study

in Black and White," in *The Perfect Medium: Photography and the Occult*, ed. C. Chéroux and A. Fischer (New Haven, CT: Yale University Press, 2005), pp. 92–96.

46. Blavatsky's conception of eternity was close to that of the *Bhagavadgita*, chap. 2, v. 19: "If any man thinks he slays, and if another thinks he is slain, neither knows the ways of truth. The Eternal in man cannot kill: the Eternal in man cannot die. He is never born, and he never dies. He is in Eternity, he is for evermore. Never-born and eternal, beyond times gone or to come, he does not die when the body dies." This is also very similar to *Kasha Upanishad*, chap. 2, v.19.

47. Charles J. Ryan, *H. P. Blavatsky and the Theosophical Movement: A Brief Historical Sketch*, 2nd ed. (San Diego, CA: Point Loma Publications, 1975).

48. Philip Larkin, "Aubade," in *Collected Poems* (New York: Farrar, Straus & Giroux, 1989), pp. 40–41.

49. Stephen Hawking and Leonard Mlodinow, *A Briefer History of Time* (New York: Bantam Dell, 2005), p. 142.

50. Nieremberg, p. 224.

51. Nabokov, *Speak, Memory*, pp. 19–20.

52. William Hazlitt, "On the Fear of Death," in *Table Talk: Essays on Men and Manners* (London: Bell and Daldy, 1869), pp. 455–56.

53. Sigmund Freud, "On Transience," in Matthew von Unwerth, *Freud's Requiem: Mourning, Memory, and the Invisible History of a Summer Walk* (London: Continuum, 2006), p. 216.

54. Pascal, *Pensées*, trans. Roger Ariew (New York: Hackett, 2005), p. 64.

55. Ibid., p. 216.

56. Henri Poincaré, *The Value of Science*, trans. George Bruce Halsted (New York: Science Press, 1913), p. 355. For similar sentiments from another twentieth-century Frenchman, Pierre Chaunu, see footnote 1 of the introduction.

57. See Lawrence J. Hatab, *Nietzsche's Life Sentence: Coming to Terms with Eternal Recurrence* (New York: Routledge, 2005); Ned Lukacher, *Time-Fetishes: The Secret History of Eternal Recurrence* (Durham, NC: Duke University Press, 1998); Karl Löwith, *Nietzsche's Philosophy of the Eternal Recurrence of the Same*, trans. J. Harvey Lomax (Berkeley and Los Angeles: University of California Press, 1997); and Adam Frank, "The Day Before Genesis," *Discover*, April 2008, pp. 54–60.

58. See Brian Leiter, *The Routledge Guidebook to Nietzsche on Morality* (London: Routledge, 2002), and also his concise summary in the online *Stanford Encyclopedia of Philosophy*, "Nietzsche's Moral and Political Philosophy" (2007) (http://plato.stanford.edu/entries/Nietzsche-moral-political/#Bib).

59. See Joan Stambaugh, *The Problem of Time in Nietzsche*, trans. John F. Humphrey (Philadelphia: Bucknell University Press, 1987).

60. Friedrich Nietzsche, *The Gay Science*, 341, trans. Walter Kaufmann (New York: Vintage, 1974), pp. 273–74.

61. Milan Kundera, *The Unbearable Lightness of Being,* trans. Henry Heim (New York: Harper and Row, 1984), p. 5.

62. Ibid., p. 4.

63. See John Paul II's encyclical *Sollicitudo Rei Socialis*, December 30, 1987, sect. III: "Survey of the Contemporary World"; sect. IV: "Authentic Human Development"; sect. V: "A Theological Reading of Modern Problems."

64. Pew Forum on Religion and Public Life/U.S. Religious Landscape Survey, Final Topline; May–August 2007; questions 30, 33, 34, 35, and 36 (http://religions.pewforum.org/reports#).

65. CBS News (http://www.cbsnews.com/stories/2005/10/29/opinion/polls/main994766.shtml).

66. The Harris Poll no. 11, February 26, 2003: "The Religious and Other Beliefs of Americans 2003" (http://www.harrisinteractive.com/harris_poll/index.asp?PID=359). This Harris poll and the CBS poll cited above differ little in their findings. Life after death: eighty-one percent; ghosts: fifty-one percent.

67. ABC News (http://abcnews.go.com/US/PollVault/story?id=3440869); The Vegetarian Society (http://www.vegsoc.org/info/statveg.html).

68. Raymond Chandler, *Playback* (New York: Ballantine, 1975), p. 137.

69. Library Index:Death and Dying: End-of-Life Controversies: Public Opinion About Life and Death (http://www.libraryindex.com/pages/3164/Public-Opinion-About-Life-Death-LIFE-AFTER-DEATH.html); Harris Poll no. 11, "The Religious and Other Beliefs of Americans 2003."

70. David Klinghoffer, "Hell, Yes," *National Review*, November 9, 1998 (http://store.nationalreview.com/archives).

71. Alfred, Lord Tennyson, *In Memoriam*, ed. Vernon Squires (New York: Silver, Burdett, 1906), pp. 30, 71–72.

72. Klinghoffer, "Hell, Yes."

73. See William Lane Craig, "Time, Eternity, and Eschatology," in *The Oxford Handbook of Eschatology*, ed. Jerry L. Walls (New York: Oxford University Press, 2008), pp. 596–613.

74. Augustine, *Confessions*, X, drew much inspiration from two biblical texts. Psalms 90:4 "For a thousand years in thy sight are but as yesterday when it is past, and as a watch in the night." 2 Peter 3:8 "one day is with the Lord as a thousand years, and a thousand years as one day." See Jaroslav Pelikan, *The Mystery of Continuity: Time and History, Memory and Eternity in the Thought of Saint Augustine* (Charlottesville: University Press of Virginia, 1986).

75. "Twenty Things You Didn't Know about Time," *Discover*, March 2009, p. 80.

76. Tim Folger, "Newsflash: Time May Not Exist," *Discover*, June 12, 2007 (http://discovermagazine.com/2007/jun/in-no-time). Another theory proposes that the universe itself is "nothing." See Russel Standish, *Theory of Nothing* (Author: BookSurge Australia, 2006).

77. Julian Barbour, *The End of Time: The Next Revolution in Physics* (Oxford: Oxford University Press, 1999), pp. 10, 14.

78. Kurt Vonnegut, *Slaughterhouse Five* (New York: Dial Press, 1995), pp. 34, 109.

79. Adam Frank, "The Day Before Genesis," *Discover*, April 2008, p. 58.

80. Adam Frank, "The Discover Interview: Max Tegmark," *Discover*, July 2008, pp. 38–43. For an introduction to multiverse cosmology and theories other than Tegmark's, see Alex Vilenkin, *Many Worlds in One: The Search for Other Universes* (New York: Hill and Wang, 2007).

81. Paul J. Steinhardt and Neil Turok, *Endless Universe: Beyond the Big Bang* (New York: Doubleday, 2007).

82. Laurence Marschall, "What Happened Before the Big Bang?" *Discover*, July 9, 2007 (http://discovermagazine.com/2007/jul/books-coming-soon-the-big-bang).

83. Pascal, *Pensées* (Ariew trans.)., p. 64.

84. Ibid., p. 224.

CHAPTER 6 NOT HERE, NOT NOW, NOT EVER

1. Pascal, *Pensées* (Ariew trans.), p. 132.

2. Thomas W. Clark, cited by Jesse M. Bering, "The End? Why So Many of Us Think Our Minds Continue On After We Die," *Scientific American Mind*, October–November 2008, p. 36.

3. Stephen Barr, "Theories of Everything," *First Things* 92 (April 1999), pp. 48, 50.

4. Martin Heidegger's *Being and Time* (1927), one of the most influential philosophical treatises of the twentieth century, is also among the most difficult to comprehend, in any language.

5. See Julian Young, *Heidegger, Philosophy, Nazism* (Cambridge: Cambridge University Press, 1997), and Tom Rockmore, *On Heidegger's Nazism and Philosophy* (Berkeley and Los Angeles: University of California Press, 1992).

6. Luis Buñuel, "Swang Song," from *My Last Sigh*, trans. Abigail Israel (New York: Knopf, 1983), p. 99.

7. *The New Yorker*, April 18, 1953, p. 28.

8. Tom Stoppard, *Rosencranz and Guildenstern Are Dead*, act 2 (1967).

9. Arthur Rimbaud, "L'Eternite," "Nuit de l'enfer," *Une Saison en enfer & Le bateau ivre*, ed. Louise Varèse, pp. 62–63. Translation mine. For another example of eternity as a feeling, see Charles Simic, "The Garden of Earthly Delights," in *Return to a Place Lit by a Glass of Milk* (New York: George Braziller, 1974), p. 41.

10. Ibid., pp. 26, 28; translation mine.

11. Blake, "Eternity," in Erdman, *The Poetry and Prose of William Blake*, p. 462.

Eternity

~

A Basic Bibliography

Almond, Philip C. *Heaven and Hell in Enlightenment England*. Cambridge: Cambridge University Press, 1994.

Ariès, Philippe. *The Hour of Our Death*, trans. Helen Weaver. New York: Knopf, 1981.

Audretsch, Jürgen, and Klaus Nagomi, eds. *Zeit und Ewigkeit: Theologie und Naturwissenschaft im Gespräch*. Karlsruhe: Evangelische Akademie Baden, 2001.

Baudry, Jules. *Le problème de l'origine et de l'éternité du monde dans la philosophie grecque de Platon à l'ère chrétienne*. Paris: Sociète d'édition "Les Belles lettres," 1931.

Beemelmans, Friedrich. *Zeit und Ewigkeit nach Thomas von Aquino*. Münster: Aschendorff, 1914.

Behler, Ernst. *Die Ewigkeit der Welt: Problemgeschichtliche Untersuchungen zu den Kontroversen um Weltanfang und Weltunendlichkeit im Mittelalter*. Munich: Schöningh, 1965.

Brabant, Frank Herbert. *Time and Eternity in Christian Thought*. London: Longmans, Green and Co., 1937.

Caes, Charles C. *Beyond Time: Ideas of the Great Philosophers on Eternal Existence and Immortality*. Lanham, MD: University Press of America, 1985.

Camporesi, Piero. *The Fear of Hell: Images of Damnation and Salvation in Early Modern Europe*, trans. Lucinda Byatt. University Park: Pennsylvania State University Press, 1991.

Candel, Miguel. *El nacimiento de la eternidad: Apuntes de filosofía antigua*. Barcelona: Idea Books, 2002.

Canetti, Luigi. *Frammenti di eternità: Corpi e reliquie tra antichità e Medioevo*. Rome: Viella, 2002.

Chaunu, Pierre. *La mémoire de l'éternité*. Paris: R. Laffont, 1975.

D'Anna, Nuccio. *Il gioco cosmico: Tempo ed eternità nell'antica Grecia.* Milan: Rusconi, 1999.

Dales, Richard C. *Medieval Discussions of the Eternity of the World.* Leiden: E. J. Brill, 1990.

Delumeau, Jean. *Sin and Fear: The Emergence of a Western Guilt Culture, 13th–18th Centuries,* trans. Eric Nicholson. New York: St. Martin's Press, 1990.

Eire, Carlos M. N. *From Madrid to Purgatory: The Art and Craft of Dying in Sixteenth Century Spain.* New York: Cambridge University Press, 1995.

Fischer, Norbert, and Dieter Hattrup, eds. *Schöpfung, Zeit und Ewigkeit : Augustinus: Confessiones 11–13,* Paderborn: Schöningh, 2006.

Fox, Rory. *Time and Eternity in Mid-Thirteenth-Century Thought.* Oxford: Oxford University Press, 2006.

García Astrada, Arturo. *Tiempo y eternidad.* Madrid: Gredos, 1971.

Granarolo, Philippe. *L'individu éternel: L'expérience nietzschéenne de l'éternité.* Paris: Vrin, 1993.

Greenblat, Stephen. *Hamlet in Purgatory.* Princeton, NJ: Princeton University Press, 2001.

Guitton, Jean. *Temps et l'éternité chez Plotin et saint Augustin.* Paris: Boivin, 1933.

Jackelén, Antje. *Zeit und Ewigkeit: Die Frage der Zeit in Kirche, Naturwissenschaft und Theologie.* Neukirchen/Vluyn: Neukirchener, 2002.

Jaritz, Gerhard, and Gerson Moreno-Riano, eds. *Time and Eternity: The Medieval Discourse.* International Medieval Congress, 2000, University of Leeds. Turnhout: Brepols, 2003.

Jüttemann, Veronika, ed. *Ewige Augenblicke: Eine interdisziplinäre Annäherung an das Phänomen Zeit.* Münster: Waxmann, 2008.

Küng, Hans. *Eternal Life?* trans. Edward Quinn. London: Collins, 1984.

Le Goff, Jacques. *The Birth of Purgatory,* trans. Arthur Goldhammer. Chicago: University of Chicago Press, 1984.

Leftow, Brian. *Time and Eternity.* Ithaca, NY: Cornell University Press, 1991.

Leisegang, Hans. *Die Begriffe der Zeit und Ewigkeit im späteren Platonismus.* Münster: Aschendorff, 1913.

Longo, Giulia. *Kierkegaard, Nietzsche: Eternità dell'istante, istantaneità dell'eterno.* Milan: Mimesis, 2007.

Manzke, Karl Hinrich. *Ewigkeit und Zeitlichkeit: Aspekte für eine theologische Deutung der Zeit.* Göttingen: Vandenhoeck and Ruprecht, 1992.

Marenbon, John. *Le temps, l'éternité et la prescience de Boèce à Thomas d'Aquin.* Paris: Vrin, 2005.

Mayer, Fred Sidney. *Why Two Worlds? The Relation of Physical to Spiritual Realities.* Philadelphia: J. B. Lippincott, 1934.

McDannell, Colleen, and Bernhard Lang. *Heaven: A History.* New Haven, CT: Yale University Press, 2001.

McGrath, Alister E. *A Brief History of Heaven.* Malden, MA: Blackwell, 2003.

McManners, John. *Death and the Enlightenment: Changing Attitudes to Death among Christians and Unbelievers in Eighteenth-Century France.* New York: Oxford University Press, 1981.

Meijering, E. P. *Augustin über Schöpfung, Ewigkeit und Zeit: Das elfte Buch der Bekenntnisse.* Leiden: Brill, 1979.

Mesch, Walter. *Reflektierte Gegenwart: Eine Studie über Zeit und Ewigkeit bei Platon, Aristoteles, Plotin und Augustinus.* Frankfurt: Klostermann, 2003.

Minois, Georges. *Histoire des enfers.* Paris: Fayard, 1991.

Mondolfo, Rodolfo. *Eternidad e infinitud del tiempo en Aristóteles.* Cordoba, 1945.

Muessig, Carolyn, and Ad Putter, eds. *Envisaging Heaven in the Middle Ages.* New York: Routledge, 2007.

Neville, Robert C. *Eternity and Time's Flow.* Albany: State University of New York Press, 1993.

Padgett, Alan G. *God, Eternity and the Nature of Time.* London: St. Martin's Press, 1992.

Pike, Nelson. *God and Timelessness.* London: Routledge and K. Paul, 1970.

Russell, Jeffrey Burton. *A History of Heaven: The Singing Silence.* Princeton, NJ: Princeton University Press, 1997.

Reinke, Otfried, ed. *Ewigkeit? Klärungsversuche aus Natur- und Geisteswissenschaften.* Göttingen: Vandenhoeck and Ruprecht, 2004.

Ryan, Mary Imogene. *Heaven: An Anthology, Compiled by a Religious of the Sacred Heart.* New York: Longmans, Green and Co., 1935.

Simon, Ulrich E. *Heaven in the Christian Tradition.* New York: Harper, 1958.

Swedenborg, Emanuel. *Heaven and Its Wonders, and Hell,* trans. by John C. Ager. New York: Citadel Press, 1965.

Walker, D[aniel]. P[ickering]. *The Decline of Hell: Seventeenth-Century Discussions of Eternal Torment.* Chicago: University of Chicago Press, 1964.

Walls, Jerry L. *Heaven: The Logic of Eternal Joy.* New York: Oxford University Press, 2002.

———, ed. *The Oxford Handbook of Eschatology.* New York: Oxford University Press, 2008.

Index